To Michael ^ Christmas 2022

In case you want a change
from AI!
No where in the world
like Liverpool ♡.
Hope you enjoy reading
a different perspective on
your lovely city, which is
part of your history.
lots of love
Debra N Chris
X X

THE TALK OF LIVERPOOL

PADDY SHENNAN

m
B

MIRROR BOOKS

For Sandra and Tom

MIRROR BOOKS

1

First published in Great Britain and Ireland in 2022 by
Mirror Books, a Reach PLC business.

www.mirrorbooks.co.uk
@TheMirrorBooks

Hardback edition ISBN: 9781915306067
eBook ISBN: 9781915306074

Photographic acknowledgements:
Paddy Shennan personal selection, Reach Plc, Mirrorpix.
With thanks to Natalie Jones.

Every effort has been made to trace copyright.
Any omissions or oversights will be rectified in future editions.

Design and production by Mirror Books.

Printed and bound by CPI Group (UK) Ltd,
Croydon, CR0 4YY.

Contents

Foreword by Brian Reade of the *Daily Mirror*   9

Introduction   11

Chapter 1: Face-to-face with a killer   17

Chapter 2: Confessions of a feature writer   20

Chapter 3: A right royal soap opera   31

Chapter 4: 'Look! It's those people from the telly!'   44

Chapter 5: Hilda and Gordon   70

Chapter 6: Singing a different song   76

Chapter 7: With(out) The Beatles   126

Chapter 8: Heysel   153

Chapter 9: Quite a bit of politics (well, it is Liverpool)   162

Chapter 10: Laughing matters   199

Chapter 11: James Bulger   232

Chapter 12: A Blues medley   239

Chapter 13: Voices of peace in the face of hatred   263

Chapter 14: In search of Madeleine   269

Chapter 15: This Is My City   289

Chapter 16: Jim Beglin is not amused 301

Chapter 17: Never listen to a PR person 305

Chapter 18: Banned by The La's 308

Chapter 19: Nerys Hughes 1 Geoffrey Hughes 0 311

Chapter 20: 'Take your Echo and shove it up your arse!' 313

Chapter 21: There was fan mail, too – honestly! 316

Chapter 22: Hillsborough 318

Acknowledgements 376

Foreword by

Brian Reade

ONE OF the first thoughts I had on joining the *Daily Mirror* in 1994 was that certain colleagues I'd left behind at the *Liverpool Echo* could make the step up to national newspapers with ease. Especially one: Paddy Shennan.

And I told him so. But he was happy to stay where he was, on a newspaper and in a city he loved.

In a way, I was pleased. Not because it meant I had less opposition at the *Mirror* (OK, maybe partly) but because Fleet Street's loss was my home town's gain.

Paddy became the go-to chronicler of Liverpudlian tales for more than three decades, as those of us who have dabbled in cultural, social or sporting causes can testify.

If you wanted to get a good show in the *Echo* for your new book, film, play or social justice campaign, you rang Paddy. He'd always agree to meet you in a pub (enthusiastically) and grasp the essence of what was needed quickly, before sinking a few pints as he filled you in on the latest newsroom gossip or Half Man Half Biscuit story. Then go back to the office, occasionally half-cut, and turn out another cracking piece.

After an astonishing 33 years of sterling service at the

Echo, Paddy has created a unique body of work which he's pulled together in this wonderful book. Including the hate mail, which I can testify is in a class of its own from *Echo* readers, who never hold back in telling its journalists how far they can ram their "Tory/Kopite" rag up their jacksey.

It's his take on every major event that has affected this city since the late '80s, from the most soul-crushing tragedies to the most joyous celebrations.

And at its heart is a celebration of the power of the Scouse spirit. All told with compassion and a deadpan wit.

Reading it was a lovely trip down memory lane for me. And hopefully it will be for you.

Shame he's a bleedin' Blue.

Brian Reade, 2022

Introduction

IT WAS a lunchtime drinking session like no other, and made me wonder – are all work experience days like this?

Alcohol played a starring role during my 33 years at the *Liverpool Echo* as, alongside Mike Chapple, I launched and wrote the newspaper's much-loved (especially by us) pub column. It eventually became a book – the *Liverpool Echo* Pub Guide (we knew an original and sophisticated title when we saw one) – which won two national awards.

And it was the sometimes demon, but more often delightful, drink which was responsible for starting my journalism career.

The 1980s were not as bad a decade as many have painted it, because it was still the era of the liquid lunch – as opposed to an overpriced sandwich and bottle of water at your desk.

"Are you applying for the reporter's job?" asked *Lancashire Evening Post* deputy news editor Tony Skinner, as a group of understandably jolly journos began their fourth pints of bitter (lager for the non-drinkers) in The Welly (Wellington Inn) in Preston.

Explanation/confession: I was born, and spent the first 19 years of my life, in Preston, after my Liverpool-born parents had the audacity to move there before I was born – though my dad retrieved many brownie points by bringing me up as an Evertonian.

I told Skinner I was only halfway through a one-year journalism course in Sheffield. Never mind that, he replied. But I was either really keen to avoid having to start work before it was strictly necessary, or a great respecter of tradition (you know – start a course, finish a course, apply for jobs), because I then said: "I thought the current interview process was over – and anyway, one of those who was interviewed is a friend of mine who, unlike me, has been to university. Oxford, no less!"

"He won't get the f****** job," said Skinner, with more than a hint of disdain, before adding, this time with disdain dripping from his mouth: "We brought him to the pub and he'd only drink orange juice! You've had four pints."

I was interviewed by the editor and the news editor about an hour or so later (I can't be sure on the exact time, because I was pissed) – and got the job.

Three years, a great many pints and a few news stories later, I was in my spiritual home – starting my 33-year stretch at the *Echo*.

On day one, after go-getting reporter Keith Kendrick had quizzed me about my career ambition – I told him: "Er, I've achieved it. I always wanted to work here, not least because it will be easier to go and watch Everton" – he shouted out: "F*** me, lads, we've got a lifer!"

By the way, there's no need to shed any tears for the man who went to Oxford, and thought I had stolen his job.

It wasn't too long before Andrew Hobbs was working at the *Post* himself (the "no lightweights" policy had obviously been relaxed), and, before leaving to launch his own magazine, the *Preston Other Paper*, and going down all sorts of other interesting avenues before selling out to academia, he easily overtook me on the career ladder by winning a specialist role on the paper – education reporter.

And in the years since I got pissed that lunchtime, our friendship has grown. I was even Hobbsy's best man, proving that he didn't hold his initial grudge too long – while he also soon swapped orange juice for ale!

* * *

Trainee journos are told to avoid cliches – like the plague.

Early in my career, one of my mentors, the *Evening Post's* Peter Richardson (a brilliant reporter who went on to become a brilliant feature writer and features editor – while he has always been a brilliant man, and drinker), told me: "Never complain about being a journalist, because it beats working for a living."

This sounded like an old industry cliche to me, so I ran for the hills (didn't really).

I had always had a deep distrust of work – the 9 to 5. The best thing I ever wrote at school was an anti-work essay. I was 15 and hadn't done a day's graft in my life. My favourite sitcom, meanwhile, was The Fall and Rise of Reginald Perrin, in which the hero, played by the Liverpool-born, Everton-supporting Leonard Rossiter, was a downtrodden and disillusioned wage slave looking to escape his life of daily drudgery.

Peter's line didn't convince me, and I didn't really give it any more thought – until now. I think he was right all those years ago, when he spoke to me in the Wigan office of the *Lancs Evening Post*.

What, really, did I end up doing to earn my living? I talked to people, mostly. Talked to people one-to-one (always the best way, especially for a shy person like me), wrote down or recorded what they said and then typed it up – to enable other people to read what they had told me. I talked to people. That's all. Usually interesting people, who had something to say.

Writing – feature writing – was all I wanted to do, really. I thought it was more interesting than being a news reporter – and far, far more interesting than working on a news desk or being a more senior executive.

I've never been able to understand anyone who went into journalism because they wanted to end up answering phones or attending endless, mindless meetings. The money is better, but is that enough? I didn't think so.

Talking to people. Talking to people about Liverpool - and life. And writing. That's what it was all about for me.

I think I was one of the lucky ones. I arrived in the promised land of *Echo* features (Kendrick christened it the cocktail lounge, the cheeky bastard) after three years as an *Echo* district reporter, to add to the three years of news reporting at the *Lancs Evening Post* (mostly spent living and working in the severely underrated town of Wigan).

The joy of being a feature writer is that you can write about any and every subject, which may or may not be in the news. As such, I was often able to stray into so many different worlds – including music, football and politics, without needing to have a music column or be a full-time football or politics reporter. My apologies to any former colleagues who thought I was invading their territory!

But it wasn't all beer and skittles – there was a certain amount of unpleasantness, like that time I was sent shit in the post (more of which later). Hey, you digi kids of today's newsrooms – never mind all those mean Tweets, this was old school trolling!

Paddy Shennan, 2022

Chapter One

Face-to-face
with a killer

I WASN'T expecting to find myself in an otherwise empty pub car park, casually chatting to a murderer.

Then again, I didn't know at the time that I was talking to a cold-blooded killer. On Tuesday, February 9, 1988, Helen McCourt, a 22-year-old insurance clerk, caught her usual bus at the end of another working day in Liverpool. But she never made it to her home in Billinge, near St Helens.

At the time I was a district reporter covering Ormskirk, Skelmersdale and Southport for the *Liverpool Echo*, but I was asked to team up with Harry Dean, the *Echo's* St Helens reporter, so I could help him on this big story. I'm not sure how much help I ended up being, though things could easily have been dramatically different.

The news desk wanted me to see if I could find out any background information which could be added to Harry's reports. I assumed the pub closest to Helen's home, the George and Dragon, would be a good place to start – perhaps the landlord or landlady knew her, and could give me some quotes.

It wasn't yet opening time and immediately after I arrived a man parked up in the car park and headed around the corner towards the front door – it had to be the landlord. I stopped him in his tracks, explained who I was and asked if it was his pub. Yes, he said.

And did he know Helen McCourt?

Yes, he said.

So could we go inside for a quick chat?

Yes, he said.

But the landlord was then greeted by detectives in the doorway – maybe two or three of them.

It was clear they wanted to talk to him. Nothing unusual in that, of course, as the police were gathering information from a great many people at that time. But, not sensing the potential importance of these particular enquiries, all I could think of was the story that I could see slipping away.

Which is why I blurted out something like, "Excuse me, but am I OK to have a quick chat with him for the *Echo* first?"

No, I was told.

Quite bluntly.

Obviously.

I wouldn't have to wait too long to find out why.

The police ended up charging the landlord, Ian Simms, with Helen's abduction and murder, and he appeared before St Helens magistrates on Monday, February 15.

In March, 1989, at Liverpool Crown Court, thanks to overwhelming DNA evidence, Simms was found guilty and jailed for life – with a minimum tariff of 16 years.

It is believed he killed Helen inside that very pub, although he has always refused to say what he did with her body.

As well as continuing the heartbreaking search for her daughter's remains, Helen's mum, Marie, tirelessly campaigned for a change in the law which would deny killers parole if they did not reveal where the remains of their victims were located.

In November 2020, 'Helen's Law' gained Royal Assent, and it was enacted in January 2021. And in October 2021, it was reported that Glyn Razzell, from Somerset – who is serving a life sentence for the murder of his 41-year-old wife Linda Razzell, and has refused to reveal the location of her body – had his parole bid turned down under the new law.

But the change to the legislation came too late in Helen's case – Simms had become a free man in February 2020, after serving 32 years in jail.

Chapter Two

Confessions of a feature writer

THERE IS never any shortage of hard news for journalists to get stuck into – you don't have to look too far for it.

I've never gone along with those who believe newspapers ought to ignore bad news, but it's impossible to overstate the importance of having some light to go along with the dark – and the feature pages were always a good place to shine this light.

My long-time colleague and friend Joe Riley – who starred in the *Liverpool Echo* Pub Guide as Big Fat Joe – always said features (interviews, columns and so on) provided a paper with its personality. And every personality, of course, should include a sense of humour.

I wrote about anything and everything during my time at the *Echo* – including the hardest of hard news stories – but I was always keen to insert a little lightness and humour into the working day, whenever possible.

***

Behind The Scenes at Ann Summers, April 13, 2012

My behind the scenes trip into the previously unknown was for a series called – you aren't going to believe this – 'Behind The Scenes'. It was subtitled 'Interesting people, interesting jobs'. And *Echo* photographer Colin Lane and I had an enjoyable and entertaining time at Ann Summers, though, to be honest, I think Col got more out of it than me.

Here's an extract from my feature...

***

I was picking up good vibrations as I walked around the Ann Summers store in Liverpool One. It was all to do with the F word – the word which, let's be honest, this High Street company seems to be all about.

Fun.

This being a family newspaper, there was no need for myself and *Echo* photographer Colin Lane to be whipped into line, although a PR woman at Ann Summers HQ did stress there were to be no photos taken near the sex toy area (discreetly positioned at the back of the shop, if you're an Ann Summers virgin and want to know where they keep their cute little, and not so little, 'rabbits').

Anyway, let's crack on.

Wow, look at that! There's a bloke behind the counter, to the right of the Pasta Boobs.

Mmmm, yum yum, what man can resist pasta?

Manager Vicky Grant introduces me to her assistant manager, the Alex James from Blur lookalike, Tom Fowler.

Come on Tom, what's the best thing about your job?

He tells me: "Your customer service skills here have to be a notch above everywhere else, so it's the satisfaction you get from making customers feel more confident in themselves and about their bodies."

And the worst? A big smile appears on his face, and some very specific memories flood into his mind: "When people bring a sex toy back and you have to get your gloves on! One person told me 'The dog chewed it!'"

Later during our visit, area manager Nicola Collins told me: "There is no need for any customer to feel embarrassed because we have heard it all before – nothing can shock us! But in Liverpool, people are often very vocal and not scared to say which products they did and didn't like."

But one or two people have asked questions the staff weren't expecting. Manager Vicky Grant said: "One person asked if we sold umbrellas!"

There were one or two things I saw on my tour of the store which I wasn't totally sure about, but they definitely weren't umbrellas.

Confessions of... a funeral director, February 26, 2015

My 'Confessions of...' series was a variation on the 'Behind The Scenes' theme, and saw me putting a dozen customised questions to people with fascinating jobs. And, in some cases, it was shown that you can be totally serious about, and dedicated to, your work, but still retain your potentially sanity-preserving sense of humour.

I wasn't particularly expecting to smile, and certainly not laugh, at any of the answers from Andy Bannon, managing director of Desmond L. Bannon and Sons, which has funeral homes in Stoneycroft, Gateacre Village and Smithdown Road.

I was, therefore, in for a nice surprise.

Andy told me about some of the more unusual choices of songs to be played at a loved one's funeral. They included Happiness by Ken Dodd, Paddy McGinty's Goat – and a song called Bugger Off by Fiddler's Green. It includes the line, "Bugger off, you bastards!" And I asked Andy to tell me about anything that had gone wrong...

He revealed: "Around 30 odd years ago, we took a guy home to his family in Liverpool 8. The coffin was placed in the living room and we were coming back the next day for the funeral. So that next day, my late dad, Des, and my Uncle Bernie were shown into the living room and saw the coffin was empty. It was a case of 'He was there last night, wasn't he?'

"Then they opened the curtains which separated off another part of the room and saw the fella was being propped up on the sofa in between his two brothers, who wanted a last picture taken of them all together.

"On another occasion, also about 30 years ago, there was a funeral in Childwall on a very icy day and two of our former pallbearers, Tom and Charlie, were struggling because of the conditions.

"Old Charlie fell into the grave, but said 'It's OK, I've still got a hold of the coffin.' And then old Tom looked down at him and said 'It hardly seems worth you coming up, Charlie!'"

Confessions of… a pub landlady, February 12, 2015

The 'Confessions of…' series was full of interesting insights.

Fiona Hornsby, then licensee of Thomas Rigby's on Dale Street (she and hubby Dom today have their own places – The Bridewell on Campbell Square and the Denbigh Castle on Hackins Hey), told me: "Lots of people seem to want to have sex in the toilets – why would you?!

"I'd say, while checking the toilets to make sure they're clean and tidy, we would catch a couple every eight to 12 weeks – and there will be others we don't catch.

"Sometimes you can tell before they're in the toilets – there's a walk and a kind of look. So then you leave it a minute, let them get going and then walk in and say 'Hey!' The reaction is usually denial, with one of them saying they were 'helping' the other because he or she wasn't feeling well. And, of course, they're totally embarrassed."

***

I wondered later whether that article, and Fiona's remarks, made people think twice about having sex in pub toilets.

Probably not, the dirty beggars.

Confessions of…an A&E worker, March 5, 2015

Later, it was the turn of Rob Jackson, an emergency nurse

clinician at the Royal Liverpool University Hospital, to inform and entertain our readers.

What were the funniest/oddest things he had seen in A&E? He told me: "People from time to time come in with things stuck in different orifices. Many have slipped while in the bathroom and impaled themselves on shampoo bottles or deodorant cans. We've also seen people with milk bottles, cans of hair mousse and even a butternut squash, which have mysteriously made their way into their cavities. We've heard all the excuses, and we believe none of them."

Harsh. And, err, ouch!

Happy 800th birthday, Liverpool, 2007

There were laughs to be had at the expense of the great and the good – together with the likes of Margaret Thatcher, Kelvin MacKenzie, Norman Tebbit, Jeffrey Archer and Robert Mugabe – courtesy of The Paddy Shennan Birthday Letters, which asked them to wish Liverpool a 'Happy 800th birthday.' Basically, the more unpopular the recipient the more piss-taking my letter – and then we printed my letters and, if they came, the replies.

The letters idea was the brainchild of *Echo* deputy editor Andrew Campbell (a very good DJ as well as a journalist, by the way), who had been inspired by The Timewaster Letters by Robin Cooper – which were in the same, wonderfully absurd vein as the earlier Henry Root Letters (the work of William Donaldson). I loved both, and was therefore more than happy to get writing.

August 14, 2007

Dear Baron Norman Beresford Tebbit... Great name!

Listen Norm, Liverpool will be celebrating its 800th birthday this summer and the Echo is contacting 'The Great and The Good' to ask them if they would kindly wish this proud city many happy returns.

We also wanted to get in touch with leading members of the Conservative government which had such an amazing impact on the city, especially in the dark, dismal and depressing days of the 1980s.

As Secretary of State for Unemployment between 1981 and 1983 and Secretary of State for No Trade and No Industry (1983-1985) – proud days in the Tories' factory-closing, dole-queue expanding programme, I'm sure you'll agree, Tebbo! – your name was certainly on many people's lips in this city.

*Your dad got on his bike and looked for work, then you came along, took all the work away and, just for good measure, said "Oi, you, hand over them f*****g bikes, or I'll stop your dole!" What larks.*

Anyway, to show you no longer wish us any harm, we'd like to give you the chance to wish Liverpool a very happy 800th birthday. Go on, Norm, be a sport and we'll say no more about the bad old days – and your part in them!

Paddy Shennan

And it was so nice to get a reply...

Dear Sir,

Lord Tebbit has asked me to acknowledge your letter of 16th March. Lord Tebbit does not reply personally to childish and abusive correspondence.

Yours faithfully, Private Secretary (illegible signature)

***

Childish? The cheeky bloody sod. At least Tebbit replied, though, if not personally. Thatcher didn't. No idea why not. A day earlier, we carried the following charming request of mine...

Thatch,

They say time is a great healer and I guess, over the years, you've often hoped the city of Liverpool (yes, we're still here despite the Tory Blitz – Hitler had a go, too!) has found it within its famous, big, open, warm and generous heart to forgive you your sins. Well, it hasn't.

But never mind, hey, because we'd like to give you the opportunity to try and repair just a miniscule amount of the shocking damage you inflicted on this city during your reign of terror while you were, truly, the enemy within, by inviting you to wish Liverpool a very happy birthday – we're 800 in August. Even older than you!

Your place in history is assured – but there's no use crying over spilt milk – so come on Maggie ("Maggie! Maggie! Out! Out! Out!"), send us your best; we've already seen your worst.

Paddy Shennan

In the same edition, we printed kind and courteous replies from the likes of Sir Alex Ferguson, Jose Mourinho and Sir Cliff Richard – but no, there wasn't even so much as an insult from The Thatcher or her lackeys.

Blimey, even Jeffrey Archer replied to the following piece of piss-taking, which we ran on the same day as our Tebbit exchange.

Yo Jeffrey,

And to think so many know-nothing nincompoops continue to insult us by claiming David Cameron is "down with the kids." Bloody heck, you are so down with the kids you actually taught some of them how to read and write while you were in choky!

Talking of which, it must have been hard for you in there. And for what, exactly, were you sent down? Simply telling a few whoppers. What's the world coming to when you can't tell a porky or two, while under oath, in court? Ridiculous.

But never mind that, because we'd like to invite you to say a very happy birthday to Liverpool. As we're sure you already know (you know everything and have done everything!) we're 800 years old this summer.

We know you love Liverpool with a passion. You were a close personal friend of all the Beatles (well, there was that one picture you posed for with them) and a close, personal friend of Frank Smith of Frank's Café on the Dock Road (well, there was that one picture you posed for with him during a by-election campaign – May 9, 1991).

Incidentally, your party (why do so many of its members

seem ashamed of you, Jeff – jealousy?) obviously touched many a Liverpudlian's life between 1979 and 1997. Don't worry, we've still got one or two factories left, which is more than can be said for Tory MPs!

Only joking! So come on, Lord, you strike us as a great sport, send us a birthday greeting... and we promise to read your books.

Paddy Shennan

Dear Paddy,
Many thanks for your letter regarding the great city of Liverpool's 800th birthday. Happy 800th Liverpool. I salute the city that will never walk alone and which will be triumphant long after all of us are dust.

With best wishes. Yours ever, Jeffrey

***

I hate to give the man a compliment, but that's the way to do it. I obviously wasn't really bothered about Thatcher's snub, but I had hoped for a reply from Professor Stephen Hawking – not least because I had asked him a very important question.

August 16, 2007

Dear Professor,
You are, without doubt, a very clever man. No, don't be

modest! You know loads and loads about cosmology and quantum gravity, especially in the context of black holes.

You have also provided theorems regarding singularities in the framework of general relativity and made studies in the fields of quantum cosmology, cosmic inflation, helium production in anisotropic Big Bang universes, large N cosmology, the density matrix of the universe, topology and the structure of the universe, baby universes, Yang-Mills instantons and the S matrix, anti de Sitter space, quantum entanglement and entropy and the nature of space and time (including the arrow of time), spacetime foam, string theory, supergravity, Euclidean quantum gravity, gravitational Hamiltonian, Brans-Dicke and Hoyle-Narlikar theories of gravitation, gravitational radiation and wormholes.

But can you tell me the answer to the following...

Richard Madeley – why?

Even if you can't answer this very tricky question, we would be delighted if you could send Liverpool a special birthday greeting... the city will be 800 years old this summer. That's what I call cosmic!

Paddy Shennan

Ah well, you can't win 'em all.

Chapter Three

A right royal soap opera

"THE LORD Mayor of Liverpool, Councillor Jack Spriggs, requests the pleasure of the company of Mr Paddy Shennan at the Golden Jubilee Luncheon at Liverpool Town Hall in the presence of Her Majesty The Queen and His Royal Highness The Duke of Edinburgh, Thursday, 25th July, 2002."

I still don't know whose idea it was to put my name forward for this arduous assignment but, really… what were they thinking? There was no way I was going to look a free lunch (or "luncheon") in the mouth. It would make a nice change from my usual Sainsbury's or Tesco meal deal and, if I was feeling greedy, steak bake from Greggs.

And then there was the joy to be had from writing a tongue-in-cheek feature documenting the delightfully indulgent afternoon I had enjoyed at other people's expense (though it would have been more satisfying if it had been at the Queen's).

It wasn't a straightforward process, though. Apart from an awkward encounter with Phil, I remember there was some last-minute unease about my two-page feature.

That morning after the luncheon, I had spoken to someone in the city council press office who didn't believe an *Echo* employee, having been graciously invited to dine with Her Madge, should be writing an irreverent piece about the occasion.

Then, having relayed this information, I was told editor Mark Dickinson had the willies about going ahead with it. If this was the case, his deputy, Jon Brown, who I had been liaising with over the feature and had no qualms, must have been able to calm any nerves as my piece of harmless nonsense duly appeared.

It was headlined, "The day I had lunch with Her Majesty – What happens when a republican is invited to a royal lunch? Paddy Shennan reports."

***

Snubbed by the Queen!

That's the last time I buy any stamps.

And I'd been so looking forward to hearing who she's voting for in tonight's Big Brother final (you don't think she's a Jade fan, do you?)

I would have asked Prince Philip, but I was thrown when he walked towards me and opened his plum-filled mouth… I just couldn't get his Spitting Image puppet out of my head. Then, it happened. As she was apparently saying "Oh, really" to a succession of people in the other line (five times in a minute, I was told) the Queen's gaffe-prone partner shook my hand weakly – and made an equally feeble "joke."

After being introduced to myself and my colleague,

Liverpool *Daily Post and Echo* IT business manager Paula Beer, Phil said: "I see. So she does something in the *Post* and you *Echo* it!" As I grinned an embarrassed grin and muttered "Err, no, not really," the Duke moved onto Canon Neville Black, who spoke to him about Liverpool's Strategic Housing Partnership.

"I used to be President of the National Federation of Housing Associations," said Phil, who was then asked by the clergyman: "And did you enjoy it?" There was a long pause before His Dukeness replied: "What a silly question."

He then moved along but, having noticed that the Queen was still saying "Oh, really" a couple of yards behind him (it's not done to walk in front), he turned back and had another go at me. "There must be more than a couple of newspapers in Liverpool," he said, with a hint of abrasiveness. Though tempted to say that the national papers were also available, but few people bought them, I told him about Merseyside's weekly papers and, in response to a follow-up query, explained how far and wide the *Post* and *Echo* are sold. He nodded and wandered off. Although it looked like he might nod off at any minute. God, it must be a tedious life being the Duke of Edinburgh. And the Queen. He's 81. She's 76. It may not be work in the traditional sense, but being choked by the air of formality at stuffy function after stuffy function can't be much fun either. Rather them than me. Even though she didn't speak to me, I can tell anyone who is likely to be impressed by these sorts of things that the Queen and I did have lunch together. Well, it was the Queen, me and more than 200 others.

It was interesting to see how the other half lives. Well, not "half," more like a tiny fraction. The glittering venue for this glittering occasion was Liverpool Town Hall's main ballroom and the Royal party was joined by community representatives, business leaders, councillors and the Lord Mayor.

Why was I there? Why shouldn't I have been? I pay my taxes. Why should it only be arch-royalists who are treated to a spot of top nosh with the "big" nobs and nobesses?

In a very helpful letter, Jean Evans, head of the Lord Mayor's office, said: "May I remind you that, if addressed by Her Majesty, the initial response is 'Your Majesty' and thereafter 'Ma'am' (pronounced 'Mam' to rhyme with 'Jam'), and, for His Royal Highness, 'Your Royal Highness' and 'Sir' thereafter."

I had a problem with this. Just like I have a problem when England's football fans sing "Rule Britannia, Britannia rules the waves." Let's face it, she doesn't.

And Betty and Phil are neither higher nor better than you and me. But I've been brought up well. I'm a man of manners. The danger – if, that is, I could have got close to the Queen – was that I'd lose face with fellow republicans by saying "Your extremely high and much-better-than-me Majesty. I am not worthy. Who am I? What am I? I'm nothing. I'm the dirt on your shoe – or I would be if you ever got your shoes dirty."

The letter of advice continued: "Gentlemen bow from the neck and ladies adopt a bob curtsey, although I am advised that The Queen has let it be known that this is no longer considered essential." Oh, has she now? How wonderfully generous and selfless of the planet's most pampered pensioner.

As the Queen and Prince Philip entered the room and stood just feet away, I realised how close I was to infamy. My picture could be on the front page of every newspaper in the world – all I had to do was swear at them or say something outrageous.

Thankfully, I kept my mouth shut – until Prince Philip spoke to me. Did I bow? I don't think so, although Paula, who was wearing a camp brooch featuring Queenie's head, thought she saw some movement. She can't have.

Sitting between Liverpool city council chief executive David Henshaw and Mayor of Liverpool, Cllr Jack Spriggs, Her Madge seemed happy enough and she ate all her grub. I'm not surprised, because head chef Roy Aidoo and his team did a sterling job.

The Prince was on table two, as was Yoko Ono (is this why Sir Paul McCartney wasn't at the lunch?). She was sandwiched between the Recorder of Liverpool His Honour Judge David Clarke QC and Merseyside Chief Constable Norman Bettison.

I wonder what they talked about. Sex and drugs and rock 'n' roll? Or perhaps Yoko asked Norman whether he knew that John Lennon's mum, Julia, was knocked down and killed by an off-duty police officer.

There was also a Yoko Ono lookalike (well, sort of) serving, which was a bit confusing – as were all the women of a certain age who were wearing the Queen's pastel green.

In her short speech, the Queen – who was struggling with a frog in her throat – talked of the "once tense" relationship between Merseyside and Greater Manchester. If she goes to a Liverpool-Man United game next season, she may remove the word "once" next time. It was a wonderfully strange and ridiculously unreal day for me but, I imagine, a pretty common one for them. My God, so that means they must have thought this was normal! You have my deepest sympathy.

FREE THE BUCK HOUSE TWO!

And the answer to the BIG question – what did we eat?

– *Combination of fresh crab and mango encased in smoked halibut, served with sweet chilli dressing.*

– *Breast of Barbary Duckling served on a bed of sweet potato rosti, surrounded by rich rosemary jus. Selection of market fresh vegetables and roast barrel potatoes.*

– *Mousseline of passion fruit set on raspberry coulis, garnished with Langues de Chat. Coffee and petit fours.*

Like the Queen, I cleared my plate – though I found the food so rich, I recall craving the simple goodness of Heinz spaghetti hoops on toast for tea that night.

***

What the butler saw, June 14, 2004

One of the most enjoyable things about interviewing people is that you have the final word – you are the person who, after talking to your subject, goes back to the keyboard and types in whatever you want to say (within reason), presenting it in whatever way you want (within reason). Interviewing Paul Burrell, the late Princess Diana's controversial former butler, was a brilliant assignment. I was convinced it was going to be a thoroughly entertaining and enjoyable experience.

After all, the butler had seen all sorts of apparently high and mighty things and loved to talk about them – while I loved taking the mickey. It was a perfect combination! I saw an open goal ahead, and was determined not to miss it.

***

Loose-lipped Paul Burrell, the former butler-turned-international-best-selling author, just can't stop talking balls…

And I'm not referring to Euro 2004.

We're having a chinwag in Liverpool's Crowne Plaza hotel, a couple of hours before the amiable chatterbox – former job description: Princess Diana's "rock" – is to sign copies of the new paperback edition of his 1.1million-selling book A Royal Duty in a city centre store. Cue balls… Burrell's balls, Prince Charles's balls and, bless my soul, the Queen's balls. "I couldn't believe the Queen had bigger balls than her son," says Burrell, referring to Her Majesty's 11th hour intervention, which led to the collapse of his trial at the Old Bailey, where he had pleaded not guilty to the theft of items belonging to Diana. "That is a crude expression, but it's true. She came forward and saved me, and it should have been her son or somebody else. I didn't expect the monarch to do it." Took her time, though.

"But it was an unprecedented situation. No reigning monarch had ever intervened in a criminal court case before. And she is the law, it's Regina versus you."

New balls, please.

"My wife, Maria, always said the princess had me by the balls in her lifetime and still has me by the balls now. And that's true, in a way. You don't forget the people who made you who you are." The way Paul Burrell, a 46-year-old father-of-two, from Farndon, near Chester, talks about the late Diana, Princess of Wales, you would think she was more than a mere mortal while she was alive and, in death, an archangel.

He's either an incredibly good actor, or he really did worship this woman – and still does. "Take away the fact that she was a princess, she was an extraordinary human being," he says. "And when you've been touched by magic, it does change the rest of your life. People say, 'Oh God, you're obsessed with her.' I'm not obsessed. I have a passion. She was a very special lady.

"Wasn't I a lucky man? I know that and every day of my life I used to say that to her when I served her breakfast. I used to look at that fresh face scrubbed clean, with that white towelling robe wrapped around her, and she'd say 'Pull up a chair and have a cup of coffee.' And I'd say to her, 'Do you know how lucky I am?' And she'd reply, 'Oh Paul, get out. Just stop it.'"

Did you fancy her, then?

Sadly, he skilfully sidesteps this and takes the conversation to a higher plane – and the word "love."

He says: "It means different things to different people, love. She was a very beautiful woman and I defy any man to have not lost their heart to her because she was so special and such a funny, charismatic creature. Her lifeforce was the attraction; the way she flirted with her eyes, the way she'd look at you, the way she'd respond to you and the touch – that very special sort of human touch."

Right, so has your missus ever been jealous – or is she superhuman?

"Jealousy is the wrong word. She resented it sometimes, that the princess took me away, when I should have been at home with my children (sons Alexander and Nicholas are now 19 and 16, respectively). But she is very unselfish and she knew the princess came first in my world – and that's very selfish of me as a father and husband. But Diana did come first because she needed me more than anyone else needed me. She was a very needy person and I was needy – I needed to be needed by her, in a strange way. And the more we needed each other, the more we cemented… it was like superglue, you couldn't tear us apart."

Did she fancy you, then? Sorry, was there a chemistry between you?

"There had to be some kind of chemistry there. I'd like to think a little bit of me rubbed off on her and a little bit of her rubbed off on me – and I think that says it all."

Say no more. No, actually, please say some more!

"It was a platonic relationship which went beyond the boundary of friendship and blood relations. You can choose your friends but you can't choose your family."

Diana and her rock even went kerb-crawling together. No, really...

"She did this to me all the time. She'd drive me down to Paddington Station and round the corner to where all the girls were working. She'd then wind the window down on my side, so the girls would come and lean in the window and chat to me – and she would be wetting herself in the driver's seat. I was horrified and would say 'One day we're going to get arrested!' and she'd say 'Chill out!'"

If she could speak to you today, would she be saying 'Chill out – and please switch off that word processor, for the sake of my kids'?

"I can tell you honestly, she would be shouting at me from the highest rooftop, 'Get on with it. Don't let them squash my memory.'"

But what of the former lights of her life, her children, William and Harry? They have described your book as a "cold and overt betrayal."

"I am not the betrayer. Prince Charles betrayed the princess first. He went on TV and admitted adultery to the whole world. How do you think she felt? She didn't have a voice. She wrote things down on paper and she told me. There are things that happened behind those closed doors which, quite frankly, I haven't got the stomach to repeat, because they're so sad. That woman was a tortured soul."

Yes, Charles went on TV and Diana went on TV, but do three wrongs make a right? "I've only written a loving tribute to the princes' mother. It's a matter of defending her memory.

"Anyone who loved the princess will love the book." And he adds: "The boys' mother has become an icon, and people will be writing about her in 20, 30 years' time. They have to come to terms with that."

Burrell has had no contact with William or Harry since their mother died in 1997, although there have long been rumours of a, no doubt frosty, reunion – will there be a meeting, as has been suggested? "I'd like to think so. If it did happen, it would be behind closed doors and what we had to say would never be repeated. People will say, 'How can we know that?' Because, quite frankly, their mother trusted me, the Queen trusted me and, I think, William and Harry can trust me."

But can we trust you not to write another book?

"I've no plans to write one. I'll never say 'Never' because I've said that once before. I said I'd never write this one, but I had to set the record straight."

Is there enough material for a second?

"It's possible to write 10 books," he says, before laughing.

But Mr Burrell, this is not a laughing matter. What would be a laughing matter is if "staunch monarchist" Paul Burrell declared that his experiences had persuaded him to adopt the republican cause. Strangely, they haven't…

"That surprises most people – although I might become a republican if Charles and Camilla ascend the throne! But I do feel the monarchy needs to be reshaped, so it is in tune with modern-day thinking."

He adds: "I'm a huge supporter of the Queen and long may she reign, for as long as she's on the throne it's safe. I personally don't think we'll ever see King Charles III and Queen Camilla on the throne of England."

What about Charles as King and Camilla lurking, as usual, somewhere in the shadows?

"I don't think it's going to happen. The princess said she didn't think he was fit for the top job, and I think she's right."

Oh blimey, I feel another book coming on. And a film, and a T-shirt and…

Paul Burrell. You are a charming man and have done much, I feel, for the republican cause but… have you ever considered early retirement?

Scouser Queenie

Calm down, calm down, because it's true: the Queen can do a mean Scouse accent…

Paul Burrell, who began working as a footman at Buckingham Palace when he was just 18, says: "The Queen does a fantastic Liverpool accent.

"When she returns from a visit to Liverpool, everybody will be standing around asking 'How did your day go?' and she'll say 'Did you see that man who said 'You alright there, queenie?'

"And she'll do the Liverpool accent and everyone will have their mouths open and be thinking 'That's hilarious, because that's our monarch!'

"But she means it in fond respect, because she loves going around the country listening to what people have to say. You might think she's got this hard, straight face but, inside, she's soft and squidgy." And of Princess Diana, he says: "I know she had fond memories of being in Liverpool and the people in Liverpool, because this is a place where you find characters.

"It's a part of the world I know well, because my in-laws are from Liverpool. They grew up in the Scottie Road area. My mother-in-law, Betty, who now lives with us, has fond memories of going down to the docks and spins such stories about the characters she's known."

And the man who owns a flower shop in Holt, near Wrexham, adds: "I see Liverpool characters on a regular basis. I go down to the flower market in Edge Lane and they all shout 'Alright, mate?' to me.

"They're honest and forthright and don't mind what they say – and you don't get that in London."

Chapter Four

'Look! It's those people from the telly!'

Legacy of the Blackstuff, October 21, 2002

I'VE ONLY written to the BBC on one occasion – and Alan Bleasdale was the reason.

It was in the autumn of 1982, when Alan's Boys From The Blackstuff made its TV debut, on BBC2. I was 18 and on the dole.

I loved it and thought it was important – so much so that I fervently believed it had to be repeated as soon as possible, and this time placed before a wider audience, on BBC1. Furthermore, this had to happen before the next General Election (which turned out to be in June, 1983) because – and this is how naive I was – its repeat screening would surely mean that Margaret Thatcher and the Tories would be unceremoniously thrown out of office.

Alan and I discussed all this when we met up in the Crowne Plaza Hotel on the Liverpool waterfront – just down the road from where George Malone took his "last ride" around the then derelict Albert Dock – to mark the 20th anniversary of Blackstuff.

***

Alan Bleasdale, who's currently working on a feature film, describes himself as a refugee from British television.

I think British television – all soft soap, soft drama and gormless reality shows – should be begging him to come back. The man from Mossley Hill – who gave the world classic TV series including GBH, The Monocled Mutineer, and, of course, Scully – is sitting in a Liverpool hotel talking about the 20th anniversary of his groundbreaking five-part drama Boys From the Blackstuff.

But only because I twisted his arm.

Alan only had a vague idea the anniversary was looming: "I don't look back," says the 56-year-old. "I swear to you it's 20 years since I've seen any of that series." You should put the videos on, Alan, it's pretty good stuff, you know.

"But because I don't think about it, it is nice to sit here and recall the events."

Oh, it's more than that. Boys From The Blackstuff (which grew out of Alan's 1980 BBC2 play The Black Stuff) was first shown on BBC2 in October and November 1982, having been "knocked back" by BBC1. But then, just nine weeks after it finished its run, the series was repeated... on BBC1. It was a record, and it still stands.

Jobs For The Boys, Moonlighter, Shop Thy Neighbour, Yosser's Story and George's Last Ride. Five incredible, inter-linking plays which provoked a massive reaction. Britain was freefalling into a chronic state of recession and unemployment. And industrial cities like Liverpool, in particular, were being hit hard. Where it hurts.

Boys From The Blackstuff, which won the BAFTA for best drama series, told the human stories behind the economic misery, focusing on the former tarmac-laying gang of Chrissie Todd (Michael Angelis); Logo Lomond (Alan Igbon); Dixie Dean (Tom Georgeson); Yosser Hughes (Bernard Hill) and George Malone (Peter Kerrigan).

Julie Walters played Chrissie's wife, Angie; Gary Bleasdale (the son of Alan's cousin) played Dixie's son, Kevin, and Alan's children – Timothy, then 11; Tamana, then eight, and Jamie, then seven – played Yosser's children.

It was emotional, powerful and passionate stuff. Harrowing, heartbreaking but, somehow, occasionally hilarious. Alan says: "I think we all knew what we were doing was good but I don't think any of us knew the effect it would have and the reception we were going to get. People I met in the street were great, as they were later with GBH. The worst response I've ever had to anything I've done was for The Monocled Mutineer. I got some real hate mail from retired colonels in Bognor Regis."

But while they may not have been delivered personally, there were, for Blackstuff, some brickbats to go with the bouquets: "There were some letters in the *Echo*, but I never respond. I've had the opportunity to give my opinion and people have then given theirs. So it's a one-all draw. And if someone is a right-wing fascist, one conversation or letter isn't going to change his or her mind."

Recalling the Liverpool of the late '70s and early '80s, Alan says: "It was a city built on casual labour, which meant we were going to be among the first to suffer. They just looked around and thought 'Well, they can go.' You knew Liverpool was going to take a terrible battering. That battering hadn't occurred while I was writing it, but you would have been a fool not to know it was on the way." But he stresses: "I knew the series wasn't going to change anything. I just hoped it was going to open people's eyes and make them think.

"People have asked 'How important do you think it was to British political life?' I just point to the next General Election result – a landslide victory for Margaret Thatcher in 1983."

What, though, of the Boys From The Blackstuff?

Chrissie Todd (Michael Angelis). Alan says: "I knew the Yosser part would be the unforgettable one, but the true, main character of the whole piece, for me, was Chrissie – because he was your common man. I adored what Michael and Julie Walters (Angie) did in that famous scene (in which she's yelling at him to 'fight back'.) It was shot at 6.58pm on a Wednesday in my brother-in-law's house in Wavertree. We had to be out at 7pm. It wasn't my brother-in-law saying 'I want my house back,' it was union rules. This was before Thatcher really got a grip!"

George Malone (Peter Kerrigan). George was based on two other Georges in the writer's life; his uncle, George Grant, and father, George Bleasdale: "George Malone had the same attributes. It was that kind of tremendously dignified and quiet compassion and understanding of people – and also generosity of spirit. My uncle, for example, ran an unofficial citizens advice bureau in the Dingle." Peter Kerrigan, meanwhile, was an ad-libber. In the final episode, George's Last Ride, he delivered the defiant words of a principled, dying man – ending with the famous "I can't believe that there's no hope." That line was not Alan's, it was Peter's: "He kept saying to me 'There's got to be hope.' He came out with such gems. With Peter, you got the real thing."

Yosser Hughes (Bernard Hill). Bernard Hill was nominated for a best actor BAFTA and received the Press Guild Award for Achievement of The Decade, for his portrayal of Yosser, the maniacal man in black whose lines – including "Gizza job. Go on, giz it. I could do that!" – became national catch-phrases. But although proud of his performance, the actor is always keen to remind journalists, when they dare to mention the 'Y' word, that it was all a long time ago. Is Alan upset when he reads such interviews, or does he have some sympathy?

"It doesn't upset me, but I have no sympathy. He gave an extraordinary performance and won all sorts of awards. All I can say is that Bernard was the finest actor I'd ever seen in my life.

"I can understand that he would always worry about being only known for one part, but his career has been such that he shouldn't think that now. But I could never hold a grudge against Bernard. He gave the great, definitive performance of his generation."

Loggo Lomond (Alan Igbon). "I thought that Alan Igbon's performance was so underrated. It wasn't an easy part to play. Here was a character who could only get through his problems by putting a brick wall around himself. He was hurt and he was upset but he didn't want to articulate it. He was going to pretend nothing had happened. He would never show his true feelings."

Dixie Dean (Tom Georgeson). "Tom Georgeson's performance was fantastic. Dixie's tragedy, in a way, was bigger than the others. He believed in a hierarchical society. If people were at the top he thought it was because they deserved to be at the top. He'd been a foreman, but once that role was taken from him he wasn't a man any more."

I wonder where they would have ended up. Alan doesn't...

"I never thought about where I could have taken them, because I just thought I shouldn't touch them. And the actors agreed. We all said we weren't doing it again. There's never been a temptation. Everything fell into place in that series. It was perfect at times. The deep irony is it was about one of the most imperfect times in our society."

A walk on the wild side with our Ricky, November 12, 2008

Ricky Tomlinson was a great friend to me and the *Echo* during my time on the paper. I was delighted to be invited to the party he threw in Ma Boyle's pub in the shadow of Liverpool Parish Church, to celebrate the publication of his autobiography, and to his 70th and (surprise) 80th birthday parties (sorry I couldn't make the 70th, Rick). He also invited me to a memorable afternoon in his company – and at his expense – at a Good Turns Society bash at the police club in Fairfield, Liverpool (the society was founded by Ken Dodd, and held lively afternoon dinner shows for entertainers and celebrities). Ricky was such a generous host that day, I genuinely did fear for my health. After sinking several Guinnesses, I knew I couldn't face another pint – but Ricky was insistent that more alcohol be ordered for everyone on his table: "Err, just the smallest glass of dry white wine then, please, Rick." He turned to the waitress: "A bottle of white wine for Paddy!" But at least I fared better than a colleague (my "plus one") – he ended up falling asleep after the onslaught of generosity and ale.

Ricky also got me involved when he appeared on BBC1's Who Do You Think You Are? I ended up being filmed giving him some information about his family tree – information that came from someone else. It was my friend, genealogist Karen Murphy who had unearthed it, but she wasn't available for the filming, so the programme-makers asked me to pretend I'd done the research.

I did countless stories and features with Ricky over so many years, but there is one that always stands out for me. I thought it would be interesting for *Echo* readers to see the world through the eyes of the incredibly popular star of The Royle Family – by going on a Royle walkabout between Church Street and the *Echo* offices in Old Hall Street, about a 10 to 15-minute walk. But things didn't quite work out as I had planned.

***

A 69-year-old man is standing by a bin opposite Primark in Liverpool city centre. But this is not an ordinary, everyday scene. This is a soon-to-be extraordinary scene, as the pensioner is quickly swamped by hordes of admirers.

This is because he is Ricky Tomlinson – man of the people, Scousers' Scouser and one of the most popular and recognisable faces in Merseyside and the UK.

The plan was simple but the plan, in hindsight, was simply stupid. We wondered what it must be like for someone as famous as Ricky to walk through their city centre, and decided to walk with him from Church Street to the *Echo* in Old Hall Street.

We really should have known better. And so should Ricky, despite him modestly telling me on the phone: "I really don't think anyone will stop and talk to me."

"That's fine," I told him. "We'll just say it shows your career is over."

But the planned 30-minute walk – allowing for time spent signing a few autographs and posing for a few photographs here and there – never happened, because Ricky wasn't able to move. That's right. Rickymania struck somewhere between Schuh and Primark. It was an incredible sight. Think bees around a honey pot. Or crowds of men, women and children of all ages swarming around that big, bearded bloke off the telly who says "My arse" a lot.

First, a small group of teenage lads approach him and politely ask for autographs, as others say – or shout – things like "Hey, it's him from The Royle Family. My arse!" And "I know him! Who is it?"

Interest is growing, as are the number of little groups gathering. A gaggle of girls get in a tizzy: "Gizza pen! Quick, quick!" "You go!" "No, you go, I'm shy!" "Jim! I mean, Ricky, can you sign this please? Can we have a photo?"

Then it's a couple of old ladies – "I've never had so much attention, God bless you, girls!" Then a middle-aged couple. Then some builders. Then some more students. Then some parents with young children.

We're 15 minutes in and the planned walk hasn't started. We try a couple of times, but it's just not going to happen. It was never going to happen.

Taking a brief break from his adoring public, Ricky tells me: "I love the people of Liverpool. Southerners are amazed I still live here, but there is nothing in London I want – everything I want is up here. This is the best city in the world, and I'm proud of the fuss people make of me here." It was, indeed, a right Royle occasion – and there was probably more intense interest and affection in the air than there would be for any member of our official Royal family.

Long live Rickymania!

"No champers for me, Cilla?" September 1, 2003

I was in a bit of a state when I arrived, hot and bothered, in a swish hotel room in London's Covent Garden, to interview Cilla Black, who had recently celebrated her 60th birthday and was about to mark 40 years as an entertainer.

My train had been late getting into Euston, and, fearing I may anger the megastar by not turning up on time, I ran the last leg of the journey. It was a hot day and though I turned up on time, I was sweating profusely.

After Cilla, the second thing my tired eyes spotted was a bottle of bubbly. Oh lovely, me and Cil are in for a sesh... or so I thought.

***

She's a multi-millionaire who loves living the high life and basking in the glory of being the undisputed Queen of Showbiz... but Cilla Black is one very angry woman.

We are sitting in an elegant hotel in London's Covent Garden, an opened bottle of Moët is chilling nicely in an ice bucket on a table (you could have offered me a glass, chuck) and Priscilla Maria Veronica White is here to talk about her wonderful life – and plug her new autobiography.

I have been requested by the publishers not to ask about the recent break-in at her mansion in Denham, Buckinghamshire – Cilla also has pads in London, Spain and Barbados – and shortly after the interview begins, eldest son Robert, who took over as her manager following the death of her beloved Bobby in 1999, comes into the room to ask his mum to "please" stop talking about it.

Cilla – who is supposed to be saving these sort of quotes for her appearance on her good friend Michael Parkinson's BBC1 show on September 20 – looks, for a moment, like a naughty schoolgirl. But she can't help herself and she can't hold back.

***

Back to the champers, though, so I can make a point of clarification…

Yes, it is true that I had my eyes on Cilla's Moët and was hoping for a thirst-quenching and spirit-lifting guzzle, but, to be fair to my hostess, she did ask for someone to fetch me a bottle of water when she saw that I was sweaty, knackered and, most probably, very thirsty. The water was nice and much appreciated, but no, it wasn't Moët.

Right, let's return to Cilla and her anger (and the quotes that should apparently have been exclusively Parky's)…

***

She wants to tell the world what she thinks of the balaclava-clad robbers who raided her home of more than 30 years just over a fortnight ago – and why she's set to sell off all her pricey and previously precious possessions.

A gang of three men burst into her home and attacked the youngest of her three sons, 22-year-old Jack, with a crowbar. They threw him to the ground, put handcuffs on him and threatened to slash his throat with a hunting knife unless he told them where Cilla's valuables were stored. Jack's attackers, who also had plans to kidnap him, eventually made off with £1m worth of Cilla's cash and jewellery, including gifts from Cilla's late husband and her mother's wedding and engagement rings.

"I'm very, very angry. Jack is OK, thank God, although I keep expecting it to hit him any time," says Cilla, who was on holiday at the time of the robbery. "I can't get over the fact that I could have been flying back for a funeral. And I can't get over my anger."

***

Shocking stuff – and it had quickly taken my mind off Cilla's champers.

It was a wide-ranging interview, and I was fascinated to later hear the daughter of Scottie Road talking about her great friend, Paul O'Grady, aka Lily Savage (Cilla just called him "Savage") – who hadn't always been her great friend.

***

Paul had called Cilla that morning to say he'd just had his first decent night's sleep since the break-in.

In her book, Cilla explains how she and "Savage" have been firm friends since they appeared on Parky together in 1998, even though she knew he held a "rather uncomplimentary opinion of me."

Four years earlier, Lil had said of Cil: "I'm sure they bow their heads in shame in Liverpool over her, because no-one speaks like her in that ridiculous accent."

Dismissing her as "a professional Liverpudlian," Lil/Paul also uttered words such as boot-licking, Tory, champagne, monster and guzzling and put them all together – but not in that order. At the time, he said he was being heavily baited by journalists and eventually cracked. But didn't Cilla, the self-respecting superstar, ever tackle the young upstart about his unkind words? "No, I didn't, because my kids and other people, Liverpool people, were telling me how good he was. And I always give people the benefit of the doubt."

***

Many years later, following her death, I was asked to write a piece about Cilla for the *Echo* – and I referred back to that interview in 2003 because one short quote from it really leapt out.

August 3, 2015

She may have been the Queen of Showbusiness, but there was a vulnerable and insecure side to Cilla Black.

To many, she was the consummate professional whose steely determination to succeed, allied to her natural talent, took her to the top and made her seem untouchable – maybe even a little fearsome.

But the girl from Scottie Road once told me: "To be loved is all I ever wanted." Of the latest down – that break-in – in a life of so many highs, she had said: "It's going to take a long time for me to get over what happened to Jack, but I know, when I look back, that I have been blessed in my life. I've been blessed with love, from Bobby, my family and my fans – and to be loved is all I ever wanted. But I believe that to have a great life, you've also got to taste a lot of sorrow."

Maybe I just expected too much on some jobs – like Champagne with Cilla, and a little fine dining with superchef Marcus Wareing.

Heaven's kitchen, May 24, 2004

It was a late lunch and a perfectly enjoyable one. But it could have been so different... my feast was a £1.39 hamburger from Euston station, as opposed to anything off the menu at the restaurant where I had just spent more than three hours in the entertaining company of one of the country's finest chefs.

Still, all I gave him was a £1 stick of Southport rock to remind him of his birthplace. And my host, Churchtown boy Marcus Wareing – business and swearing partner of Gordon "F*** me!" Ramsay – could probably charge people much more than a quid for the privilege of simply smelling his fine food.

It was also remiss of me not to plan ahead and stake my claim for something like caramelised breast of Gressingham duck on white cabbage and sage a' l'Alsacienne with confit lemon, potato fondants, foie gras port veloute, or Arjou pigeon, poached and pan-fried, on a liver and truffle crouton, confit pigeon leg with garlic, red wine shallots and pigeon sauce. There is, after all, around a one-week waiting list for a lunch table at the chef patron's Petrus restaurant at the Berkeley Hotel in London's posh Knightsbridge.

Marcus and I first sat and chewed the fat, metaphorically, in his crisply clean, classy, comfortable and deliciously designed restaurant. Lots of deeply rich claret textures. Mmm, nice. Not to mention the waiters steam-ironing the tablecloths – I've never seen that in a Burger King. We later moved into the gleaming (and calm, rant-free) kitchen, where we sat on the squashy sofas at the Chef's Table, which parties of eight can book for £800 (12 food courses and a bottle of Dom Perignon thrown in, although not literally).

But before my nostrils were to be distracted by the aromas of adventurous-sounding dishes, which have delighted the palettes of a host of la-de-da London food critics, not to mention Madonna, Diana Ross and the not-so-grand and not-so-old Duke of York, I had to establish something of staggering importance. Is Marcus Wareing capable of swearing as well as Gordon Ramsay, his former mentor and now best mate and business equal?

Too f****** right he is! Triumphantly waving his stick of rock (£1, don't forget), he jokes to a waiter: "You f*** around and this goes up your arse!" His employee, David, showing commendable cool, replies: "I never f*** around."

Excellent, I thought. We were cooking on f****** gas.

Later in the interview, I asked him what it f****** was with all the f words: "It's the language of the kitchen. No disrespect to chefs, but most haven't been to university and the ones that have are no f****** good anyway. But what are you supposed to do in the middle of serving in a busy kitchen – politely say 'Excuse me, but can you please tell me when the pigeon will be ready?'?"

Yes, that was an enjoyable f****** morning.

Keith Chegwin, March 14, 2006

I loved Cheggers. I loved his boundless energy, enthusiasm and optimism – and I loved his honesty and openness.

***

The Bootle boy who made his name as a chirpy, cheeky and chubby presenter on the likes of Swap Shop and Cheggers Plays Pop, before he spectacularly fell off his wagon after drinking too much pop, has more bouncebackability than a squad of Olympic trampolinists. Boing! After admitting to being an alcoholic in 1992, Keith, whose parents, Colin and Margaret, live in Rainford, turned his life around and relaunched his TV career, courtesy of his bright-eyed and bushy-tailed appearances on The Big Breakfast.

Boing! After taking his kit off and exposing his wee willy winky on Channel 5's Naked Jungle in 2000 – "That killed my career, and my mum wasn't happy about me doing it" – Keith again fought back, partly through his appearances on GMTV as the bloke who knocks on people's doors and gives them money (some of them have even been known to answer the door). And now the 49-year-old who refuses to stop bouncing is again claiming headlines after launching his own bingo website ("I bloody love bingo" – yes, Keith, but you bloody love everything).

***

How honest was Cheggers? He also told me in that interview, regarding those long-gone, booze-drenched days of utter misery: "I very rarely reflect on it now, but I am so lucky. People often say it must have been the worst thing that ever happened to me. But now, nearly 14 years down the line, I think it's one of the best things that ever happened to me. I know people will knock me for saying that but, in the long term, it did me the world of good. Now, I realise life is so precious, and what I do every minute of every day I enjoy."

Later that year, we saw Cheggers play a homophobic racist in BBC comedy Extras. You may remember the tribute he earned from Ricky Gervais: "I worked with such international megastars as Orlando Bloom, David Bowie, Chris Martin of Coldplay, Sir Ian McKellen, Daniel Radcliffe and Robert Lindsay, but for me the performance of the series comes from a little fat Scouser called Keith Chegwin. It's the most excruciating cameo we've done, including Les Dennis. I don't know why he doesn't act full-time. He was remarkable."

After he died in 2017, I wrote a tribute to Keith in the *Echo,* in which I recalled something he said to me during that 2006 interview: "There is so much trouble in the world and I sometimes think 'Why are we fighting? Why can't we all just get on with life?'

"And I always go to bed with a little thought in my head, 'Let me make people laugh.' I think if you can make people smile, it's such a great thing. I love it."

Cheggers was a man who couldn't help but smile, and make others smile, too.

Gatecrashing The Antiques Roadshow, April 12, 2002

I made my own TV debut in 2002, after turning up at St George's Hall when The Antiques Roadshow came to town.

I was armed with some very old photographs of presenter Michael Aspel, borrowed from the *Echo* library.

***

Michael Aspel. This is NOT Your Life. This is The Antiques Roadshow – and these are some very embarrassing (and antique) photographs.

Of you.

They had been taken between 1959 and 1989 and could, together, be called "Aspel: Those Hair and Fashion Disasters Through The Decades."

The idea was simply to get a picture of Aspel and an expert looking at the old photos, before the expert announced what they weren't worth. But this is television, darlings. And nothing is simple in television.

And so it came to pass that, with the top man filming elsewhere in the building, the Roadshow's Clive Stewart-Lockhart tried to stop laughing long enough to talk me through these quite amazing artefacts: "My God, look at his hair! It looks like it's glued on. Ha ha ha! These are funny!"

Then things got silly. Stewart-Lockhart was unable to resist showing the ageing Aspel pics to members of a film crew working at the next table. They fell about laughing and offered to buy them off me. And then a very important-looking man wearing headphones, perhaps realising this could be one of those Roadshow Moments, said: "Don't move. We're going to film you next."

When everybody was happy that the light wasn't bouncing off the balding expert's bonce, the cameras (well, camera) rolled. It was stop-start stuff. Take. Retake. Close-ups. Sadly, however, I wasn't "made-up" by a make-up artist, unlike most people who were being filmed for possible inclusion on the programme.

Then the call went out: "Get Michael!"

As I made a mental note to watch the programme All The Way Through for the first time, the presenter appeared at our table. After having a quick look and laugh at the pictures, he received his directions. And so, come the autumn, you may or may not see Mighty Michael interrupt the expert and I with a "What's all this, then?" (or something similar – we did a couple of takes). Asked how much one of Aspel's crazed stalker fans (if such people exist) might pay for the set of photos, Stewart-Lockhart said "perhaps between £30 and £40."

What a bargain.

P.S. Yes, this scintillating segment did make it onto the show!

Being served by Michael Portillo… in Asda, April 12, 2003

Michael Portillo is a man who has had many contrasting TV lives – including terrifying the nation as a Tory minister and then delighting it by making train journeys for TV while wearing ridiculous clothes.

But it shouldn't be overlooked that for one week in 2003, while a backbench MP, he lived the life of a single mum in Wallasey.

His host family had declined pre-programme publicity,

while the BBC was trying to keep the programme – to be called When Michael Portillo Became A Single Mother – and the MP for Kensington and Chelsea under wraps.

We heard that the smarmy face of the barmy right, who had famously had the smug grin wiped off his face when he lost his Enfield Southgate seat in the 1997 General Election (he sadly returned to Parliament in 1999), was "working" in Asda's Liscard store, and so set out to film him being filmed.

***

It was the four-letter word on his bright green Asda T-shirt which made me laugh the most. What did it say? It said "Mike." Ha ha ha. Meet Mike Portillo, the newly-reinvented man of the people. The "Portillo buzz" at Asda, when *Echo* photographer Martin Birchall and I arrived to hunt down A Man Called Mike, was… non-existent. In fact, the majority of shoppers probably didn't even know he was there, because he was in the store's George section away from the hurly-burly of the main supermarket.

A waiting game began as we sought permission from the BBC, via a helpful Asda employee, to photograph Mike in his unnatural habitat. Then, suddenly, there he was on the shopfloor. The BBC didn't want to give us a photo opportunity, so out came the long lens. Our man Mike was now in position at the till and so was I, queuing up behind another customer. I was not to be denied.

I've never previously wanted Portillo to serve me. But this was different. He was behind a counter, not pontificating in Parliament. With apologies to the two female assistants who could have taken the £7 George T-shirt off my hands, it had to be "Mike."

And it was. He looked smart and businesslike enough but he got off to a bad start on the customer service front: "I thought I'd get a nice blue shirt," I said.

Silence.

Perhaps he was just busy concentrating, as he struggled to remove the security tag. I tried again: "How are the wages, then, Mike?" And then… he spoke: "Tight, very tight." I bet they are. Well, relatively.

Interestingly, my money was taken by the full-time member of staff looking after him. You would have thought the former chief secretary to the treasury could have coped with handling change for a tenner.

But hey, thanks Mike. And, seriously, it was good to see you doing something useful for a change.

***

"How I saved your city" (yeah, right), April 7, 2005

Horse-racing pundit John McCririck was an interesting character – full of himself and full of obnoxious and offensive opinions, but also touchy and sensitive.

I drove over to Doncaster racecourse to interview him – and got a speeding ticket on my way back.

Was it worth it? Yes, because I quite enjoyed ridiculing the toxic terror.

***

Ladies and gentlemen of Liverpool, allow me to introduce the saviour of our thriving city... John McCririck!

Er, hang on.

Big Fat John, weren't you the man who, in 1985, called Scousers "Grousers" when claiming they did "absolutely nothing to save the Grand National" when it was in danger?

"Yes, that was me."

Weren't you also the man who, in 1988, said of Liverpool: "It's the land of Gizza, as in 'Gizza something,' all of the time?"

"Yes, that was me."

And weren't you the man who was offered police protection at the 1990 Grand National, the day after telling viewers of Granada's Up Front programme: "Liverpool is a cancer on the face of England"?

"Yes, that was me."

And your message to *Echo* readers today, oh great one?

"Well done for listening to me! You knew, in your heart, that what I said was right and you went and did something about it."

There's no stopping the 64-year-old motormouth. I spent a day with the pompous windbag at Doncaster racecourse, where he was on duty for Channel 4, but, to be honest, I quite enjoyed it. The trick? Don't take him seriously.

More McCririck "wisdom", please, mutton chops: "In fairness, Liverpool has changed – and I helped to change it. In the mid-1980s I used to say it was as if the Luftwaffe had been there the night before. It was absolutely terrible. But you got rid of people like Derek Hatton and the Militant

Tendency and, to give you credit, Liverpool has tried to stamp out the image that people had of the place."

A cancer on the face of the country. Bit strong, wasn't it?

"A lot of people did think that if you could cut off one part of the United Kingdom and have it floating in the Atlantic it should be Merseyside. The morning after that TV programme I went to Aintree and a police sergeant asked 'Do you want police protection?' I said 'What on earth are you talking about?' and he told me there had been threats made on my life. That was awful to have to think about – that this was happening in a part of the UK, because of something I said that was perfectly logical."

Perfectly logical? Or an outrageous, ill-informed attack which defamed an entire city and its population?

"It was not directed against all Liverpool people," he protests. "It was against a minority – and most people now agree it was right and that things have changed in the city." Yeah, we know, and it's all down to you. As is our European Capital of Culture status, no doubt…

"I was very surprised you got that, but I was delighted. You have turned it around, like Glasgow did. And it's all because of people like me standing up and saying things like I did in the '80s." We're all dead grateful, honest (but I wonder why he won't tell me where exactly he'll be staying in the Merseyside area tomorrow night).

You don't interview McCririck or have a conversation with him. You can get a few questions out, but have to simply sit back as he spews out a tidal wave of occasion-ally entertaining, occasionally poisonous points of view masquerading as statements of fact. But, as the Surrey-born, Harrow-educated old blusterer has said himself, he's merely a pub bore with a microphone. Just because he's a "celebrity" (isn't everyone these days?) doesn't mean we should value his prejudices any more than those of the next pub bore.

And despite some of his now kind words, he's still got a knife in his hand – and bile in his mouth: "There is still this maudlin self-pity, worship of death and blame culture in Liverpool. Carla Lane's got a lot to answer for, but what she wrote in Bread struck a chord. And there is still a depressingly aggressive element in the city."

On and on the pub bore drones. So what happened back in 1997 – the Grand National bomb scare year – when so many Merseysiders forgot they were aggressive, self-pitying, death-worshipping lovers of the welfare state and opened their homes, hearts, fridges and spare bedrooms to stranded racegoers? "People were taken in and there was a great wartime spirit – of course there are contradictions."

So anyway, overall, we're not the worst city in the country any more in your eyes? "No, no, no. Liverpool has become an acceptable part of the UK once again – all it needs to do now is start voting in Conservatives!"

***

John McCririck loves horses – when he speaks passionately about his hatred of the use of the whip, you'd swear he was a caring human being – but I reckon he loves women more. Or is it just lust? Decide for yourself …

He says: "What helped turn Aintree around is the

Liverpool women. They come in their fantastic, skimpy outfits, showing all they've got – it's absolutely fantastic. Everyone hates rain at racecourses, but when it's raining at Aintree you see the women carrying their high heels in one hand and a glass of champagne in the other – while the rain is making their dresses transparent and they're tottering around totally out of control. It's one of the great sights in sport, isn't it?"

Something tells me he must agree with legendary trainer Ginger McCain, who recently dismissed the chances of female jockeys in the Grand National: "Ginger is absolutely wrong. So many horses go better for having women jockeys. There is no reason why a woman shouldn't win the National, but they've had so few chances. One of the appalling things about British racing is that there is this sexism."

You read it here first: John McCririck is a feminist.

But whatever I call him, I'm under orders not to call him nice. As if. "It makes me very angry when journalists write 'He's actually got a heart of gold and, underneath all the bluster, he's a nice chap.' He's not a nice chap. I make no pretence about it. I'm not a pleasant person!"

***

There you go, then. McCririck knew exactly who and what he was – and he didn't want things sugar-coated.

But between me interviewing him and the piece going in the paper, he seemed genuinely anxious as he asked me over the phone: "Not an awful piece, is it?"

God bless Leon and June

Retired teachers Leon and June Bernicoff proved that you never do know what's around the corner.

For he was 78 and she was 75 when they achieved national fame – as millions of viewers fell in love with watching them watching television on Channel 4's Gogglebox.

After getting to know the friendly, welcoming, delightful and down-to-earth couple over the course of a few entertaining interviews, I was honoured to be invited to True Blue Leon's 80th birthday bash at Everton Football Club – and it was a great night!

"We're going to be stars!" Leon had told June, after returning home from Liverpool Bridge Club one day in 2012. Two young researchers, looking for people of a certain age to appear in a new programme, had paid a visit to the club… and Leon's hand went up immediately!

He was soon calling Nigel Farage a "dickhead" on national television, and famously showed his sweet and loving nature while the couple were watching the film Gladiator, and the scene where Meridius (Russell Crowe) is reunited in the after-life with his wife and child. Leon told June: "I'll join you. You'll see. Always, June."

Leon died in 2017 and June died in 2020.

I loved them and I miss them.

Chapter Five

Hilda and Gordon

"The Street has changed," December 17, 2007

Coronation Street's Hilda Ogden and Gordon Clegg reunited thanks to this book! Well, not really – but I thought it would be nice to include, alongside each other, extracts from interviews I did with Jean Alexander, who played Hilda from 1964 to 1987, and Everton FC chairman and West End theatre producer Bill Kenwright, who played Gordon Clegg from 1968 to 1969 (although he made occasional appearances up until 2012).

***

I was still watching Coronation Street – my favourite programme for so many decades – when I interviewed Jean, ahead of her presenting a celebration of Christmas at the Philharmonic Hall in Liverpool.

It was six years later, in 2013, having clocked up 45 years as a Corrie fan (I started very young) that I finally decided to give up on it. There were just too many people in Weatherfield that I couldn't get on with, but I was very sad to have to write about the end of what had been a very special association.

Jean was ahead of me, regarding her unease about the modern-day Corrie, saying: "The programme has changed. Nowadays, I think a lot of the characters are similar. You don't get too many individual characters – they are very good, but it's a different style. And, unfortunately, most of the stories are very similar."

Though she recognised the major changes there had been since her day. "It's a different show, and the hours the actors now work must be punishing. When I was in it, we did two episodes a week, not five, and we had three days of rehearsal."

***

Jean was 81 when I interviewed her – and at the time I recalled (but didn't mention) meeting the Corrie legend at a book signing for her autobiography, The Other Side of The Street, in Preston in 1989. On that occasion, I overheard a photographer asking the actress: "How are you enjoying your retirement, love?"

Fortunately, hard-working Jean didn't hear him. For Hilda Ogden, as we all now know, was just part of a very long story with many different chapters. As well as Last of The Summer Wine (Jean made the first of two guest appearances playing Auntie Wainwright in 1988, the year after leaving Corrie, and was a regular from 1992), she also appeared in the likes of Heartbeat, Barbara and Where The Heart Is, and the films Scandal and Willie's War.

***

I asked if her post-Weatherfield career had gone just as planned. "Yes, it has. I was lucky enough to get a part that suited me (Auntie Wainwright) – it was right up my street. And I'm now in the fortunate position where if I don't like a script and don't want to do it, I don't have to. I can pick and choose, which suits me very well now."

By God, woman, you're 81 – your work ethic probably puts some people half your age to shame! So what's the secret of being one of Merseyside's – perhaps the world's – healthiest-looking octogenarians?

"I think it's just hard work," she says, laughing. "And if you can still remember lines and not fall flat on your face, you can go on forever as an actor!"

Inside Story on a "Private Man", October 6, 2003

Bill Kenwright – as was the case with Jean Alexander, who died in 2016 – is a workaholic.

Here, ahead of his latest show opening at the Liverpool Empire, he spoke to me about a side of his life that people rarely see – and about Gordon Clegg, of course!

***

If the *Echo* launched a word association game, starting with the name "Kenwright," answers on a postcard would probably include enthusiastic, effervescent and ebullient. Then there would be loud, proud and even, perhaps, over-the-top and in-your-face. And yes, of course, there would be the obligatory "impresario" ("What does that actually mean?" asks Bill) and "luvvie" (well, he does work in the heart of luvvie-land and did say "Bye love" at the end of our conversation).

Bill, 58, is well aware of his public image, but insists: "There are very, very few people who know me, because I am incredibly quiet and private. People don't understand this about me because I will shout about my productions to the rooftops and I love talking about Everton Football Club. I am very private, but I can only talk in one way – though I don't want to come across as a passionate buffoon."

Don't be silly, luvvie.

He adds: "If you knew how many requests I get every week – to make documentaries, to write my biography and so on. But I turn them all down."

This aversion to the spotlight can be traced back to the late '60s when Bill played Gordon Clegg, briefly, in Coronation Street (although he did make occasional return visits). "You've got to remember I was 20 (I make it 22, Bill, but let's not quibble) when I was on the programme, at a time when it was hotter than it is now. I remember Pat Phoenix (who played Elsie Tanner) telling me on day one 'You're a good-looking lad from Liverpool – and you've got no idea what will happen to you when you appear on that screen.'

"I was really shocked. My character was the first teenager specially written into a soap to attract teenage viewers. It was an extraordinary situation to be in and I really didn't like it. That's one of the reasons I left."

***

Later in the interview, after Bill had detailed his days of work, work and a bit more work, I said it didn't sound like he had much opportunity to go for a swift half down the British Legion… "I don't actually miss not having any free time, because I've never had it – I was on the stage at the Liverpool Playhouse at the age of 12, worked in my summer holidays and went to London when I was 17 to join a youth theatre.

"I never see myself retiring – not at all. Maybe there is something in having a yacht and other things which I don't have, but I've never aspired to that lifestyle."

***

At the time of the interview, Bill was celebrating a very special anniversary – 10 years with the love of his life, actress Jenny Seagrove (and they're still together).

***

"It's my longest relationship. It started when she was starring at the Liverpool Playhouse in the Noel Coward play Present Laughter."

But he confesses that Jenny has to share him when they go to bed…

"Poor Jenny," he laughs. "I'll get to bed at about 1am – and read through some scripts. We'll have the TV on or a DVD and I never get to sleep until about 3 or 3.30am… I'm always working.

"I really don't go out much. And Jenny is a hard-working actress… and an extremely committed person, who is very much into her health and animal charities. She also comes to a lot of Everton games – and she always knows where I am!

"The great thing is when you find the person you've been looking for. That relationship gives you freedom because there's absolute trust."

Bill and Jenny are not married, but Bill has been, briefly, to New Zealand-born former actress Anouska Hempel, whose films included the James Bond flick On Her Majesty's Secret Service. She later became an internationally-renowned designer and hotelier.

They married in 1978, but sadly it was all over by 1980 – and Bill's voice lowers as, for once, words don't come easy: "That was painful – any divorce is painful."

Bill, meanwhile, has one daughter, Lucy, 30, by actress Virginia Stride: "Lucy, who's a mad Evertonian, is a very successful producer with the BBC. And she's got all her dad's attributes; she's hard-working and shy. I'm so proud of her.

"Liverpool means family to me. Liverpool means home. I've lived in London for 39 years, but I only start to feel at home when I arrive at Lime Street station."

Chapter Six

Singing a different song

IT ALL began with The Sweet, aka Sweet.

The glam rockers were my first music heroes, and the first band I saw live (Southport Floral Hall, August 23, 1974).

Blockbuster, scandalously, was their only number one single. I remember feeling especially cheated when Teenage Rampage became one of five Sweet singles to only make it to number two (so God knows how singer Brian Connolly, guitarist Andy Scott, bass guitarist Steve Priest and drummer Mick Tucker must have felt). Fast forward many years and I almost interviewed Connolly in November 1996, ahead of Sweet, Slade and John Rossall's Glitter Band Experience performing a Merry Xmas Show at the Liverpool Empire.

Connolly, I was informed, was scheduled to team up again with guitarist Scott – but this wasn't the case, the singer told me in no uncertain terms during a very brief exchange on the phone. He sounded in a bad way, and so it was not as big a shock as it might have been when I heard he had died, aged just 51, the following February, due to kidney failure, liver failure and repeated heart attacks. Tragic.

Months before my ill-fated "interview" with Connolly, I

did have a brief and very enjoyable chat on the phone with Andy Scott, when Ballroom Hitz: The Very Best of Sweet was released. Here's part of it…

January 26, 1996: Scott was born in Wrexham, and played his first gig at the Cavern in Mathew Street as a 14-year-old in Guitars Incorporated, before winning Opportunity Knocks in the mid-'60s with The Silverstones and going on to work with Mike McCartney's Scaffold. Then he joined Sweet – formerly Sweetshop – and found that glamour and glitz equalled hits. Songwriters Nicky Chinn and Mike Chapman penned the pop classics, but the band was less lightweight on stage and wrote their own rockier material, which initially appeared on B-sides and LPs.

"In the early days, we would have done anything to be successful," says Wiltshire-based Scott, 46 – and still on the road with Andy Scott's Sweet (which doesn't include any other original members). "The plain fact of the matter, though, is that we had a bit more to offer." Scott's own favourite Sweet single is their last top 10 hit, Love Is Like Oxygen, which he co-wrote with Trevor Griffin. It was released at the start of 1978 – and by the end of the year, Connolly had left, with Scott explaining that the group was pulling in different directions much earlier: "Three of us wanted to leave the girls' pin-up magazines behind – Brian didn't.

"Looking back at those days, it just wasn't real… but it was special." Hear, hear.

***

Then came punk and – post-punk!

And when new scenes emerge, there need to be influential people around who help make things happen.

I was lucky to interview several of them: John Peel, Malcolm McLaren, Tony Wilson, Geoff Davies and Doreen Allen.

John Peel

I interviewed Peel, whose late night radio show was responsible for an enormous amount of my record collection, in April 1997 – a chat over the phone specifically about the forthcoming Hillsborough Justice Concert at Anfield, at which he would be the master of ceremonies. It was only a brief conversation as he was one of many subjects for the article, but I made sure I said a very specific "thank you" to him – as I explained in a column written seven years later, following his death.

Teacher who made a lasting impression, October 27, 2004

A year or two ago there was an advert on television in which various famous faces named and praised a teacher who had made a lasting impression on them. Me? I couldn't think of one who was worthy of such an affectionate accolade. But yesterday afternoon, as I tried to get my head around the shocking news of his sadly premature death, I realised my memorable mentor did his teaching with a turntable. Earlier this year, I eagerly rifled through my record collection to find the 80 seven-inch singles worthy of a place on the jukebox which my wife had given me for my 40th birthday.

And I may as well rechristen it The John Peel Jukebox, as I heard the vast majority of the songs on it for the first time on his show in the late 1970s. As many of my peers were probably drifting off to sleep while thinking sweet thoughts about their favourite teacher, I was lapping up previously unknown pleasures played by a balding, gruff-sounding man who kept going on about Liverpool FC. But I never held that against him, because Peel provided the soundtrack to my teenage life.

I was glad to be able to interview him in 1997, as he looked forward to being the MC at the Hillsborough Justice Concert at Anfield. At last I had the chance to say: "Thanks for playing Rowche Rumble by The Fall on your show in August 1979 – I think it may have changed my life."

Although he must have received a million similar bouquets, I like to think the man who was worthy of a much grander job description than the demeaning "DJ" sounded quite moved.

For his 65th birthday, he was presented with a unique two-track single featuring The Fall and another of his – and my – favourite bands: Birkenhead's Half Man Half Biscuit, who, fittingly, provided a cover version of Roy Orbison's A Legend In My Time. The Legend, for his part, described the Biscuits as a "national treasure" – well, he should have known.

Many acts now swimming in the mainstream were once up a stinking creek with Peelie as their only paddle. Johnny

Rotten may now be considered wholesome enough for I'm a Celebrity, but if you wanted to hear him in the late '70s, the John Peel Show – weeknights, 10pm till midnight – was the only place to go. As it was if you enjoyed the likes of (refers to jukebox): The Slits, Subway Sect, Desperate Bicycles, Dead Kennedys, The Prefects, Steve Miro and The Eyes and so on.

He may have been cruelly robbed of the long and happy retirement he deserved, but John Peel really did have a wonderful life.

And heaven knows I'd be miserable now if he'd been, say, a bank clerk rather than a broadcaster. My jukebox and record collection would probably be full of the most appalling garbage by artists too many and mediocre to list.

Cheers John, you were the best teacher I ever had.

Malcolm McLaren

There is some dispute about the true extent of Sex Pistols manager Malcolm McLaren's influence (ask Johnny Rotten/ John Lydon!) – but one thing is certain, he was a brilliant interviewee.

February 4, 2000: Sometimes you can't get a word in edgeways, but sometimes it doesn't matter – step forward mouth almighty Malcolm McLaren, the godfather of punk, who is now campaigning to be Mayor of London.

The colourful and entertaining entrepreneur, in Liverpool to give a two-hour lecture to students at the Liverpool Institute for Performing Arts (LIPA) – "Paul McCartney threw the gauntlet down, saying I'd be the biggest a******* on the planet if I didn't come up" – still hasn't lost his voice after all these years.

I know, it's a miracle.

"This has been practice for being on Question Time the week after next," said the man who has sparked many a "genius or lunatic" debate. Only the planned Q&A session never happened, because the top talker ran out of time.

McLaren, who caused the first of many storms with former partner Vivienne Westwood as the owner of the outlandish fashion store Sex on London's Kings Road, believes we are now living in a karaoke world: "We have to promote the artisan and the artist's spirit, before everything turns corporate," he says.

"Entertainment is something Liverpool can reinvent itself on. It's a cliche to talk about The Beatles but at least it's something that's better than the Millennium Dome. The Dome is karaoke, The Beatles were real."

McLaren – all wild hair, wild eyes and wild gestures – is in full flow now. And it's an impressive sight. At times, you wonder what on earth the man is going on about – then he says something so simple, sensible and homespun you could be talking to your wise old granny.

Although busy concentrating on London, the man who has been dubbed a pop Svengali and cultural manipulator believes all cities – not least Liverpool – should have their own elected mayor. (He was certainly way ahead of the game here – Liverpool didn't get its first elected Mayor until 12 years later): "People in Liverpool and elsewhere have got to reclaim their identities and take over their own cities. And culture is what is important and is what cities are remembered for – they don't go down in history because of their bank rates."

He dismisses his own political rivals as "part of an old soap opera; poor actors in a re-run that we have seen a million times."

He says London has been "going down the pan at a rapid rate" for the last five years: "You realise all the artisans that originally inhabited places like Soho – the local tailors and so on – are no longer there because the rates are going up and the only people who can afford them are those boys from America... Starbucks and McDonald's!" Some have dismissed McLaren's ideas as crazy, others have hailed them as utterly sensible: allowing libraries to sell alcohol; scrapping museum charges; a lottery to help the homeless; adult education available for £1 a year; electric tram routes; 24-hour opening for pubs and restaurants; Amsterdam-style cafés licensed to sell cannabis... and brothels to be set up opposite the Houses of Parliament. "The response to my plans has been humour, fun and 'He's a lunatic! He's not serious.' Politicians can't stand the thought that someone other than them might be serious. It's as if they've invented and own the word."

Booze in libraries, then. Tell us more...

"Libraries have become places for the elderly to go and read newspapers and get out of the cold. They use it as a form of community spirit and that's good, because they should be big community centres. They should be able to put in bars, not least because they don't have any money to buy books. Why can't you have a glass of Guinness while reading Dickens? Why does anything to do with education or intellect have to be joyless and grim? Why can we only walk around galleries until 6pm – don't they realise people don't finish work until 6pm?"

Much of what McLaren was advocating back in the punk era of the late '70s – from language through to attitudes through to fashion and hairstyles – is now part of everyday life in Britain.

Back then, he was vilified and demonised – today, the BBC is asking him to appear on Question Time. What happened, Malc? And why did it take so long?

"You're never going to get credit at the time for something the Establishment thought was pure and utter trouble," he explains.

Changing the world and the way it thinks, it seems, takes a while. So it could be many years before people can walk into a library and say something like: "Two pints of lager and a packet of crisps, please – oh, and have you got the latest Maeve Binchy in yet?"

Tony Wilson, aka Anthony H. Wilson

What?!? "Mr Manchester" in the *Echo*?

The truth is, Manchester was lucky to have him – and we could have done with him in Liverpool.

I met and interviewed Tony for an article which ended up being headlined "Mr Liverpool."

August 20, 1999: This can't be happening. It has to be some kind of bizarre dream. Or an elaborate wind-up: Mr Manchester, otherwise known as Scouse-baiting Tony Wilson – or Anthony H. Wilson, take your pick – is praising Liverpool to the heavens.

And slagging off Manchester.

Amazingly, it isn't a dream. He really is saying all these things. And it's music to the ears.

But let's be fair. This is the man who, love him or hate him, has repeatedly followed up his enthusiasms by putting his money where his mouth is – and, at times, his comfy Granada job on the line. This is the man who went out on a limb to put punk and new wave acts like the Sex Pistols, The Clash, Blondie and Elvis Costello on TV in the late '70s and who later invested in a groundbreaking record label (Factory), a groundbreaking band (Joy Division, who became New Order) and a groundbreaking club (the Hacienda).

And this is the man who is now bringing, together with his business and romantic partner Yvette Livesey, a prestigious international music convention to Liverpool.

In The City – dubbed the Urban Glastonbury – will base itself at the Crowne Plaza Hotel and bring about 1,500 music industry movers and shakers to the city between September 18-22.

Over five nights and in 40-plus venues across the city, 500-plus bands, artists, singer-songwriters and DJs will be taking part in "The Biggest Live Music Party In Europe." The "Unsigned" section of In The City is now recognised as the ultimate breeding ground for new talent – old boys and girls include Oasis, Catatonia, Placebo, Stereophonics and Kula Shaker.

Since being launched in Manchester in 1992, it's been an event synonymous with the city (only Glasgow and Dublin have also hosted it). But a glorious love affair, it seems, is over. How so, To'?

"Manchester, in the last two years, has lost the plot," he says. Yvette adds: "People within the town hall originally had a vision and understood the communities that were happening in Manchester – like the music community. They supported it but, suddenly, they lost it – they lost that understanding." Tony, now warming to his new role as Mr Anti-Manchester, explains: "They don't think the music business is important any more. They think 'We've done our bit'."

***

Later in the article, I pointed out that Tony had once told the *Echo* that Liverpool people didn't understand him – and that this was a chance for him to explain himself.

***

Tony says: "Liverpool went on the skids in the mid-'70s. There have been occasional blips that have lasted six to eight months and then tailed off. But this isn't a blip. This feels as if it has been going on for about two years and it's different, so different.

"I get this 'Wilson – the bloke down the motorway who keeps having a go at Liverpool' thing, but I've always said

'Liverpool is a great city.' I've always loved it and its people. "But as a local journalist covering this area, I have to be allowed to make two points – that to react to the problems created by the stupidity of the '50s and '60s leadership of this city with pure negativity was not the answer. The reason it is different now is that, sod everyone else, you are doing it for yourselves – making the city come alive.

"My other point was always that your tragedy, with the exception of a few bloody wonderful men like Alan Bleasdale, was that if you make it in Liverpool you go to London. The Beatles are the most significant example of that – and that's something that should be said. People should stay and reinvest in their towns."

Back to Liverpool being great, Tony adds: "I am so pleased it's different now. It's great to be here and it's going to be great to show people from the south of England the new Liverpool."

So is he expecting any hassle in the city, during In The City?

"I don't find much resentment. I think people know that what I was moaning about was Liverpool moaning. But that's in the past. We have now got to get back to this idea of two great cities – a twin capital of Lancashire."

Ladies and gentlemen, I give you Tony Wilson... the new Mr Liverpool.

***

Five days after he died, I devoted my weekly opinion column to him. Here are some excerpts.

August 15, 2007: What would we give for our own Tony Wilson?

He was a man of many strongly-held opinions, a man who provoked many strongly-held opinions – and a man of many names.

Tony Wilson. Anthony Wilson. Anthony H. Wilson. Mr Manchester. And "That Tony f****** Wilson, What a ****!"

The Sage of Salford seemed to relish putting the boot into Liverpool, while we loved to mock his pretensions and pomposity (even if he sometimes took the wind out of our sails by doing this himself).

But the real story, once you stripped away all the panto-style rivalry, sniping and bitching, was that the TV presenter and entrepreneur loved Liverpool. And a lot of us were pretty fond of – and full of respect for – him, too.

I referred to his nice words about Liverpool during my interview, and then added...

In another tribute a few months later, when talking about his dreams for a futuristic centre at Liverpool's Kings Dock dedicated to fashions in music, art and industry, he said: "Popular culture started in Liverpool, which is really why it should be here." Tony Wilson did talk a lot of tosh at times and I loved laughing at him when he did, but I also loved the part he played in enriching our cultural life. He was part of the team that brought us Factory Records, the home of the wonderful Joy Division (and the pretty-good-I-suppose New Order), and the team which brought us the Hacienda club. He was also the first person to put the Sex Pistols, and many other punk and new wave bands, on TV. And I still fondly recall the day the maverick presenter urged viewers, at the end of an edition of Granada Reports in March 1979, to go out and buy The Fall's debut LP, Live at The Witch Trials.

Tony Wilson was an enthusiast. He spoke up for his region. He was a catalyst. He made things happen.

What would the city of Liverpool give for a few Tony Wilsons right now?

Geoff Davies

Geoff, who I got to know well over the years, once ran the greatest record shop in the world (Probe) – while his record label (Probe Plus) put out records by the greatest band in the world (Half Man Half Biscuit).

The following is taken from an interview Geoff (who has since retired) did to celebrate his label's 21st birthday.

September 21, 2002: "These are all my mistakes," the often dour and deadpan one says dismissively, pointing at some of the unsold vinyl cluttering up one of the upstairs rooms of his home close to Sefton Park.

He doesn't really mean it, though.

The Probe Plus success story, it could be argued, begins and ends with Half Man Half Biscuit. Their debut LP, Back in The DHSS, is thought to have sold more than 100,000 copies (their debut single, The Trumpton Riots, has sold a similar number). Probe's next biggest-sellers? All the other HMHB singles and LPs.

But Geoff stresses: "I would say about 96 per cent of what I've done on the label I have put out because I thought it was great and deserved to be heard. I'm a great believer that if I like something then other people will. I believe 'the good will out' – although it might only happen when you're dead."

Geoff is still an enthusiast. During our chat, he plays me Probe stuff old and new – an old 12-incher from Accrington band Gone To Earth ("Just listen to that combination of fiddle and electric guitar!") and the ethereal sounds of the recently released 4-20 LP ("This is completely irresistible!")

And he talks me through other Probe releases, including The Walking Seeds' Skullf*** LP – "They were Liverpool's only grunge band and reputedly influenced Nirvana. Cook Da Books sold quite well and there's still a demand for The Revolutionary Army of The Infant Jesus – they were an odd bunch. The Onset included La's founder member Mike Badger; Levellers 5, from Darwen, were real quality and a great favourite of John Peel. Then there's The Dead Poppies, Liverpool's only truly psychedelic band."

Other releases include Calvin Party, The She, Mr Amir, Kelso, Marlowe, Ex-Post Facto, Brenda and The Beachballs, Jegsy Dodd and The Sons of Harry Cross, Poisoned Electric Head, Fflaps, Fishcake Shake and The Doonicans.

And, of course, Half Man Half Biscuit... "Thank God for Half Man Half Biscuit!" says Geoff.

Doreen Allen: Queen of Clubs, March 3, 2020

Doreen Allen was the Queen of Eric's – the beating heart of

the club in Mathew Street where she did virtually every job going and was loved and respected by punters and performers alike.

She went on to co-launch Liverpool's Planet X club, which lasted 10 years in a number of different venues and is the subject of regular reunion nights.

At Eric's, Doreen, at various times, worked on the door, in the bar, kitchens, cloakroom, in the office (doing the accounts, selling posters, tickets and membership cards), and meeting and greeting the bands.

She says: "The best gig I ever saw at Eric's was by The Cramps. And at 2.15am, Roger (Eagle, who ran Eric's with Pete Fulwell and Ken Testi) asked me to walk them across to their hotel – The Stork, on Williamson Square. They were so wild – they made me look normal! All the clubs were letting out as we walked across town. It was an experience!"

Regarding characters from the Eric's audience who went on to achieve fame, Doreen says she was most surprised by Ian Astbury (founding member and lead singer with The Cult) and Wayne Hussey (The Sisters of Mercy and The Mission): "I looked after Ian and his mate when they came to the Eric's matinees, aged about 14. Ian was from Heswall, and I originally come from Irby. I looked after him because he was so small. Ian was always so quiet and in the background. When I first saw him on stage, I didn't realise it was him – but those eyes!

"Wayne was from Bristol, but came to Liverpool because of his love of Liverpool FC. He was brought up a Mormon and was another unlikely pop star – until Pete Burns put make-up on him! There were so many others, including Julian (Cope, of The Teardrop Explodes), who Hilary (Steele, his friend from CF Mott teacher training college on the Huyton/Prescot border, who soon became a great friend of Doreen's) initially had to talk into coming to Eric's, and even Ian McCulloch (of Echo and The Bunnymen). He would be on the doorstep when I arrived for work and would just follow me everywhere – whenever I turned around, he would be there. I used to have to buy him cups of tea in the Armadillo Tea Rooms – one time we were joined by my mum, and, a few weeks later, Ian was on Top of The Pops. Mum couldn't believe it!

"Pete Wylie, though (of Wah!) – he has never changed over the years, and that's why we love him. He was born to be on stage, and he's always made up when I go to his gigs – because it means there is someone older than him there!"

Doreen and Planet X: May 19, 2008

It was christened by a member of Frankie Goes To Hollywood, played host to The Stone Roses, Primal Scream and The Boo Radleys and was patronised by stars including John Lydon and Morrissey.

This was Planet X which, between 1983 and 1993, added a great deal of colour, together with a great deal of darkness and gothic glamour, to the city's club scene. Its clientele wore outrageous outfits and high-maintenance, often high-rise, hairstyles, helping to make Liverpool the unofficial Capital of Crimpers.

The club was launched by Doreen Allen – a largely unsung heroine of Liverpool's punk and post-punk music scene, who worked at Eric's and The Warehouse and for the likes of Pete Wylie and Dead or Alive – and her then partner, Kenny Dawick, with Doreen becoming sole owner in 1989.

"I just wanted Planet X to be different," says Doreen. "It's always associated with goth, but it was basically an alternative music club."

Its name came courtesy of Frankie Goes To Hollywood's Paul Rutherford, and was taken from the lyrics of The B-52s' song Whammy Kiss – with Doreen recalling: "We were really into the B-52s and had seen them at Eric's."

The woman who has been called Liverpool's High Priestess of Gothic Glamour then proudly shows me an article on Planet X from a 1983 edition of *The End*, the magazine co-edited by Peter Hooton of The Farm.

It says: "Weirdos have always been around – that's a fact of life – but, quite recently in Liverpool, they have been given a new lease of life.

"Weirdoism, the doctrine which they follow, has been given credibility by the success of bands like The Creatures, The Cramps and all the other bands who wear black and paste their faces with white make-up. Planet X has become the mecca of the Liverpool weirdo and many an ex-good guy and gal has been spotted in there, by a fact-finding crew from *The End*."

Beaming the biggest of smiles, Doreen says: "Isn't that great?"

As well as the aforementioned Lydon and Morrissey,

she reveals another famous face popped in after playing at a bigger venue in the city: "One of Hall & Oates came in once – I don't know which one is bloody which! – but he didn't stay long. He said 'It's a brilliant club, but not quite my scene'!"

The Crucial Three

Imagine The Crucial Three – Ian McCulloch of Echo and The Bunnymen, Julian Cope of The Teardrop Explodes and Pete Wylie, of Wah! Heat and loads of other Wahs! – back together in the same room! You'll have to imagine it, because it's never going to happen.

There probably isn't a room big enough to contain their giant personalities – and, yes, egos. And, knowing what we know now (and having heard all those classic songs), it was obvious that their short-lived band was never going to be able to accommodate such supreme talent – and, yes, showmanship.

I became a feature writer in 1992, and it wasn't too long before my mind turned towards Messrs Wylie, McCulloch and Cope – eventually, I got the set! I met and interviewed Wylie and McCulloch on many occasions (always in pubs, I'm pleased to say), but sadly I only interviewed Cope once, and it was on the phone. It was, however, such an enjoyable chat that I can't have any complaints.

Each, on his own, was great company – and it soon became clear, in every case, that each was destined to be The Frontman.

***

I never went to the original Eric's club. My age (I was 12 when it opened in October, 1976, and 15 when it closed in April 1980) was one factor (though I could have attended the matinees), but the biggest one was that I lived 40 miles away in Preston. But I was a prodigious record buyer, and my treasured, fast-growing collection included the debut singles by The Teardrop Explodes (Sleeping Gas), Echo and The Bunnymen (The Pictures On My Wall) and Wah! Heat (Better Scream).

I think I imagined a harmonious Liverpool scene, in which the main players encouraged, were pleased with, and proud of, each other. Then, after speaking to them all, and reading Cope's brilliant book, Head On, I realised things had been a little different. It had actually been an intensely competitive and bitterly bitchy scene – which made for great interviews and great gossip.

Pete Wylie, October 7, 1994

Pop star Pete Wylie has pulled himself back from the brink of suicide to relaunch his once-glorious career… He broke his back almost three years ago in a freak, near-fatal accident and harboured thoughts of taking his own life just 18 months ago: "I was on a real downer. I was really in the pits and I couldn't get out of it. There was nothing good in my life as far as I could see. I was really close to wanting to top myself. The weird thing about it was how calm and logical it all seemed. I just sat at home in this horrible hole thinking 'There's nothing, just nothing.'"

But thankfully, with a little help from his friends – especially Carl Hunter and Roy Boulter of The Farm – Wylie's famous lust for life returned: "Now I think 'Thank God I didn't do it!' A few weeks ago, Ian McCulloch was interviewed in the *NME* and the reporter called me a 'living legend'. In the past 'legend' would have been the important word – now it's the 'living'.

Wylie on… Julian Cope, his book 'Head On' and band, The Teardrop Explodes: "I was looking forward to getting the libel lawyers onto him and making some money at last, but I was really surprised at how generous he was. I love him but he drives me mad. The Teardrop Explodes were really good and Copey was a great bass player."

Wylie on… Eric's club: "I sold my soul to Eric's. It opened on October 1, 1976, and I started at university on October 4. There was no contest – I left university. Once Eric's opened, you wanted to be there all the time in case you missed something. The Clash gig on May 5, 1977, was the big night. That was the night me, McCulloch and Cope formed The Crucial Three."

Wylie on… Ian McCulloch: "I adored McCulloch and, as Copey says in the book, I often deferred to him."

***

My memory of my first meeting with Ian McCulloch is that I had simply faxed him (fax machines! Remember them?) – and asked if he fancied meeting up in a pub for a wide-ranging interview. I remember he was delighted with the idea of meeting in a pub, which was a great start – because everyone knows the best interviews take place in pubs. It was another great, alcohol-fuelled afternoon.

Ian McCulloch, March 13, 1998

Some pubs are born great, some achieve greatness – and some have greatness thrust upon them.

The Gardeners Arms in Vale Road, Woolton, may have long been known for its fine beer and fine service, but it can now also claim its place in rock 'n' roll history. For it was within these unassuming walls that Ian McCulloch, Will Sergeant and Les Pattinson – fuelled by Cain's bitter – decided to reform one of Liverpool's (and therefore the world's) greatest bands: Echo and The Bunnymen.

And now McCulloch is back in the boozer – this time to do several rounds with the *Echo* and talk about his 19 years as a living legend. It's an invigorating journey which will end several hours later outside the White Star pub in the city centre, when several *Big Issue* sellers will unexpectedly find themselves on the guest list for the Bunnymen's forthcoming gig at the Royal Court...

"The 18 months since we started demo-ing have been the best 18 months of my life... I felt fit in my mind more than anything and thought 'I'm gonna have this!'... Our role has always been to provide an alternative – U2 are a fine rock group, but they are ten-a-penny. File under The Eagles and Simple Minds." Yes, the Mouth is undoubtedly back. He's slagging off U2 again!

But Mac is no stranger to being slagged off himself. On BBC2's Rock Family Trees, for example, guitarist Will Sergeant said of the singer during the Bunnymen's darkest days: "He was beginning to think he was God."

Today, McCulloch says: "Will's had me in tears. We were in a Milan club a long time ago and I was in a bit of a state. He said 'Why do you do this? I don't like you when you're like this.'

"And when he said that, it was like 'He likes me! And he's chosen this moment to tell me.' We do like each other a lot and probably love each other. But the friction between us is what makes things tick. And I've got no plans to make it easier!"

Mac on... Pete Wylie: "I've got a lot of time for Pete. I've known him since I was 13; we used to live about half a mile from each other and both went to the same school – Alsop in Walton... Better Scream is my favourite Wylie/Wah! song. That was the only thing I heard in a two-year period that made me stop and think 'I'm not happy about this.' It's a really, really good song...He once said 'I want to be your guitarist. Just once, on one song.' The day will come. We will be The Crucial Two. He's loved. I still love him."

Mac on... Julian Cope: "He was always striving for a

personality. I don't even think about him. I haven't seen him for years. If he ever records Bloody Sure You're On Dope – which is one of the greatest-ever song titles (and something my mother once said to me) – I'll have him."

Mac on… Mark E. Smith/The Fall: "Mark E. Smith is a one-off and Julian Cope isn't fit to lick his boots… I used to go and see The Fall in Manchester and he would let me stay at his flat. He lent me a coat once, because it was raining – and I later wore it for the cover of our first LP, Crocodiles."

Pete Wylie, November 13, 1998

"One of the things that happens in adversity is that you find out who cares about you. It's like when I read that Ian McCulloch interview in the *Echo*, and he said 'I love Wylie.' That meant so much to me.

"By the nature of what we do, it's not easy to keep in touch, and so we're never going to say those sorts of things to each other face-to-face. You are our medium. You are the Doris Stokes of our relationship!"

Julian Cope, October 16, 1999

Even though I didn't get to meet Cope, this remains one of my favourite interviews. He was, like Wylie and McCulloch, hugely entertaining – and, it seems, born to be a brilliant interviewee. He's a bloody great writer, too. Oh, and then there was his magnificent music!

***

Somehow it seemed like the perfect start to the interview – Julian Cope's American wife, Dorian, greets me with the immortal line: "He says can you give him five minutes? He's just come back from Swindon." Swindon! Rock 'n' roll!

Mr and Mrs C, who met in New York in 1981, live in domestic bliss in the Wiltshire village of Avebury (just down the road from sexy Swindon). But, although he was born in South Wales and grew up in Tamworth in the West Midlands, Cope will forever be associated with Liverpool and its vibrant punk and post-punk scenes of the late '70s and early '80s... But today, Cope is probably as well known for his mystical musings as his music. To many, he is merely a professional eccentric. A weirdo with an unhealthy interest in "psychic geography" and stone circles.

His diaries, which he describes as "therapy", take no prisoners. He says: "Someone asked if I'd lost a lot of friends through writing and self-publishing Head On. But all that would have happened is that the people who didn't like me before now won't like me even more."

But nobody is belittled more than the author, who, in (new book) Repossessed, describes himself as a "self-obsessed, white, middle-class a*******." He says: "I think it's really important to keep all my neuroses in. If I was a plank for doing something, then I should say so. One reviewer said I portrayed myself as 'self-serving' when I wasn't – but I was! To get to the level of being a rock 'n' roll star, you have to be self-serving."

Ian McCulloch and Pete Wylie could easily find anecdotes in Repossessed that may offend them – so no romantic reunion for The Crucial Three, then? "I'd probably make an effort not to bump into them. I still share the same publicist as Mac, but it sounds, from what I hear and read, like he really hates me."

McCulloch has long protested that Read It In Books, a song recorded by both the Bunnymen and the Teardrops and credited to him and Cope, was actually written solely by himself – and he recently told the *Echo* that if Cope ever recorded another ancient song (Bloody Sure You're On Dope) he'd "have him". Cope replies: "It's tempting to do it, if it's going to weird him out."

Later in the interview, Cope told me, regarding a forth-coming talk here: "Coming back to Liverpool always makes me a bit nervous – but it'll be cool because I'll be wearing my five-inch platform boots and Archbishop's hat. I'll look 6ft 9!" And as we neared the end of a hugely-entertaining hour, he told me he was an "adventurer who believes in the shaman and exploring the physical geography of the land."

Then, with enormous enthusiasm, he added: "I'm out there!" I, for one, believed him.

Pete Wylie, March 24, 2000

"I'll have to give someone else credit for (calling me) 'Peteloaf' – a mate said it before me, and I thought it was hilarious. As for my word 'optimisery', people think you're either up or down, and I'm neither. It's the condition of anyone who's had a broken heart but still believes he can fall in love again."

Pete Wylie, from his "My Weekend" questionnaire, January 13, 2001

What would you pack in a picnic basket?
"It'd have to be a picnic wheelbarrow... lots of alcohol, pastry-based products and chocolate raisins."
What is your favourite hangover cure?
"Sleep and then more lager."
Do you exercise?
"Of course. I follow a very strict regime to keep myself in tip-top condition. I'm launching the Fat-Wah! Diet."

Ian McCulloch and Will Sergeant, August 17, 2001

The Bunnymen have received shedloads of critical acclaim and sold shedloads of records – so where did all the money go? That's a good question, they say. "I could do with a few more bob," says the singer. "The thing that amazes the pair of us is that we're not financially secure. But we're still doing great things and that gives me more pride than having a house in the South of France – which I wouldn't even go to because I'd be here watching Liverpool."

Ian McCulloch, November 28, 2003

It isn't a great start. Ian McCulloch isn't a happy bunnyman.

Fresh – well, jaded and jetlagged – from an international tour which took in the USA, Canada, Australia, Japan and Brazil, mouth almighty feels in need of some Liverpool medicine: a pint of Cains bitter. We head for his pub of choice: The Philharmonic, but disaster strikes: the Cains is off! "I don't bel-ieeee-ve it," says Ian.

This is swiftly followed by disaster number two: The Tuna Melt Incident. Ian wants to eat in the main bar but we're directed to the lounge/dining room at the back of the pub. "Would you like a side order?" asks a nervous young chap. "Yeah, I'd like to eat it on that side of the pub."

He can't, so cancels his Tuna Melt. Then, after a few more uncomfortable seconds, the nervous young chap says: "Well, you can't drink in here if you're not having any food." "Good," says Ian. "Because I didn't want to drink in this room in the first place!" We head for The Brewery Tap, next door to the Cains brewery, where there is plenty of Cains bitter and, for Ian, a plate of Lamb and Mint Pudding, chips and peas. He is a happier bunnyman.

***

The Crucial Three loved The Fall – and so did I. In fact, between 1979 and 1983 I was probably obsessed with them.

The man who made his Mark with The Fall, November 24, 2000

A wise person once warned: never meet or interview your heroes – you'll only be disappointed. But after several near misses, there was now no escape... the time had finally come to speak to the unpredictable Mark E. Smith, leader of The Fall for the last 23 years. And, according to some, not the easiest of interviewees.

Smith, to my ears, is responsible for some of the greatest records ever made (most of them many years ago). But, to my and many other Fall fans' ears, there have been several dodgy spells – although the band's new LP, The Unutterable, is widely viewed as a return to form.

There have also been spells of disharmony. The Fall have released about 35 albums – and Smith has used a similar number of musicians.

One of many incarnations disintegrated on a New York stage in 1998, when ex-drummer Karl Burns vaulted his drum kit and pinned a tired and emotional-looking Smith against a wall. All, you could tell, was not well. End result: drummer, guitarist and bass guitarist (long-time servant Steve Hanley) left the band. And Smith? He just dusted himself down and carried on with keyboard player Julia Nagle and another set of hired hands.

The Fall's delightfully named producer Grant Showbiz says of the singer: "Always being slightly crazy is one of the brilliant things about him; he is from Planet Mark. But what doesn't come over is that he's a lovable, wonderful guy, not a curmudgeonly old git who sits in the pub and rambles on about how much he hates everything."

Smith spoke to me, for about eight minutes, from the restaurant of a London hotel. He wasn't curmudgeonly, but he certainly came across as slightly crazy. And, erm, merry.

Producer Showbiz says the new album is your best for at least a decade. Smith: "He's the producer, he would say that! Ha, ha!"

But isn't he implying that previous releases haven't been up to scratch?

Smith: "Ha, ha, ha, ha, ha, ha, ha!"

Right, so how do you rate The Unutterable?

Smith: "I like this one… I like the middle bit best. Does that make sense?" The singer then launches into a rambling explanation about how the band no longer uses Pete Waterman's Manchester studios – and that part of the LP was instead recorded in a "cubicle." By The Fall's standards, this latest line-up has been together some time. Have you managed to mould them yet?

Smith: "Yes, but it's taken me two years. They're about 10 years younger than me; they're brats… I always recruit people who haven't been in groups before."

So you don't want anyone with baggage?

Smith (as if I'd just uttered the word that had been on the tip of his tongue for the last 12 years): "Baggage! Yes! That's right! That's right!"

We talk about tonight's gig at the Lomax and he says: "Liverpool was the first town to recognise us. We played lots of gigs at Eric's in the late '70s. Sorry, they're all giggling here…"

Finally (although it wasn't intended to be my final question), I asked whether he feels vindicated as none of the many musicians who have left The Fall have gone on to greater things – with the possible exception of Marc Riley, though it could be argued that has merely been as a sidekick to Radio 1's Mark Radcliffe, rather than as a musician.

Smith: "Ha, ha, ha, ha, ha!"

So, do you feel vindicated?

Smith: "Yes, Paddy. It's good to talk to you, Paddy. It's nice to hear a Scouse accent (I haven't got one)… I'm down in London. I've got to go now."

Cheers.

***

But I can't leave things there. The following is taken from a column I wrote, following his death.

Mark E. Smith of The Fall, thanks for the memories: January 31, 2018

If you love music as an adult, it's likely it first grabbed you by the scruff of the neck when you were a teenager. And it probably moved you more intensely then than it has ever been able to do in later life.

I fell hook, line and sinker for The Fall when I was 15. I liked, even loved, them during various parts of my adult life, but nothing rivalled the passion I felt during my first three or four years as a Fall fan.

It all started when I first heard Rowche Rumble during the school summer holidays in August, 1979 (thank you, John Peel). This was their third single. I bought it – then bought a second copy, just in case something happened to the first. I caught up by buying their first and second singles and first LP. Their second LP, Dragnet, was released in October of that year and I saw them play live for the first time in November. I can't match comedian Stewart Lee's gig total of 52 (I did fall out of love with them at various times), but still saw them on 14 occasions – not bad. I remember day-dreaming about becoming a member of The Fall in 1980. I was 16. Then I heard they had recruited a new drummer – Paul Hanley. He was 16. I was disappointed but, to be fair, I couldn't play the drums. Or any instrument! In the summer of that year, claiming to be a bedroom band called The Ambitious Merchants, me and my mates living next door recorded a number of "songs" which we released on a cassette I christened Eating Apple Crumble Whilst Listening To Rowche Rumble (I wrote to Mark E. Smith, who wrote back telling me he loved the title!)

I last saw The Fall at Liverpool's East Village Arts Club, in 2013. One of those former next-door neighbours was playing in support band Evil Blizzard. It seems fitting that this was the last time I saw the frontman whose band moved me like no other during my formative years. Mark E. Smith, rest in peace.

Half Man Half Biscuit

Regular *Echo* readers will have noticed that below my name, on my column every Wednesday, were the words "Likes: Pubs, Everton and Half Man Half Biscuit. Hates: Everything else." Stewart Lee may have watched The Fall on 52 occasions, but there's one band I'm pretty sure I've seen more times than that – the mighty Half Man Half Biscuit, who were formed in 1984 by Nigel Blackwell (singer and guitarist) and Neil Crossley (bass guitarist).

And this despite me being a late starter, having only seen them for the first time in 1994 (though I wasn't a late convert, as I already had the records).

The first time I interviewed the band's frontman, Nigel Blackwell, was in 1998, and I went on to interview him a few more times – but knowing that he had very little interest in being promoted in this way, I stopped asking him in the end, and we just started enjoying a regular drink together instead. It's grown into a friendship which I cherish.

But no, Nigel could never be described as "publicity hungry" – as you might gather from the following interview and column extracts…

Halfway home, July 17, 1998

The Biscuits' story is one of what might have been, what still could be, and what frontman Nigel Blackwell would quite happily live without.

This is the man who split up the band – a split which lasted more than three years – at the height of its early success. Dickie Davies Eyes, the follow-up to The Trumpton Riots, was top of the independent singles' charts and the group was on the eve of a seven country tour of Europe and America.

But after a date in Holland, the only country Nigel's ever visited, he realised that touring wasn't for him: "I've got to wake every morning in my own bed," he says today.

Since reforming, the Biscuits have played only one-off gigs and the band remains as wilfully underexposed and anonymous as ever: no names or pictures on album sleeves and no pictures in the *Echo*, please.

Over the last six years, they have bypassed Liverpool because Nigel felt uncomfortable playing in front of so many familiar faces, including lads he sees as he follows his beloved Tranmere Rovers around the country.

He feels more comfortable about that prospect today – hence the gig planned for somewhere in Liverpool in September – but Nigel would never feel comfortable playing the pop music game. He says: "I love the idea of big bucks. A common misconception is our so-called stubborn independence, but it's just this 25-date tour thing... I've never really had any money, but it's probably not as much of a problem as people think. I'm very easily pleased. I have no material aspirations. I can't drive. I don't go on foreign holidays. I've never flown and don't like sailing. I gave up smoking and I don't drink.

"At the moment I'm doing my damnedest to get a mortgage for a little terraced house. If a big label came along and said 'Here's a load of money; do this, this and this', I'd probably take the money, buy a house, and then get myself dropped on purpose and go back to Probe. We've got so much freedom with Geoff (Davies). I've got control over everything we do."

At a recent gig in Cheltenham, a poster advertising future gigs explained the type of music played by each visiting band. After one, it said "blues/funk", another said "punk."

Then came Half Man Half Biscuit: "We just had a load of question marks," says Nigel.

Doesn't he look like...? April 28, 2000

Thousands of wannabe pop stars would sell their own granny (and throw in grandad) for one column-inch of publicity.

But, should they perish in a freak road accident on their way home from one of their almost secret gigs, this band's collective tombstone would probably read: "Here lie Half Man Half Biscuit. They couldn't be bothered."

If life was a little less complicated, word and tunesmith Nigel Blackwell would be hailed as one of the great comic writers of this and the last century. But that would be a nightmare for the man himself.

"Anonymity is everything," says the bard of Birkenhead, whose label owner, Geoff Davies, has the unenviable task of promoting their new CD, Trouble Over Bridgwater. Following a rare sighting on a Liverpool stage 18 months ago, one reviewer likened Nigel to Manchester United superstar Jaap Stam (appearance, not footballing ability) and the singer says today: "When I go and get my *Echo* the kids in the street shout 'Alright Jaap?'" Quality of life and the freedom to do what the hell he likes, rather than over-exposure and a bulging bank account, are what is important to the singer: "What I cling to is to be able to wake up most days and think 'What should I do today?'"

The attraction with any Biscuits' CD begins with the title

and Nigel says: "I was thinking of calling it Merseyrail Stinks of S***, after graffiti spotted at Leasowe Station. I loved the nightly Merseyrail cancellation bulletins you ran in the *Echo*, but they should have been used bigger."

What will interest Nigel-watchers is how on earth he ended up in the recent edition of lads' mag *Loaded*: "I only did it because it's so untrendy these days and no-one seems to read it. I also like the writer, Johnny Cigarettes. But I've always wondered why the people who buy *Loaded* and *FHM* don't go the whole hog and buy Fiesta or Razzle instead."

HMHB play irregular (very irregular) gigs all over the country, but their last Liverpool show was their first in six years.

Any chance of going mad and playing another one soon? "We've no plans to, but I'm not averse to it. It's just that thing about everyone I know coming to see us, because I'm not a natural performer. It's not that it fills me with dread, it's just that I can't really be bothered with it."

Nigel Blackwell. He may not be bothered, but he's still a genius.

Nigel unmasks plans for Biscuits future, September 21, 2002

If they played the game and hung out with the music industry's posers and parasites, HMHB would be bigger than Beelzebub. And Will Young.

Instead, singer Nigel Blackwell, the publicity-shy wordsmith and sometime tunesmith (fellow founder member, and demon bassist, Neil Crossley supplied the music for five of the 13 tracks on new CD Cammell Laird Social Club), is again trying to avoid having his photograph in the *Echo*.

The Guardian Weekend magazine? That was different. People wouldn't see that. But his mug in the *Echo*? That would definitely blow his much-prized anonymity. Well-meaning souls might collar him and say: "I thought you'd packed in for good after The Trumpton Riots single and Back In The DHSS album in the mid-'80s."

Still, progress is being made: four years ago, the *Echo* simply used the Four Lads Who Shook The Wirral CD sleeve alongside a Nigel interview; two years ago it was the Trouble Over Bridgwater sleeve and a picture of Nigel lookalike Jaap Stam.

But now, we present Nigel... in shades and a cycle helmet: "Well, I do write most of my songs while cycling along country lanes – and it would be irresponsible not to wear a helmet," he explains.

Andy Kershaw recently dubbed HMHB "Britain's greatest folk band." Nigel, typically, says: "That's a bit over the top, isn't it? Nice of him to say so, though."

Apart from a new CD, fans can also look forward to seeing their most recent gig released on video. Allegedly.

It took place in Manchester... 10 months ago.

Nigel says: "It's out of our hands, but apparently it's very close now! But the people putting it together can't include our version of Joy Division's New Dawn Fades, which is a shame because I was practising my golf swing during that one."

Achtung Liverpool! Ahead of a rare Liverpool gig, Paddy Shennan talks to Half Man Half Biscuit's Nigel Blackwell, September 30, 2005

Since the last time we interviewed Nigel Blackwell, he has been voted the 57th Greatest Ever Merseysider by *Echo* readers and Radio Merseyside listeners (in the 2014, *Echo*-only poll, he would shoot up to number 10).

He says: "Obviously the whole thing was a bit silly, but it did at least astound my parents, whom I feel had hitherto deemed me a bit of a tramp. Which I am, of course."

John Peel loved HMHB and the late, much-missed broadcaster once said of the band's gifted lyricist: "He's a shrewd observer of life and genuinely funny – a man who rejoices in the use of language."

Nigel loved Peel, too, and says: "What is often overlooked about him is his writing, although his forthcoming book should go some way to redressing the balance. And he was someone who had the attitude of 'F*** the visitor centre, let them explore' – I don't know why Radio One doesn't just simply replay a load of his old shows."

As for Nigel's shrewd observations and rejoicing in the use of language, there's a new body of evidence on the latest HMHB CD, entitled – sorry, U2 fans – Achtung Bono. What kind of mind is it, for example, that marries a seminal band with an everyday household item – producing the classic track Joy Division Oven Gloves?

Nigel, who's fond of telling big fibs in his rare interviews (he once told *The Guardian* there was a HMHB tribute band called It Ain't Half Man, Mum), says: "I received the idea for this song from a powerful inspirational force that comes from somewhere outside myself – a theory of creation somewhat similar to that of the poet Shelley. Or possibly our drummer wrote it." Letters Sent, meanwhile, celebrates the letters pages of local newspapers. But does Nigel believe those people who pen made-up, mickey-taking missives have got too much time on their hands (see CD's inner sleeve for examples)? Or should it, instead, be an Olympic sport? "To be fair, it's probably a tragic reflection of my life. I merely got to wondering one day how many letters of an equine nature I could get printed in the local freesheet and it sort of went on from there."

Then there's the sublime For What Is Chatteris, which isn't intended as an insult to the Cambridgeshire town, whatever its local paper might think. Of its inspiration, Nigel says (fibs?): "I got it from Frankie Baldwin in Coronation Street who, in relation to moving up North to be with husband Danny, said something like 'What's Dagenham if you're not in it?' It may not have been Dagenham, but it was certainly Essex-based."

Column: "Ground Control to Monty Don" – HMHB should be on the NHS, May 2, 2018

There is a new release by the band, due out later this month. It's called No One Cares About Your Creative Hub So Get Your F*****' Hedge Cut.

Nigel Blackwell, the band's frontman, was number 10 in

the *Echo*'s Greatest Merseysiders of All Time poll in 2014. Well, he is our greatest living lyricist. No offence to David Bowie, but I can't think of a better opening line to a song than "Ground Control to Monty Don" – from the new LP's masterpiece, Every Time A Bell Rings (chorus: "Every time a bell rings, I hate you some more.") So many of Nigel's delightful and delicious lyrics drip with disdain. He has an extremely healthy contempt for ridiculous people and institutions, and his righteous indignation hits the bullseye every time.

Column: Let's hear it for these fine words of wit, wisdom and wonder, September 26, 2018

You can't overstate the importance of lyrics, and Nigel Blackwell's one-liners, wordplay and flights of fancy are things of beauty, and, often, hilarity: "There's a man with a mullet going mad with a mallet in Millets."

"Twin town said we just weren't cool, so now we've got a suicide pact with Goole." He is a keen and shrewd observer of life: "Never trust a crown green bowler under 30." "Not long now before lollipop men are called Darren."

Always articulate, sometimes angry and vitriolic, he wants people to get things right: "If you're going to quote from the Book of Revelation/Don't keep calling it the 'Book of Revelations'/There's no 's', it's the Book of Revelation/As revealed to St John the Divine/See also Mary Hopkin/She must despair."

"Opinionated weather forecasters telling me it's going to

be a miserable day. Miserable to who? I quite like a bit of drizzle, so stick to the facts."

He is full of sound advice: "Quick, run, hide – here comes Dave Stewart…" He has an eye for the absurd: "Oh, Geraldine, we were so laissez-faire/Every other day was a non-sequitur: Hadron Collider/Who's there?/Knock knock."

He can take you aback: "Midge Ure looks like a milk thief!"

And he knows what is truly important: "She's the main man in the office in the city and she treats me like I'm just another lackey, but I can put a tennis racquet up against my face and pretend that I'm Kendo Nagasaki."

"There is nothing better in life than writing on the sole of your slipper with a biro." It's a wonderful world. Why not step inside, if you haven't done so already?

Never too old to pogo – Buzzcocks interview, May 28, 1993

I loved Buzzcocks. I loved Pete Shelley – his perfect pop songs, and bittersweet lyrics about unrequited love.

In 1993, the born-again band was due to play the Royal Court in Liverpool, and I took the opportunity to go and see them in Birmingham so I could interview Shelley and do a preview piece (guitarist Steve Diggle ended up joining in on the interview).

***

Before taking the stage at a sweaty nightclub in Birmingham, Pete Shelley sips a can of lager backstage and says: "I'd love to talk to the *Liverpool Echo*. It will help relieve the boredom. "Touring involves 23 hours of tedium and one hour of panic. Mind you, we once enjoyed some exciting and Beatle-esque scenes in Liverpool."

Steve Diggle takes up the story: "We were playing the Empire in 1978. I remember the hotel was only a short walk away, but there were hundreds of screaming kids outside and we had to be driven around the city centre in a police car to get to it."

The group is unlikely to get such a reception next week and many would suggest it was a big mistake to reform: "When I sing the line 'I'm already a has-been' from Boredom, it does raise a few chuckles," admits Shelley. "We had a rejection letter from an A&R man who said he had been a great fan of ours and was very upset that we had reformed. I think he felt that we were running the risk of tarnishing the image. But when you start believing the image rather than the actuality, you're in trouble. It's my life and I can do what I want with it. There's no sell-by date on anyone. As long as we are enjoying ourselves, why shouldn't we carry on?"

***

Later in the interview, he tells me: "This is still better than working behind a desk all day. And it's more enjoyable the second time around because there's less pressure and fear." And it is soon clear which songs the crowd have come to hear…

As your parents always tell you: "The old songs are the best!"

***

I referred to this interview again following Pete's death, many years later. Here's an extract from that column...

Sublime songs, brilliant lyrics: nostalgia for an age that's come, December 19, 2018

I was lucky enough to interview Pete Shelley on a couple of occasions – once face-to-face, before a gig in Birmingham in 1993, ahead of a gig at Liverpool's Royal Court, during the tour to promote their first album since reforming in 1989.

It was a meeting which threw up an anecdote I've been boring people in the pub about ever since. After the interview, we were chatting in the bar of the venue – and I asked Pete if I could buy him a drink. He offered to buy me one, but I insisted I do the honours – so I could tell my friends and family: "I bought Pete Shelley a drink!" Pete didn't give up easily, telling me: "But, if I bought it, you could tell them 'Pete Shelley bought me a drink!"

Many people have since disagreed with me, but I'm still proud to be able to say "I bought Pete Shelley a bottle of beer!"

A little earlier, during the interview with Pete and fellow Buzzcock Steve Diggle, he again showed he was a man of wit and wisdom. I brought up a quote of Steve's, who had likened Pete's lyrics to Mills and Boon and his own to a Jackson Pollock painting. Pete gave me a knowing smile and said: "Mills and Boon sell more!"

Years later, Steve told *The Guardian*: "I say his (songs) are like Mills and Boon. And he says mine are like Ralph McTell." Pete then said: "And I'm not trying to be particularly kind to Ralph McTell."

Postie Vic put his own stamp on punk, December 2, 2005

One of my favourite singles of all time is Ambition by Subway Sect – and sometimes, I love its B side, Different Story, even more, which explains what a special single it is. I was delighted to be able to interview the band's genial, laid-back singer, Vic Godard, on the phone, ahead of a gig at the Magnet in Liverpool. It only made a short piece in the *Echo*, but I still treasure the cutting.

More than seven years later, I went to see Subway Sect in Preston – but I was travelling back from London in the early evening and was worried I might miss at least some of the set. I'd kept in contact with Vic around this time, and mentioned this to him – and he responded by telling me the band would delay their start time! What a gent. When I arrived (not as late as I had feared), I thanked him again – and he simply said: "I'm just glad you made it!"

Here's a decent chunk of the short article…

***

He has been described as the greatest lost soul of the punk era, a man more interested in being a postman than a pop star. But despite having disappeared from the music scene for spells, Vic Godard is still recording and performing today, work permitting (he's been a postie since 1986 – "I hate it, but it's in the blood and you can do it on auto-pilot").

His band, Subway Sect, was at the forefront of the punk revolution in 1976, and the current line-up will be in Liverpool tomorrow night. It represents a return to a city which left a lasting impression on Vic – who is from south London – after riotous gigs.

When Vic was wearing tuxedos during his swing phase, his then band shared a bill with Bauhaus and The Birthday Party at the Royal Court and faced a barrage of bottles from fans of the goth rockers: "We played our entire set as normal," recalls Vic, with pride. "The bottles just bounced off us. That must have been 1980 – it was the most satisfying rebellion I've ever been a part of."

On May 5, 1977, Subway Sect joined The Slits and head-liners The Clash for a legendary gig at Eric's, which inspired three young men in the audience to make their own music: Ian McCulloch, Pete Wylie and Julian Cope. In his book, Head On, Cope wrote: "I watched, spellbound, as Subway Sect played... These guys were my new heroes."

Vic says today: "I remember Eric's well, because it was such a small venue and the ceiling was amazingly low. I think I kept hitting my head on it."

On that same tour, Subway Sect also inspired the formation of Scottish bands Orange Juice, Josef K and Fire Engines – Orange Juice's singer, Edwyn Collins, later produced a Vic Godard album and described him as "the best songwriter of his generation."

***

I asked Vic if he'd be playing Ambition at his forthcoming gig at the Magnet, and he said: "We've tried it, but can't get the hang of it yet."

But it's OK, because I did see him perform it in Preston.

And I have a great memory of an enthusiastic punter at the Liverpool gig getting up on stage and leading the tentative band in a spirited rendition of Don't Split It (the B side of Subway Sect's debut single, Nobody's Scared), after Vic had politely explained that he and the band wouldn't be able to reproduce that particular song.

A surprised but delighted Vic watched the fan sing the song, while playing Vic's own guitar, and then asked him: "Could you come and do my next postman's round?"

Frank? He's fantastic, actually! June 18, 1992

The night I didn't meet Frank Sidebottom after all – but still managed to interview him.

***

Nobody has a bigger or better head for showbusiness than Frank Sidebottom. Frank's two favourite words perfectly sum up his rapid rise to stardom: "Fantastic, actually!" The man with the papier-mache bonce has amused – and irritated – millions of viewers on a myriad of TV shows ever since Five Star ("Or was it Abba?") caught his imagination on Top of The Pops.

"I thought 'Blimey! I could do that!'" says Timperley's favourite son.

"But the golden rule of showbusiness is that you need a gimmick... luckily, I have my pink tie!" The pop star-cum-comic-cum-ventriloquist is busy all this week at the Liverpool Festival of Comedy. He is hosting six nights at Club Magico in the Hardman House Hotel on Hardman Street (by the way, what a great lost Liverpool venue. I also remember seeing Inspiral Carpets play there – when Noel Gallagher was a roadie for them, I think).

But the shy superstar was in a Frank Sinatra mood when I turned up to interview him. I was told by an intermediary that he couldn't speak to me as he had a sore throat – though this didn't stop him belting out his musical "tributes" to Kylie Minogue and Freddie Mercury. I had space to fill in the next day's *Echo* and, fortunately, the great man bowed to my begging letter, slipped backstage, and answered my questions with pen and paper. Phew!

"I've played Liverpool loads... in between shopping for me mum. I love the whole place. It's ace and top."

Looking ahead to his Desert Island Books interview tomorrow at the Central Library, he didn't want to give too much away, but said: "It will include the TV21 1968 Annual – it's got Thunderbirds and Captain Scarlet in it, and a Lucozade stain on it."

He also exclusively revealed that he is working on his very own show for ITV: "It will be called Frank's Fantastic Shed Show and will be filmed in my back garden shed. And my advice to anyone who wants to follow me into showbusiness is 'don't let your mum know! And try to be better than Paul McCartney.'"

Football fan Frank, meanwhile, is still reeling from Altrincham FC's decision to sack him as club mascot – because he was a "jinx on the team."

He said: "I now have my own Sunday football team called Timperley Big Shorts FC, who last season were runners-up in the Manchester Sunday League Division Three... but I have been banned for life after another side said I was dangerous in the box going up for headers. But that's what they pay Ian Rush for... isn't it?"

Henry Priestman: "I'm enjoying myself more than ever now," July 29, 2015

Some misguided souls who are involved in the music industry might not consider it cool, but there's nothing wrong with being a nice bloke – and Henry Priestman is one of the nicest I met while I was at the *Echo*. I'd been listening to his music since 1977 – and first met him in 2015!

***

He's sold millions of records and played stadium gigs in front of tens of thousands of people – but Henry Priestman says: "I'd rather play Thornton Hough Village Club than Wembley Arena." And the man who was a regular fixture on Top of The Pops in the late 1980s as the keyboardist and songwriter for The Christians also loves playing places even smaller than Thornton Hough Village Club, as he hires himself out – alongside fellow musician and great friend Les Glover – for house parties across the country.

I met Henry at Junction Coffee on Aigburth Road, and it was a poignant time to discuss his life in bands such as Albert Dock (who supported the Sex Pistols at Eric's on October 15, 1976), Yachts, It's Immaterial and The Christians. For he would soon be heading to Barnstaple in Devon to attend the funeral of former Yachts drummer Bob Bellis – who, along with the rest of Yachts, Henry met while at Liverpool College of Art in 1975 – and then, afterwards, in tribute, play Yachts songs Suffice To Say, Yachting Type and Love You Love You. Of Bob, who was from Rock Ferry and 61 – he had fallen ill in April when he suffered a heart attack – Henry says: "He was a wonderful, larger-than-life character; a hilarious man who was always full of great stories."

With Henry having been gigging for nigh-on 40 years, I thought it was a good time to get his top 10 venues.

Yachts and The Christians played some massive gigs, not least when the former supported The Who on a European tour in 1980 and the latter supported Bruce Springsteen in Paris "in about 1989, in front of about 100,000 people." And Henry says: "My smallest solo gig was playing in someone's kitchen in Ibrox, Glasgow, in front of about 25 people. Someone once said to me 'It's sad that it's come to this – I saw you playing Wembley Arena.' But I don't remember Wembley being that good because I was so full of nerves, whereas I'm now enjoying myself more than ever. It's like when The Christians reformed in 2000 and played in front of 200 people in small arts centres – I enjoyed those nights more than all those big gigs." So, in no particular order, here are Henry's favourite places – from 1976 to today…

Eric's, Liverpool: "Without Eric's, I wouldn't have ended up doing what I'm still doing today."

Thornton Hough Village Club: "It's fabulous! The audiences aren't saying 'Go on, impress us!' There's a lot of love."

On board the Royal Iris, Liverpool: "Yachts launched our debut album on the Royal Iris and Elvis Costello was the surprise guest. There were some great gigs on the boat, including by Wah! And Magazine – and captive audiences!"

The Processed Pea Folk Club, Etton, near Beverley, Hull: "I was born and brought up in Hull and love playing here."

Hammersmith Odeon, London: "It was just the fact that, in The Christians, we were able to play a place like this. Garry (Christian) was great at making these big venues seem more intimate because he used to run into the audience with his roving microphone."

Green Note café bar, Camden/The Hope and Anchor, Islington, London: "Green Note may hold something like 70 people – it's got a really good atmosphere. I played there the other night and it was possibly my most enjoyable London gig in 38 years of playing the capital. Yachts played the Hope and Anchor loads of times. It was a pub rock venue and then became a punk venue. It was a lot smaller than Eric's and always really sweaty."

The Lantern Theatre, Liverpool: "I played there last December and will be playing again this Christmas. It's a fabulous place."

A canal boat on the Kennet and Avon Canal: "I played to 36 people and, after 20 minutes, the boat stopped and took on a delivery of fish and chips."

The Olympia Theatre, Dublin: "The Christians played there twice, I think. There would be a play on in the evening and then we would go on at midnight, by which time everyone was tanked up. It was great!"

CBGB/Max's Kansas City, New York: "Yachts played them both – and they're too cool not to mention!"

Mark King of Level 42, October 31, 2003

Talking of nice blokes… I wasn't really a fan of Level 42 (OK, I admit it, I've got the 12-inch version of It's Over), but I loved interviewing singer and bassist Mark King, not least because of his nice anecdote about niceness…

It's hard to shake off a bad reputation – and it can be just as hard to get rid of a good one. But perhaps it's about time Mark King accepted that he may actually be "The nicest man in pop," as a music writer once claimed.

"That's a scurrilous thing to say!" moans Mark, in mock protest. "It's on a par with an interview I once saw Cliff Richard giving to Annie Nightingale on TV. Cliff was saying punk rock was the most disgusting thing that had ever happened and Annie asked him 'So, which bands do you like?'

"I sat up in bed and started shouting 'Please don't say us! Please don't say us!'… and he replied 'I really like Level 42.'

"Why? I'd never done anything to him!"

Chapter Seven

With(out) The Beatles

THERE WAS always plenty of excitement in the air when one of my colleagues secured an interview with Paul McCartney. With no disrespect to Macca, I was never that bothered. Perhaps I've just read too many interviews with the Fab Four over the years, but what intrigued me more were the stories around The Beatles – including those told by family and friends.

How it all REALLY began, January 13, 1995

If you wanted to know the truth about John Lennon – including what actually happened on the day he met Paul McCartney – you couldn't do much better than interview Pete Shotton. Then again, as Pete pointed out to me, even the people who were central to the story have different memories of how things unfolded at the summer fete at St Peter's Church in Woolton on July 6, 1957. Pete (who died in 2017, aged 75) was John Lennon's best mate. They were so close John jokingly referred to them as "Shennon and Lotton."

"Over a period of almost 30 years, from the time I first met him at the age of six to our last meeting in 1976 at his home in New York, I probably spent more time with him than anyone else," said Pete, who attended Dovedale Primary and Quarry Bank High schools along with the future Beatle, and was a washboard player in John's first band, The Quarrymen. He was made a director of The Beatles' company Apple Corps and, later, John's personal assistant.

A successful businessman, his first venture – a supermarket and sub-post office on Hayling Island, near Portsmouth, in 1965 – was financed by his famous pal to the tune of £20,000 (equivalent to more than £400,000 today).

Pete went into the restaurant business in the early '80s. He is now chairman of Fatty Arbuckle's Ltd and currently presides over an empire of 14 restaurants. He set up shop in Edge Lane Retail Park last year.

In Pete's 1983 book, John Lennon In My Life, John is quoted as saying of his growing waistline on one occasion: "I'd better do something about it before I turn into a real Fatty Arbuckle!" Despite being fed-up with talking about The Beatles, Pete kindly agreed to meet me at his Fatty Arbuckle's restaurant in Edge Lane – following the publication of a book by American author Jim O'Donnell called The Day John Met Paul: An Hour-By-Hour Account of How The Beatles Began.

It's probably fair to say Pete – who was great company and was only giving this interview because it was for his hometown paper – wasn't a great fan of the idea behind the book, which apparently took eight years to research and runs to 143 pages. In his own book, Pete devoted a mere nine paragraphs to the meeting that revolutionised music.

He told me: "Nothing like this surprises me. We'll probably end up with a book about the moments John and Paul were conceived and their ancestry will be traced back to a couple of gorillas in Woolton Woods!"

Pete did not give an interview to the author, but told me: "I would have really wound him up if I'd met him. I'd have said that on that fateful day, Paul wore a pink floral tie, belt and braces, high-heeled shoes and a diver's helmet. You never know, if I'd have kept my face straight, he might have believed me!"

But Pete stressed there was no need to make things up as far as the events at the summer fete at St Peter's Church in Woolton are concerned… because even the people who were there have wildly differing versions of what happened!

He said: "The mind is a very strange thing. It is very easy to forget things and get confused about the sequence of events. I was talking to The Quarrymen's tea chest bass player, Len Garry, about the day and he is convinced that Paul got up on stage with us, which he didn't. And I didn't even realise that Colin Hanton was our drummer at the time!"

Rod Davis, meanwhile, the group's banjo player, didn't even recall Paul being there at all. He said: "The greatest moment in rock 'n' roll history and I must have been in the toilet!" So what really happened that day – as far as Pete could remember?!

He explained: "It was a big event for us in so far as it was our first paid public performance. We had previously just played in people's houses. All this, at the time, was far more important than the fact we met a young lad known as 'Macca.'"

That John met Paul and The Quarrymen were paid – "I think we were, although I can't actually recall getting the money" – was all thanks to Pete's mum, Bessie (who was 82 at the time of my interview and living near Pete in Winchester).

"Yes! The Beatles would never have happened but for my mum! She was very well-known in Woolton and had been connected with St Peter's Church for a long time. She booked us."

The Quarrymen played two sets, the first in the scouts' field behind the church, and later at a dance in the church hall. After moving their rather basic equipment to the hall, they were joined by a friend, Ivan Vaughan, who thought John might be interested in meeting one of his classmates from the Liverpool Institute. He had a guitar in his hand and his name was Paul McCartney.

"I liked him instantly," said Pete. "He had an aura about him. He was very cool and calm. He had charisma. He seemed like a nice, friendly kid. John was a bit wary, but he was always like that. He checked people out very carefully before he offered anything of himself. When he met Paul, he basically saw the opportunity to learn something from someone he didn't feel antagonised by. If he had felt threatened by him, he wouldn't have let him near."

The meeting "probably lasted between 10 and 15 minutes – 20 at most."

Recalling how he played Eddie Cochran's Twenty Flight Rock in front of him, Paul later said: "When I met John, I knew all the words to this song – and I think that's why I got to join the band."

Pete recalled that after Paul left, he and John had a vague discussion about the possibility of him joining the band, but nothing happened until a fortnight later – when Pete had a chance meeting with Paul.

"He was cycling into Woolton from his home in Allerton. He had been to Ivan's but he wasn't in. He was looking for this group of guys he'd met two weeks earlier, so our paths would have crossed sooner or later."

Paul joined the band and Pete – never at ease with his washboard! – decided to leave soon afterwards: "I considered myself a bigger fan of Elvis and rock 'n' roll than John, but I had no idea then just how serious he was about playing music."

What would have happened if John had never met Paul? "I don't think anyone could answer that. But I can say that John would definitely not have become a solo performer at that time. He always needed some support. I'm just lucky that I don't have a musical gene in my body, or I would have probably screwed the whole thing up!"

Fab Forthlin, July 22, 1998

Yesterday… the world's media trampled through the house which used to be home to Sir Paul McCartney. But tonight, a nation of nosy parkers will be given a detailed tour of 20

Forthlin Road, Allerton, Liverpool 18, in BBC2's Birthplace of The Beatles.

My fellow journalists and I were fascinated by the original hallway lino, Belfast kitchen sink, packets of Omo and recreation of the standard McCartney breakfast: fried egg with fried bread soaked in tomato ketchup.

All nice touches – as is the tiny '50s Bush television, the old-fashioned telephone (the number was Garston 6922) and the smell of lavender (Paul and Mike's dad, Jim, grew it to counteract the smell of his cigarette smoke).

But what is really important is that this is the front room where Lennon and McCartney practised their songwriting craft while sagging off school; where they wrote Love Me Do and I Saw Her Standing There.

And, besides, it's the wonderfully evocative family pictures on the wall taken by Mike – of Paul strumming a guitar in the backyard while washing hangs on the line; reading *The Observer* in his 12ft by 8ft front bedroom, shinning down the drainpipe at the back of the house and so on – which give you the truest flavour of Macca's home life in the late '50s and early '60s. Four years ago, a charming woman called Sheila Jones, who was to sell up to the National Trust 12 months later, told me a story she'd told a thousand times before. She and her late husband, Ashley, had been allocated the maroon and cream-coloured house by Liverpool Corporation in 1964 – but the local authority failed to inform them who the previous occupants had been.

Mrs Jones recalled: "Workmen were taking out the old fireplace and one of them said to me 'Do you want to buy an old brick?' I remember giving neighbours bits of curtain. The McCartneys also left a cooker and parts of that have been sent all over the world."

She also made visitors welcome, adding: "My late husband, Ashley, also loved the Beatles' fans. The amount of tea and chocolate biscuits we must have given people!"

Bill Partington, who still lives opposite, recalls the day the McCartneys left their home: "The fans used to sweep up the road looking for anything of Paul's – like his underwear from the washing line. Jim would say to me 'I don't know how long we can stay here with all this hassle. I don't like the neighbours suffering.' Then he came over to my house one afternoon and said 'I'm doing a bunk tonight. Paul has fixed us up with a place over the water.'"

The removal van arrived at midnight. Forthlin Road was ghostly quiet.

It wasn't yesterday…

Baker's days with Macca. An afternoon at Abbey Road studios with Geoff Baker, Sir Paul McCartney's right-hand man for the last 14 years, November 17, 2003

Paul McCartney's representative on earth lights up one of the 60 cigarettes he will smoke today and pours scorn on the notion that he could ever commit the ultimate betrayal… "There is as much chance of me writing a book about Paul as there is of me taking life seriously," says Geoff Baker, who has served his lord and master as press officer for 14 eventful, newsworthy years.

"I could write hundreds of books about Paul, but I'd never do it – even if someone put a gun to my head. It would cheapen everything; I think it's entirely wrong to work for someone and then write a book about him."

But you could do it? There would be nothing stopping you?

"Of course I could do it. But it isn't a consideration. It's never going to happen." It would be letting Paul, and himself, down. Although Geoff, in his own self-deprecating words, did "f*** up" and let his boss down quite recently. And he is big enough to bring up "That David Blaine thing" just a few minutes after we meet, as he prepares to oversee an afternoon of promotional TV interviews at Abbey Road studios with two of the producers who remixed a born-again Beatles album: Let It Be… Naked.

He was fired by Paul – though reinstated within hours – after it emerged that he had tipped off a *London Evening Standard* photographer that his boss would be visiting the scene of a Blaine stunt by Tower Bridge.

There were reports of a certain amount of unpleasantness, including a scuffle between Paul's pals and the snapper, although Paul later played down the incident as "a group of friends on a night out" and dismissed the "sacking" as a joke.

Anything you'd like to add, Geoff? "Yes, I'm a ****."

So, the conspiracy theories were wrong and it wasn't a Baker/McCartney stunt to generate even more headlines? "We're not that f****** mad!" Further explaining their relationship, he adds: "There has been the odd barney over the years, but it's always me – I cause them. It's me being hot-headed, because I just am. It doesn't matter if I'm working for Paul McCartney, the Pope or whoever. I'm a bit intolerant of authority. But if Paul McCartney was a dickhead I wouldn't work for him."

He pauses to consider his role: "I think it's hysterical that I work for someone who is the most famous person in the world apart, perhaps, from the Pope – although the Pope's songs aren't as good. But it'll probably end very soon – probably after Paul reads this! I really wouldn't be surprised if it ended this year."

You've been doing the job for 14 years, so why should it end now? "Because I don't presume anything. I keep having to change the remark, but when I'd worked for Paul for 10 years I said 'If you work for Paul McCartney for 10 days that would make your life.' I'm not saying that in a sycophantic way, because he gets enough of that. But it's f****** fabulous. It's a privilege; it's not work. It's been a blast. And that's what I think it's meant to be; fun and a laugh – it's only rock 'n' roll."

Non-stop Geoff – possibly powered by Duracell batteries – does wonderful impressions of a hyperactive child and a runaway train at this world-famous musical landmark in London's St John's Wood. He has, for once, agreed to step out of Paul McCartney's shadow and into the spotlight – but only because it will give him the chance to further promote the new, stripped-down version of The Beatles' album Let It Be. Geoff, who is great company and one of the most enthusiastic people I've ever met, is excited. Very excited.

Over the course of more than four hours, he will tell me and several others "The Beatles are on the f****** front cover of the *NME*, for the first time since they split up! How cool is that?"

When we arrive, he is on his knees before The Beatles, applying tape to giant posters – and praising the new (old) album to the heavens: "This is a great day for Liverpool, Paddy. And the audacity of the whole thing – remixing an album made 33 years ago! That's not a scam, it's Scouse front!"

Being Paul McCartney – and his press officer – means questions, questions and more questions. And Geoff says: "The most ridiculous thing I see in this job is when interviewers say to Paul, 'Now, I'm going to ask you a question you've never been asked before.' Because he's always been asked it before!"

Geoff rounds things off by telling me his favourite Beatles song: "Birthday from The White Album, because it was playing when I had sex for the first time – when I was 14-years-old." Very rock 'n' roll, Geoff. And I bet you lit up a fag immediately afterwards.

***

Ten months later, in September, 2004, Paul McCartney issued a statement, which said: "I find it very sad that after years of friendship, my publicist Geoff Baker and I are parting. Over the past few months, his behaviour has not reached the professional standards I had come to expect from Geoff, and it is with regret that I am forced to end our relationship. It is particularly sad that he has chosen to attempt to implicate my wife Heather in this business, and I can say now that she has absolutely nothing to do with this. In fact, she has always been a great supporter of his. This is purely between Geoff and myself, and I am sad to see it end in this way."

It was also reported at the time that Geoff declined to comment on Sir Paul's statement.

Cynthia Lennon on her turbulent life with John – and the reunion she longed for, September 30, 2005

Cynthia Lennon – Cynthia Powell when she met John – had written her second book about life with the first of her four husbands, and I kept thinking… I do feel sorry for the other three. When would it be their turn?

I didn't really.

***

We met in an upstairs office in Waterstone's in Bold Street, Liverpool…

Though friendly enough, Cynthia looked a little puzzled and preoccupied – like she'd mislaid her knitting. She spoke ever so softly and ever so quietly.

In her book, simply called John, she recalls the time John hit her at Liverpool College of Art – the day after he'd apparently worked himself into a jealous frenzy after seeing Cynthia dancing with his best pal, Stuart Sutcliffe: "Before I could speak he raised his arm and hit me across the face, knocking my head into the pipes that ran down the wall behind me… I knew I had to end our relationship."

Was that the most painful memory?

"No, I was up and down all the way through. It happened. But he didn't beat me up and give me a black eye. He slapped me."

Then she added, with another of her warm smiles: "These days I think a lot of women slap their men."

That's OK, then!

She recounts many exciting and blissfully happy times, but the overwhelming feeling, to this reader at least, is one of sadness – the love story had a nightmare ending, Julian only saw his dad a few times between the split and John's murder and, really, Cynthia should never have become Mrs Lennon.

But, most of all, the sadness which drips from the pages seems inspired by what didn't happen – but would have, Cynthia believes, had John still been alive; a stronger relationship between John and Julian and a warm reunion with his first wife in which they had the chance to look back fondly and enjoy shared memories of the good times.

"Absolutely," she says. "That would have been closure."

And she adds: "It's also very sad that there was no funeral and no memorial. That should have happened."

I ended the interview by referring to Cynthia's three other husbands, and asking if one of the problems had been that there were always three people in the marriage – her, her current husband and the Lennon legend?

"I think so," she says. "But that's another book!"

But what would it be called? How about Cynthia Lennon

Forever (Despite Having Also Been Cynthia Powell, Cynthia Bassanini, Cynthia Twist and Cynthia Charles)?

Yoko Ono, October 10, 2005

I met Yoko in her suite in the Mandarin Oriental Hyde Park Hotel in London on what would have been her husband John Lennon's 65th birthday, and their son, Sean's, 30th – Sunday, October 9, 2005.

Before turning her mind to what on earth she might wear for the following day's Q magazine awards ceremony, where John would be honoured, she happily (and, on one occasion, not so happily) answered my questions relating to one of the most fascinating men in musical history. Jet-lagged Yoko didn't need to speak to any media on this special day, telling me: "You are the only one! Because Liverpool is where it all started for John."

She arrived for our meeting via Tokyo, while I journeyed by train via Crewe and Milton Keynes (which, on a Sunday back then, could have ranked as almost as arduous a journey as flying in from Japan).

***

"Liverpool, of course, is going to be European Capital of Culture in 2008, isn't it? John would have thought that was great. John was always talking about Liverpool and saying that living in New York was just like living in Liverpool. He even said the New York taxi drivers were just like the lads from Liverpool – very down to earth."

And but for terrible fate, he would have returned to Liverpool to promote Double Fantasy, the album released just three weeks before his murder... wouldn't he?

Yoko says: "He was a very proud Liverpool lad and he didn't want to go back without a number one record – but he would definitely have gone back. And he would have been so proud to show Sean around the city."

***

Yoko did take me aback when she said of her late husband: "In his life, he was an incredibly good artist, but he felt he wasn't really appreciated. He didn't realise how well-loved he was." Really?

She explains: "As a Beatle, he was extremely successful – he knew that. But he also knew that was a lot to do with Paul. Paul was the one who knew how to deal with the world, and John was the poet. But when John was doing his individual work, I know he felt that people were not so much into his songs."

Imagine. Give Peace a Chance. Working Class Hero. Mind Games. Instant Karma! Gimme Some Truth. Jealous Guy. Power to The People.

And he still had self-doubt!? Incredible.

***

It wasn't a totally straightforward interview. Possibly because she was jet-lagged, or due to the fact she has been interviewed a million and one times, Yoko's answers could be very short. At times, I thought she was pausing, as she prepared to unleash an avalanche of words to support the four or five she had just uttered. But they were often full stops rather than pauses. Meanwhile, I wish I hadn't pressed her on one subject…

***

John's killer, Mark Chapman, was denied parole a year ago but will be eligible for it again in another 12 months. Is the fear of his possible release something which is always at the back of your mind, Yoko?

"I'm so busy that I totally forget about it, until someone says, 'Oh, it's this year now.' You have to start thinking about it, because it's next month or something."

I asked a follow-up question – perhaps I shouldn't have.

Some people feel Chapman remains unlikely to be released in the foreseeable future. Does Yoko? "I don't want to even know about it. I don't know why you are asking this question. I really think it's horrible." Point taken.

***

Thankfully, the atmosphere improved, while the interview ended positively, with Yoko telling me: "I'm very happy that Liverpool loves John because I feel Liverpool and I are brothers – and I hope I can keep that connection going."

Former Fab Four manager Allan Williams, February 24, 2010

Allan was great company, and had so many great stories. I

was, however, a touch taken aback by his choice of tipple – red wine with ice in it?

***

Some people have initials after their name, but the bloke sitting in the pub reflecting on his extraordinary life has an entire sentence.

It's been a long time since Allan Williams was simply known as Allan Williams – it's Allan Williams: The Man Who Gave The Beatles Away (the name of the book he co-wrote 35 years ago).

Enjoying a glass of red wine in the Jacaranda on Slater Street, which he opened as a coffee bar in 1957, he tells me, amid fits of self-deprecating laughter: "It's stuck with me that name. It will be on my tombstone."

But Allan, what do you think should be on your tombstone? What would you like on your tombstone?

Cue more laughter: "Er, 'The Man Who Gave The Beatles Away'!"

No, he isn't bitter. Nor is he drunk. He's just cheerfully accepting of his public image – and a man who counts his blessings.

He says: "I was just glad to have been there in the '60s, at the start of it all. People say to me 'You should be a millionaire' – and I say 'But I am a millionaire... I'm a millionaire of memories'." His smile couldn't look more genuine, as he adds: "I've always been proud of The Beatles and proud and happy to have been just a small cog in the wheel of the most famous group in the world... I wouldn't change anything.

"I'm still here – and being interviewed by the *Echo* while enjoying a glass of wine in one of my old places, a day after my 80th birthday. Fame and adulation aren't all they are cracked up to be – The Beatles were prisoners of their own popularity."

And yet there was a certain amount of unpleasantness when you went your separate ways, wasn't there? "I told John Lennon he would never f****** work again – but it ended up being me! Ha ha ha! And when I sat at home watching them on TV doing that Royal Command Performance (in November 1963) I thought to myself 'F****** hell, I used to manage those bastards!' I picked up a cushion and threw it at the screen – only because I didn't have a brick! And yes, I did tell Brian Epstein not to touch them with a f****** bargepole. But I qualified it – I did say they were good musicians."

Allan worked with The Beatles in 1960-61, getting the band gigs both here and, crucially for their future development, in Hamburg. But then they fell out: "The second time I sent them to Hamburg, I got a phone call from Stu Sutcliffe. He said 'John has decided we shouldn't pay you a commission because we got the job second time round.' I said 'You would never have smelt Hamburg if I hadn't taken you.'

"The biggest kick I got was barring them from the Blue Angel, which I opened in 1960. I cut off their whole social scene.

"Brian later came in and said 'The boys are very sorry about how they behaved in Hamburg. Can you find it in your heart to forgive them?' I said 'OK, the next time they're in town they can come in' – and Brian said 'Actually, they're outside now.' So they came in and threw their arms around me."

Bill Harry, art college friend of John Lennon and Stuart Sutcliffe and founder of the highly-influential Mersey Beat newspaper, July 22, 2011

Bill was always very helpful to me during my time at the *Echo*. I interviewed him here to mark the 50th anniversary of *Mersey Beat*.

***

A big deal – for both band and music paper – arrived on July 20, 1961, when the front page of the second edition of the fortnightly *Mersey Beat* announced "Beatles Sign Recording Contract."

And Bill says: "The article also included the first mention of an original Beatles song – George Harrison's Cry For A Shadow. Brian Epstein bought 12 dozen copies of that issue for his shop, NEMS in Whitechapel, while he became our record reviewer in the August 3 edition. His column was called 'Stop The World – And Listen To Everything In It'."

This all underlines Bill's point that Brian, who had yet to become their manager, knew all about The Beatles well before he went to see them at The Cavern that November – allegedly because he was intrigued by Tony Sheridan and The Beat Brothers (aka The Beatles). That early contract led to their single, My Bonnie.

Bill knew John the best: "To me he was Jekyll and Hyde. At art college – with me, Stuart Sutcliffe and Rod Murray – we were into the creative thing (the four christened themselves The Dissenters). We knew Liverpool had all these talented writers and artists and we wanted it to be at the forefront of things.

"But John had this other group of friends and he got drunk with them and went out stealing. Girls used to be afraid when he walked down the corridor because he came out with nasty comments. So, on one side he was creative and on another he was a drunken idiot with all these guys."

Though he could be very funny with it. Go on, Bill, remind us of a drunken John Lennon lying on the floor of Liverpool's Ye Cracke boozer with his arms and legs flailing: "A woman came from behind the bar and said 'Stop doing that and get up!' Then she asked 'What are you doing?' John replied 'I'm swimming!' To which the woman said 'Well stop it straight away.' But John told her 'I can't… I'll drown!'"

Bill went on to become a public relations guru for a series of top acts, including Pink Floyd, David Bowie and Led Zeppelin – as well as a prolific author of music books. But the memories of the paper he ran from 81a Renshaw Street – and the part he played in a Mersey-led musical revolution – will always be with him.

"I was there when John's mum died," October 3, 2007

John Lennon's childhood friend, Nigel Walley, who lived close by in Woolton, was a tea chest bass player in The

Quarrymen in 1956 and 1957 before becoming the group's manager until sometime in 1958.

***

John Lennon's life was thrown into turmoil on July 15, 1958, when his mother, Julia, was knocked down and killed by a car being driven by an off-duty policeman in Menlove Avenue, Woolton.

The accident also haunted John's fellow Teddy boy pal, Nigel Walley, who witnessed it. He tells me: "I went to call for John that evening but his Aunt Mimi told me he was out. Mimi was at the gate with John's mum, who was about to leave. We stood chatting and John's mum said 'Well, you have the privilege of escorting me to the bus stop!' I said 'That will do me fine. I'll be happy to do that.'

"We walked down Menlove Avenue and I turned off to go up Vale Road, where I lived. I must have been about 15 yards up the road when I heard a car skidding. I turned around to see John's mum going through the air. I rushed over but she had been killed instantly."

Nigel, who moved with his family to New Brighton later that year, adds: "I had nightmares about it for years. I can see it today – Julia lying there with her hair fluttering over her face. I didn't see John much after that because he became a bit of a recluse. It worried me because, deep down, I wondered whether he blamed me for the accident and was thinking 'If only Nigel Walley had stayed a minute longer talking to my mum.' But hindsight is a wonderful thing."

Of his and John's childhood friendship, he says: "We knocked around together from the age of four. We then went to Mosspits Primary but John was expelled for being disruptive when he was just five or six – I remember he bullied a girl called Polly Hipshaw.

"He then went to Dovedale Primary and, later, Quarry Bank High School, while I went to the Blue Coat, but we remained friends as we lived so close to each other. I'd say Pete Shotton was John's closest friend, with me next.

"John always had a mouth organ in his inside coat pocket and then his mum taught him how to play the guitar, although at no time back then did I think he would go on to become famous. The Quarrymen must have been one of 100 skiffle groups in Merseyside and we went into loads of competitions and didn't win one. But things developed. John and Paul eventually got The Beatles together and Brian Epstein saw something in them, which he was able to get out of them. And he was right."

Nigel was working as a golf professional at Chippenham Golf Club in Wiltshire when The Beatles had their first hit in the autumn of 1962. But he occasionally met up with John during the 1960s, latterly during the making of the Magical Mystery Tour film, while the pair exchanged Christmas cards during the 1970s when John was living in New York.

He can still remember how John, his big pal, stuck up for him during a financial dispute – after Paul McCartney had joined The Quarrymen: "Paul and I didn't get on very well in those days. I was receiving the same money as the band when I was manager but Paul thought I should be getting just 10 per cent. John supported me, saying 'You've got to look at it this way, Paul – if we didn't have Nige, we wouldn't be getting half the engagements we are getting'." Nigel adds: "When I look back now and think about John, I don't think of him as a world-famous musician. I just see someone who was a close mate. I'd feel out of place with him if he was still alive, but in those days he was just a buddy and we were just ordinary lads."

"Photographing dad makes me nervous," (well, he is Paul McCartney!) May 28, 2013

Imagine being taken on a Beatle tour – by a Beatle (and not really being that bothered – after all, it is just your old man showing you his old house!)

At times, it can't have been easy having been a member of the Fab Four – a bit like having a Beatle as a dad.

But I reckon, on balance, it must be bloody wonderful!

I'm sure Mary McCartney goes along with that, having met and interviewed her at The Lowry in Salford, where she had an exhibition of her photographs of the likes of Madonna, Marianne Faithfull and Helen Mirren.

It was a nice chat, but I did come away feeling a bit envious after she told me about those Beatle tours she used to be taken on as a child.

***

Photography doesn't run in the McCartney family, it gallops. Linda was a renowned photographer; Mary's Merseyside-based uncle Mike has been putting people (including Lennon and "our kid") in the frame since he was a young man, Stella's life as a top fashion designer goes hand-in-hand with photography – and dad is pretty keen on it, too.

Mary says: "I grew up around photography (a picture by Linda of Mary as a baby, being held inside dad's jacket, adorns the sleeve of Paul's 1970 debut solo album, McCartney). Mum and dad were always into candid, beautiful photography. But I never ever thought I'd be a photographer. It wasn't until my early 20s that I really picked up a camera. I went into my mum's archive when she asked me to help her with a book and that inspired me."

Mary has, of course, had countless camera conversations with her family, including her dad – one of the most photographed people on the planet, and she reveals: "I took pictures of him recently for his album Kisses On The Bottom. It is a little intimidating, for two reasons. One, because he has been photographed by some of the most amazing photographers and two, because he's my dad and so I feel an extra responsibility – I want him to like the photographs.

"But he's great. He's got a really playful energy and often starts messing around. He likes spontaneity and I always get something that wasn't planned – and I like that. He's interested in photography and my mum was a professional photographer when they met. They would talk about photography and she introduced him to lots of her gallery and fine art photography."

She adds: "My mum had a way of putting people instantly at ease. She would just be hanging out with you and would take a quick photo – she wouldn't put the camera in your face."

Uncle Mike, meanwhile, is always observing and always taking pictures: "He's an inspiration. Whenever we are together, he's got his camera with him. I like that kind of photography. He's always fresh and interested and smiling."

Mary might have been born in London, but she travelled the world from an early age and had parents who were so proud of their roots – and she recalls: "If people asked me, I'd say I was half Liverpudlian and half American. My accent used to be a bit of a weird mix.

"We would come up to Merseyside for New Year and stop off in the summer on our way to Scotland. I just love the warm atmosphere in Liverpool and I love the family element to it. It's beautiful too. I came up recently to do some photography on the film about (Irish philanthropist) Christina Noble, looked at the blue sky and wonderful architecture and thought 'Why don't I come here all the time?'"

This is a woman who was taken on Beatle tours from an early age – by a Beatle!

She reveals: "Yes, Dad would drive us round. We'd been in the car for six hours and he would say 'I'm just doing a tiny detour – this is where I used to live.' He would say 'Do you understand how many people would love to be shown around by a Beatle?' – but we just wanted to get home and watch TV! It was like when we were telling him to stop playing the guitar when we were watching the telly."

Hang on – you told Paul McCartney, the real-life former Beatle, to stop playing the guitar?! Mary laughs and says:

"That's what he would say! And we'd reply 'Get over it!' Now I appreciate it, but it's different when you're in your early teens."

"Barack Obama is a Scouser!" (well, that's what Mike McCartney told me), July 2, 2010

Mary McCartney was right when she was talking about her Uncle Mike – he is always interested and always smiling. I've been lucky enough to be in his company on many occasions, and interviewed him for stories and features several times. He was always great value – full of great quotes and anecdotes. Like the day he seamlessly linked his beloved home city of Liverpool to the then President of the United States...

***

A little bit of Liverpool – actually, a large part of Liverpool – was welcomed into The White House early last month, when President Barack Obama presented Sir Paul McCartney with the Gershwin Prize for Popular Song.

Paul's brother, Mike, who was also present, with his wife, Rowena, reveals that the most powerful man in the world was like one of the Liverpool family.

He explains: "It's impossible for Liverpudlians to be normal. Most people, finding themselves standing next to the President would have been, to put it politely, extremely nervous, but I told him we'd earlier gone past his house on an open-topped bus and waved. With a smile on his face, and very coolly, like a true Liverpudlian, he asked 'Did you see me wave back?'

"I found myself standing next to the boss of the world while we were waiting to have our photo taken. He put his arm around my waist – so I put my arm around his! Later, when another photo was being done, I said 'Hold on, where's the Pressie?' – that's the warmest thing you could do regarding someone who had immediately made himself family. There was a lovely Liverpool family feel, which is why I felt comfortable calling him 'Pressie'! He's one of us – Barack Obama is a Scouser!"

Mike adds: "Liverpool is the centre of the universe and an island within an island. People should see it at least once. And then, once they visit, they often find themselves trapped for life! Liverpool people are one-offs, with their razor-sharp, quick-witted and often surreal humour. Also, they're not afraid of standing up for the truth, even if it gets them in trouble.

"I was lucky and I am so grateful to have had such lovely parents – normal, lovely Liverpool people, with that sense of humour which just can't help taking the Michael out of itself. And we have such great sayings in Liverpool. I remember asking my dad questions – 'Why? Why? Why?' – and just to shut me up he'd say 'Because there are no hairs on a seagull's chest.' That is insane, but also profound, subtle and truthful.

"My family and the city of Liverpool have given me the rock on which my life is based (the 'roll' came later!) – and having that rock is how you can do things in life, because you have an inner calm and knowledge.

"Indian gurus had a fascinating concept – that we were floating around in nothing and then saw the parents we wanted to be born through. I must be a genius because I chose the best parents in the world.

"Mum and dad (Mary and Jim) taught us the difference between right and wrong, and taught us about ethics and standards like moderation and toleration. These things don't really make sense until later – like when our kid's in The White House singing Ebony and Ivory with Stevie Wonder, in the presence of Barack Obama.

"It's wonderful sitting here and saying 'our kid' without having to explain it – which I have to do all over Britain and in America. A guy in Ohio thought I was talking about one of my children!"

Chapter Eight

Heysel

HEYSEL HAS never been the easiest subject to write about in Liverpool – when I mentioned it once, it led to an unimpressed reader sending me shit in the post. He wiped his arse on the column I had written following the Merseyside derby which took place on Easter Monday, 2001. I had always assumed it was a Liverpudlian, but looking at the column again today, I now wonder whether it was an Evertonian.

In the column, I had taken to task the lone Everton fan who shouted, "What about Heysel?" – as he chose to do this during the one-minute silence for the then 96 Hillsborough victims and the 43 supporters who had lost their lives in the Ellis Park Stadium disaster in Johannesburg, South Africa, on April 11, 2001.

I wrote: "Too many commentators from outside Merseyside have already confused matters by lumping together Heysel and Hillsborough – even though Heysel involved hooliganism and Hillsborough didn't."

I always believed my anonymous critic had been a Liverpool fan who wouldn't accept that hooliganism had any role in the Heysel disaster, but maybe I was wrong. Maybe it was an Everton fan who felt the person who shouted out had just cause – though, in my eyes, there could be no excuse for disrupting the silence.

I will probably never know – as happens when people don't give you their name and address when they send you shit in the post.

***

That unpleasantness was, I am sure, in my mind when the 30th anniversary of the Heysel disaster was looming. Which is why I suggested to my friend, Liverpool fan Peter Hooton, that I interview him but use only his words in the resulting feature (apart from a short introduction and the timeline of the disaster).

Maybe this was cowardly on my part, but I was glad he agreed.

Peter got a positive response to his words – apart, he said, from "the usual loons" on social media (I don't think he received any actual shit, though).

"I would never have watched the match if I'd known fans had died," May 27, 2015

Reds' fan Peter Hooton, lead singer of The Farm, was at Heysel stadium in Brussels for the European Cup Final between Liverpool and Juventus on May 29, 1985 – and later a leading figure in the grassroots "peace trips" involving fans of the two clubs. Here, he reflects on the tragedy and its aftermath – while stressing he is only speaking on behalf of himself.

***

"You'll never bring the 39 people who died at Heysel back, and it was an absolute tragedy, but there is a lot of misinformation about this disaster.

"I've heard the chant 'Justice for the 39,' most recently in March when we were playing Manchester United at Anfield. I think it's a new generation who probably weren't even born when Heysel happened and don't really understand what went on at the time.

"There was a judicial process and there were convictions. Captain Johan Mahieu, the police officer who was responsible for Z Block, where the disaster took place, was given a nine-month suspended sentence. Albert Roosens, the former general secretary of the Belgian Football Association, was given a six-month suspended sentence.

"Belgian police officer Michel Kensier was acquitted. In a separate civil action brought by family members, four officials were found not liable for the deaths that resulted from the tragedy. They included Jacques Georges, the former president of UEFA; Hans Bangerter, former UEFA general secretary; former Brussels Mayor Herve Brouhon; and Viviane Baro, a former Brussels councillor for sports.

"And 24 Liverpool fans were extradited on involuntary manslaughter charges, with 14 found guilty, following a trial, on April 28, 1989, almost four years after the tragedy – it was a lengthy legal process.

"Those fans found guilty were sentenced to three years in prison, 18 months of which was suspended. Some might say those convicted didn't serve enough time, but that's a different argument.

"The very fact they played the match was unbelievable. We weren't aware anyone had died. When it did start it wasn't a normal match. You were thinking 'Something's not right.' People around me thought there might be people injured, with broken ribs, legs – that type of thing.

"I think the one thing that put panic into that mass movement of people which led to the collapse of the wall was flares being fired over from the Liverpool section – because on a terrace you can't really see what's happening 20 yards away. We could see people moving back en masse and then there was a massive thud when the wall collapsed. There were chaotic scenes for maybe two hours but, honest to God, no one around me thought there were any fatalities – and if we had any idea we would have walked out. We wouldn't have watched a football match.

"We'd been in the ground early, and it wasn't until shortly after 9.40pm that the game kicked off. There was an element of fatigue, everyone was fed up and you were looking at the situation and thinking 'It can't be that bad because they're playing the match' – that's the truth. All the passion had gone from the game, but the idea that anyone had died didn't enter our heads.

"It was only when we got back to the railway station – we were going to Ostend that night – that we heard rumours of two, three or four fatalities. Everywhere was shut and the police were telling people to take off their scarves and they were confiscating fans' banners.

"It was a surreal atmosphere, but during the lead-up to the game it had been so different – an almost carnival atmosphere. There had been the odd incident in Brussels city centre – I think a jeweller's shop window was smashed – but, overall, it was just a normal cup final build-up.

"In the stadium, I saw skirmishes – but you saw skirmishes like that, as an experienced football fan, over the years.

"There should have been proper segregation. That so-called neutral section – Z Block – was nothing of the sort. There is a massive Italian community in Brussels so there was never going to be a neutral section, and the authorities should have known that.

"The then Liverpool chairman, John Smith, chief executive Peter Robinson and Juventus president Giampiero Boniperti were disgusted with the state of the stadium. Why it was chosen I'll never know – it was dilapidated and anyone looking at it would know it was not fit for purpose.

"As a Liverpool fan I don't feel any culpability whatsoever. I did not choose that ground. I did not make the security arrangements. I wasn't involved in the fracas that happened by the chicken wire separating those Liverpool and Juventus fans. I watched the match and, in a way, I feel a little bit guilty that I did – but I don't feel any culpability or responsibility because, as far as I was concerned, we were going to a ground that had met safety standards. But it had a breeze block wall outside, no sign of any turnstiles and the terraces were crumbling under your feet. It was criminal to stage a cup final there.

"You just thought six Merseyside police officers with

experience of Anfield and Goodison would have sorted out what was happening in two minutes. The police, or security, seemed to react by attacking, and things escalated to a point of no return."

***

In August, 1985, 18 Juventus fans visited Liverpool after an invitation from the Liverpool 28 Improvements Committee in Cantril Farm – which included then youth worker Peter Hooton. The trip, which had actually been planned before Heysel as part of a routine exchange visit, was organised by Peter, together with Mark Fitzsimmons from Cantril Farm, who later went on to become a youth worker. It was funded by the John Moores Foundation and supported by Liverpool City Council.

The Juventus fans were led by Mauro Garino, a long-time friend of both Peter and fellow Liverpool fan Kevin Sampson, who helped organise the visit. The group attended a civic reception at Liverpool Town Hall, toured Anfield and Goodison Park and enjoyed a concert on the Royal Iris which featured The Farm, Groundpig, Jegsy Dodd and Ted Chippington. John Peel, who had been at Heysel, was the DJ.

***

Peter recalls: "The Royal Iris night was a fantastic occasion. John Peel had wanted to come up because of what he had seen at Heysel. The whole trip was successful. Initially, the hard-core Juventus fans – the Juventus Ultras – were against it going ahead, but they eventually gave their blessing. And their leader was part of the trip.

"We went to Turin the following year and got a great reception from the local people. Their attitude was that the game should never have been played at that stadium.

"When Juventus played at Anfield in 2005, some Juventus fans turned their backs when fans on the Kop displayed the Amicizia (friendship) mosaic. I just thought if they want to turn their backs that's their right. I think their attitude was 'It's too little too late' and I think that was the attitude of a lot of Liverpool fans. There's a small plaque at Anfield but I think many Liverpool and Juventus fans think their clubs wanted to move on from the disaster.

"Our peace trip was grassroots and accepted as a genuine gesture. Liverpool and Everton fans were involved and no one ever said to us 'What are you doing this for?'

"There was no attempt at saying sorry because we didn't feel any guilt. That might look bad in black and white, but we'd been having a laugh with Juventus fans all through the day of the match. Organising the visit was a way of saying ordinary people can get on. We didn't want to brush what had happened under the carpet and wanted to show the Italians they could come to our city and be welcomed.

"When people chant 'Murderers' they may say it's not about Hillsborough, but because of what *The Sun* said about Liverpool fans it will be linked to Heysel and Hillsborough.

"The 'Always the victims, it's never your fault' chant was started by Man Utd fans during the period Luis Suarez was facing allegations of racism (against then Utd player Patrice

Evra). But of course you could say it brings in Heysel and Hillsborough. It's a chant that does hurt people, especially those who lost loved ones at Hillsborough.

"Heysel was never raised by rival fans in the late 1980s. After the advent of the Premier League, I think there was a certain feeling that the European ban had affected Everton's finances. And when Everton were flirting with relegation it manifested itself a little bit more then because people were looking for reasons why they were in this situation.

"Success on the pitch pales into insignificance when it comes to life and death and to bicker about it is wrong on any level."

***

Although I heard one or two people, standing close to me in the Gwladys Street End, half-heartedly shout "Murderers!" before the start of the first Merseyside derby after Heysel, I think Peter is basically right – I don't recall it being a major and continuous talking point back then (though I have a memory of the behaviour of some Liverpool fans and the subsequent European ban being raised on Brookside during a conversation between the characters Rod Corkhill and Damon Grant).

But yes, I think the anger of some Evertonians has grown over the years – not helped, many would say, by the apparent refusal of some Liverpool fans to accept what happened on that terrible night.

It's a pedantic point regarding those fans who insist on shouting "Murderers!" about what happened at Heysel

– but, as Peter pointed out, those 14 Liverpool fans were found guilty of involuntary manslaughter and so, legally, they are classed as being "killers" not "murderers." I'm really not being facetious, it's just that journalists can't help but be pedantic.

Chapter Nine

Quite a bit of politics (well, it is Liverpool)

Johnson Flies In To Say Sorry, October 20, 2004

I DIDN'T think it would be possible to think any less of Boris Johnson than I did in 2004, when he was reportedly ordered to Liverpool by then Tory leader Michael Howard (Johnson denied this to me) to apologise for defaming our entire city, the Hillsborough victims and their families. But just look at the havoc he has wreaked since then.

In 2004 – when, like so many politicians, he obviously wasn't content to just draw an MP's generous salary – he was the editor of *The Spectator* magazine and therefore responsible for its infamous, grossly offensive editorial leader column which had been inspired by the reaction to the beheading in Iraq of Liverpool engineer Ken Bigley.

It was later claimed it had been written by Simon Heffer, who admitted he "had a hand" in it, a journalist I believe to be as abhorrent as Johnson.

The appalling piece said of Liverpool people: "They see

themselves, whenever possible, as victims and resent their victim status; yet at the same time they wallow in it."

It also repeated the lie about "the part drunken fans played" in the Hillsborough disaster – which, it was crassly and offensively stated, claimed "more than 50 lives."

I find it almost beyond belief that Johnson was able to rise to the role of Prime Minister, and therefore be allowed to make life or death decisions – but, I've never been good at predicting which politicians would enter No 10. After coming across Tony Blair – the then shadow secretary of state for employment – during the Knowsley South by-election campaign of 1990, I told a friend in the pub: "He won't amount to anything – there's just nothing to him; he hasn't got a personality or anything of substance to say."

I interviewed Johnson on the phone early in the morning. For security reasons, it had all been cloak and dagger regarding the arrangements, which I had been given by his people late the previous evening.

By the time the *Echo* hit the streets at lunchtime, it would be safe to include in my article where Johnson had stayed overnight – but I wasn't able to, because he told me he had no idea which hotel he was talking to me from, even though he had probably been there for 12 hours by this point and had also been out for a morning run (turns out it was the Alicia Hotel in Sefton Park).

What a man. What a mind.

***

Boy blunder Boris Johnson brought his one-man circus to

Liverpool today, to allow people to see a grovelling clown close-up.

With the apparently mindless motto of "speak hurtful lies and numbskull nonsense first, think later," the Tory MP and media "personality" is the kind of himbo who gives blondes of both sexes a bad name.

The unwelcome daytripper is currently so unpopular in Liverpool that his Tory minders kept the details of today's visit a closely-guarded secret until the last minute.

I interviewed him on the phone at the start of what, hopefully, would prove to be an extremely uncomfortable day for the erring editor of an obscure right-wing mag called *The Spectator*. So, after all the cloak and dagger nonsense, where are you? Go on, you can tell me. "Er, I'm... I don't know exactly where I am. But I'm in a charming hotel."

And are you excited – or scared stiff?

"Everyone keeps joking about how I'll need my gum shield but my view is that I hope people will be forgiving of our mistakes and will show the friendliness for which they are famous. If I am wrong, then I'll be disappointed, but I will have deserved it. But I will take it on the chin – whatever happens."

He adds: "One of the sad things about today is that it's a complete media jamboree. The police have said I can't go to any of the museums and that's very, very sad. I'm going to have to come back when I'm less likely to be pelted with eggs."

Come off it, Bozza. People wouldn't even waste one good egg on one bad egg. And bumbling Boris denied that he is only here – for only the fourth or fifth time in his life – because of an order from angry Tory leader Michael Howard.

"The truth is as soon as the whole thing blew up my first thought was to come here. Then I vaguely shelved the idea, thinking it was a good idea which could go horribly wrong and people would think it was a stunt. Then I talked to Michael Howard on Saturday (it was now Wednesday) and we then both thought this was the way forward."

But you didn't write the offending article, did you? And while you have overall responsibility, what about the responsibility of the man/woman who penned the poison? Shouldn't he/she be named and shamed and be visiting Liverpool, too?

Come on Boris, it's time to cough. Name the coward who's hiding behind your thick skin. "I can't shrug off the responsibility. No, no, no, no, no, no. I'm afraid I won't be doing that, because I do think there are points in the leader that bear repetition and points that I can't retract."

Yeah, yeah, so you've said. Risk and responsibility, the idea that the state is always to blame, blah de blah.

Many people are wondering how you can suddenly be so contrite about comments which you read, passed and published. Weren't you merely forced into a corner by the resulting furore – which, you have admitted, you were "stunned" by? And aren't the views expressed on Liverpool and its people still the views you and the mystery writer hold?

"No, no, let me explain. *The Spectator* is a provocative

magazine and it's full of fiery and inflammatory statements of one kind and another. When I passed this, I did think the language was strong but I must confess that it was my own error that I did not think it would cause the dismay and hurt it did. It was insensitive. It was a complete miscalculation."

Apart from accusing Liverpudlians of wallowing in their "victim status," you repeated the lie about "the part drunken fans played" in the Hillsborough disaster – which, you added, claimed "more than 50 lives."

The word "mistake" doesn't even begin to cover it, does it?

"It is an embarrassment, because it seems to minimise... it seems to neglect the deaths of 46 fans."

So it must be time to resign.

"I don't feel I should resign. I think that would be a kind of admission that the whole point of the leader was wrong. I would have to kind of perform a full frontal lobotomy on myself. I can't resign over something I don't fundamentally dissent from."

But Michael Howard says the article is nonsense from start to finish – so have you lost faith in him?

"I'm a fervent admirer of, and believer in, Michael Howard, but I don't think I am obliged by collective responsibility to agree with him about every article he writes – and vice versa. I'm sure my political career will not have been assisted by this. But Michael Howard has chosen not to fire me and I am very glad about that. There is a fascinating job to be done in the arts."

That's right, you're the shadow culture minister. Men and women wiser than you have decreed that Liverpool will be

European Capital of Culture for 2008. Did you know that? "I did know – and that adds to my pain and remorse. In the unlikely event of my being spared, I will do everything I can to help Liverpool promote its Capital of Culture status. I'm sure it does deserve the title. I know some people want me to come up at a later stage and I am longing to do that."

Someone calling him/herself "wibbler" on the bizarre website boriswatch.com asks – regarding Johnson's dual career in politics and the media – "Can Boris continue to ride two horses with one arse?"

Very difficult. Especially when he speaks out of it, as well.

The Tony Benn interviews, March 20, 1998 and February 5, 2002

As briefly mentioned in the music chapter, as a teenager I had a bedroom band called The Ambitious Merchants. We released tapes during the period, sadly short-lived, when independent cassettes were seen as being important enough to warrant columns in the *NME* (Garageland) and *Sounds* (Cassette Pets). Our two tapes – Eating Apple Crumble Whilst Listening To Rowche Rumble and Steve Ovett, Mushrooms and Bill and Ben – also appeared in Sounds' Obscurist Charts. This wasn't too surprising, as the chart was initially compiled by my pen pal Paul Platypus and, later, by, among others, me.

Anyway, our second tape included a song called I Love Tony Benn (I later released a speech by him – Tony Benn: Speaking in Bexleyheath – on my label, Apple Crumble

Tapes. Incredibly, this received a five-star review in *Sounds* in April 1983). I hadn't even been old enough to vote when I Love Tony Benn was recorded – but I just knew, even then. I just knew. Fast-forward many years, and how could I justify going down to London to meet and interview the veteran politician for the *Liverpool Echo*?

Thank God for one particular *Echo* letter writer...

***

"The only person who consistently speaks up for Liverpool," an *Echo* reader wrote recently, "is a 72-year-old man from Chesterfield."

Tony Benn, despite reports that he has been hidden in a cupboard by New Labour's spin doctors, is still going strong. As strong as his beloved cups of tea.

I met him in the basement office of his London home – to talk about his love affair with Liverpool.

***

Tony Benn takes another puff on his pipe as he reflects on the fickle finger of political fate, which points would-be MPs to their would-be constituencies...

In his case, it has been Bristol and Chesterfield (and very proud he has been to serve there), but his eyes light up as he declares: "Oh, I would have loved to have represented Liverpool!"

Sitting here in the Benn bunker beneath Holland Park Avenue, W11, it's just a touch difficult to accept that I am in the presence of the devil. Tony Benn has been demonised so often during his colourful political life that Satan himself could be forgiven for feeling a little left out. But all I can see is a man in his cardie, drinking from a mug of tea. A warm, friendly grandfather-of-nine whose hobbies appear to be talking common sense and stating the bleedin' obvious. He is a man ahead of his time. A man still waiting for the world to catch up with him. And a man who loves Liverpool with a passion.

He speaks warmly of the late Walton MP Eric Heffer (he rings Eric's widow, Doris, on the anniversary of his death and on Christmas Day), and keeps in touch with dockers' leader Jimmy Nolan and former council leader John Hamilton.

Liverpool is a city he has possibly visited for meetings and rallies more than any other. And one which has left an indelible mark: "I just love the place. I feel very happy in Liverpool. There's a real commitment among its people – and also a great sense of humour and a smashing irreverence. I also get a lot of letters from Liverpool and they are always very shrewd, perceptive and down-to-earth.

"It's a city which is never demoralised, and that is what makes it different."

***

Tony Benn joined the Labour Party in 1943, 10 years before Tony Blair was in nappies. To many, he is yesterday's man. He didn't so much fall off the New Labour bandwagon – rather, he was never on it in the first place.

He explains: "The Prime Minister has said New Labour

is a new party. It is – and I'm not a member of it." But he is not about to rip up his Labour membership card: "I have total loyalty to the Labour Party. Nearly everything I've ever had, I owe to the Labour movement. I don't link the Labour movement with New Labour.

"I am a Labour man, a socialist, and a trade unionist. I feel, within the family of the Labour Party, it's all there still – even though it isn't being represented in Parliament."

Of his public image, meanwhile, he says: "I think the media has stopped demonising me, but my danger at the moment is that I'll be presented as a kindly, harmless, old gentleman. I am kindly. I am old. I may be a gentleman – but I'm not harmless!"

As I emerge from the Benn basement into the sunshine of Holland Park Avenue, my eyes are drawn to a street scene which could probably prove the inspiration for another stirring and passionate speech by the great man. Standing close to a branch of WHSmith is a sharp-suited young businessman barking into a mobile phone... oblivious to the beggar staring at the ground just a few feet away.

The struggle, Mr Benn might say, goes on.

"Liverpool is the most political city I know," February 5, 2002

Tony was preparing to visit Liverpool to speak in memory of Archbishop Derek Worlock – so I took the opportunity to call him up for another interview. Here's an extract...

***

It's 10am and Tony Benn, who will be 77 in April, has been up and about – giving media interviews and working at the desk of his West London home – for six hours. No wonder the legendary left-winger explains his decision to step down as an MP at the last election by saying: "I wanted to devote more time to politics."

The veteran voice of dissent has, in the last few days, been spreading the gospel according to Tony Benn (and many others) in Leicester, Glasgow, Malvern, and Leicester again. And he is looking forward to the latest in a long line of visits to Liverpool later this month. He says: "I don't think I've ever refused an invitation to come to Liverpool because I'm so fond of the place. It's the most political city I know. It has such a lot of character and such interesting people. It's very, very thoughtful and there is a lot of argument – and that's because people think so much there. They are great talkers in Liverpool, and I am a bit of a talker myself – so I appreciate that!"

Tony Benn has been cast as a devil by some and a Messiah by others – possibly even by the same people, at different times: "I haven't really changed and have tried to be consistent. I spoke out in Trafalgar Square when Nelson Mandela was put in prison, I supported having a Scottish Parliament, Freedom of Information, gay rights and talking to all the politicians in Northern Ireland – at a time when you were denounced as a terrorist if you mentioned Gerry Adams' name. As recently as 1996 I was threatened with expulsion from the Labour Party for meeting Gerry Adams – now I can't get to see him because he's in and out of Number 10!

"I actually think public opinion has shifted. The public is to the left of New Labour, which I know isn't a difficult thing. People don't want the railways privatised or private companies running our schools and hospitals."

Regrets? He's had a few – and not too few to mention: "I have made a lot of mistakes. I was wrong, for example, about nuclear power. I thought it was cheap and safe and peaceful when it was actually very expensive, dangerous and all about the bomb.

"The only thing I would be ashamed of though would be if I thought I'd ever said anything or done anything just to get on."

He later says: "I thought the mail would stop when I left the Commons but it's still pouring in. And if I knew what fun it was being in your 70s, I would have done it years ago! I've got a lot of experience and energy and absolutely zero political ambition. I don't want anything from anybody and that's the sort of freedom I didn't understand when I was younger… I miss my constituency work in Chesterfield, but sitting in the House night after night being asked to support the privatisation of the Post Office; I couldn't do it."

He now sees his role as using his experience to give people confidence – he would like his gravestone to read 'Tony Benn: He encouraged us', explaining "Old men who grumble, talk about the past all the time and want to run things are a bore, but old men who are there to encourage you – you can't have too many of them."

***

Cherie Blair: "When I Had Three Men On The Go," May 27, 2008

I travelled to London for a 45-minute chat with Cherie Blair QC, who was born in Bury but brought up in Waterloo (the one next door to Crosby, not the one in the capital). Her dad was the Till Death Us Do Part actor Tony Booth, who played "Scouse git" Mike Rawlins in the sitcom. Her husband? Yes, he's quite well-known, too.

Tony Blair's missus had just had her autobiography published, and it hadn't – surprise, surprise – been every national newspaper journalist's favourite read.

***

Walking from Euston, en route to the legal eagles' lair of Gray's Inn, where I was to meet our national newspapers' favourite whipping girl in my lady's chambers, I felt it advisable to hide my copy of her autobiography.

And it isn't just the always ever-so-angry and disapproving *Daily Mail* that has been lobbing stones from a supposed moral high ground. The day before my appointment with Mrs B, a *Sunday Mirror* columnist had told us: "I don't know of anyone more openly despised than Cherie Blair."

Cherie reveals there are two things people often tell her after first meeting her: "They say 'You look so much better in the flesh than in your pictures' – thank God! The other thing they say is 'The *Daily Mail* doesn't like you, does it?'"

But she says she has taken on board advice from Hillary Clinton, who told her she wasn't going to please the Press and so should simply be true to herself. Still, until her caustic critics prove otherwise, she is only human. The verbal volleys must hurt: "I'm not Superwoman – as I think I've said in public before! – I'm bound to think 'What have I done to deserve this?' The sad thing about it often is that it's people who haven't met me and people who haven't read the book... I don't know why they dislike me. Maybe they dislike what they think I represent."

Let's talk about when you had three men on the go, posed nude for an artist friend ("Or as good as")... and that weekend in Balmoral (much had been made of her youngest child Leo's conception at the royal residence and Cherie's decision to reveal she "had not packed my contraceptive equipment, out of sheer embarrassment" because, previously, everything had been unpacked by the Queen's staff).

Cue the following fruity passages: "Tony knew about John but not about David. John knew about David but not about Tony, and poor David fondly imagined I was living a quiet life of hard work in dreary London. Oh dear."

And: "In all the time I was going to Battersea to model for Euan (the late painter, Euan Uglow), Tony never knew that I was posing nude."

As for the publication of the above, Cherie claims: "This is all Tony's fault!" – apparently for telling their kids that, while he spent his lunch hours as a pupil barrister in the pub, she stayed in the library.

"The kids said 'Mum, you are such a saddo!'"

Regarding the modelling, Cherie says: "I was trying to show I was a bit more naughty than that!"

And the kids' reactions? "I gave them a manuscript before it was published but all they did was search for their own names, so they probably still think I'm a saddo!"

As for the lack of contraception at Balmoral, she explains: "At 44 years and 11-months-old, I thought it wouldn't matter!"

***

Oh, Cherie! You can have too much information sometimes, can't you?

***

Jack Jones – a true man of the people, April 22, 2009

I was honoured to be asked to write the obituary tribute for one of Liverpool's most famous sons, who had died, aged 96, after fighting so many battles on the national and international stages. I had been lucky enough to speak to him five years earlier, when I was writing a piece about Margaret Thatcher's legacy – his views on her were illuminating.

Here is a small part of my tribute…

***

He was a true working class hero and man of the people – someone who never tired of fighting the good fight.

As leader of the then truly mighty Transport and General Workers' Union between 1969 and 1978, Jack had the ear of prime ministers and a season ticket for 10 Downing Street. But way before then, after the outbreak of the Spanish Civil War, this man of conscience was active in the Aid Spain campaign, and joined the International Brigades. He fought for many months before being wounded in the Ebro battle in 1938.

A man of many lives, Jack lived to fight another day – and he didn't see any reason to stop fighting in later life.

For many people in Merseyside and across the country, Jack was also known as the pensioners' champion – a man who fought tirelessly for the rights of pensioners well into his 90s.

Jack, who sold the *Echo* on the streets as a 10-year-old when he was a pupil at Banks Road elementary school in his native Garston, was simply "Our Jack" to generations of Liverpool workers who looked to their union leader to help secure them better pay and working conditions.

His views on Margaret Thatcher were fascinating – discussing her legacy with me five years ago, he said: "She was very divisive and had little or no sympathy for workers. I think she was unduly influenced by her husband (Denis), who had been an employer and born with a golden spoon in his mouth. I think she became more reactionary after she married him – she had previously been a member of a trade union."

Jack turned down an invitation to go to the House of Lords, explaining: "I always said it was proof positive that there is life after death. It's a totally undemocratic institution."

No spin. No grin. It's just our Mo, June 14, 2002

I talked to woman of the people and former high-ranking Labour politician Mo Mowlam about her part in the Northern Ireland peace process and, remarkably, Ian Paisley's "sense of humour" (no, really). And she couldn't have been more down-to-earth or a more entertaining and likeable interviewee.

Tragically, Mo (who had been diagnosed with a brain tumour just months before the 1997 General Election and retired from politics at the 2001 election) died, aged 55, just over three years after this interview took place.

***

She burped after breakfast and sprinkled her conversation with jokes and four letter words. I like Mo Mowlam.

Earlier, there had been a refreshingly human start to my interview with the former Cabinet minister. No more than a couple of minutes late, Mo (well, everyone calls her Mo) arrived in the hotel reception area with wet, bedraggled hair and unbrushed teeth, saying: "The bastards didn't give me an alarm call."

But these weren't the words of an arrogant, self-important individual who wanted someone's head on a plate, more a cheerfully-delivered observation from somebody who was mildly irritated.

And later, when *Echo* photographer Frank Loughlin was preparing to take her picture, she asked him, with a glint in her eye: "Clothes on – or off?"

Mo Mowlam dares to be different. Or, rather, she dares to be herself. She doesn't take part in the tedious game played in such a boring fashion by the sharp suits and stuffed shirts who populate the political jungle.

No spin. No cheesy grin. No bull.

Mo Mowlam is what she is. A woman of the people – somebody who was obviously too popular for politics. Her warmth, humour, humility and humanity were her making – and, perhaps, her breaking.

The nation loved her. And probably still does. But some of her former whispering colleagues in the bitchy and back-biting corridors of spin? Well, apparently you can be too popular.

Mo (or Po Mo, as she once nicknamed herself, in tribute to the Teletubbies) was in the region to visit the Warrington Peace Centre – the latest venue on a mammoth, 13-week promotional tour for her new book, Momentum, which documents the peace process in Northern Ireland between 1997 and 2001.

Some have wrongly labelled it an autobiography.

"I'm too young to write a f****** autobiography," says the 52-year-old, who later asked me: "You're not putting all the f**** down are you?" At this point, I should explain that Mo Mowlam did not swear like a f****** trouper. Her occasional use of "unladylike" words and her "touchy feely manner" apparently antagonised upright (and possibly uptight) Unionist politicians during her time as Northern Ireland secretary, between 1997 and 1999.

Mo's earthy style, it seems, was everything. It turned

millions of people onto politics, but turned many politicians off. The latter included the Reverend Ian Paisley, who has never been a man to mince his (very loud) words. Mr Shouty, however, is a much-misunderstood man. Mo Mowlam, please explain yourself...

"The thing about Paisley is he has a sense of humour," she says, breaking off from her poached egg on toast.

As I'm doing my best not to fall off my chair, Mo continues: "He didn't do anything helpful for the talks and was a completely negative force but, when everyone was calling for my resignation, he said to me 'Don't forget, young lady, I was the first to call for your resignation!'"

She's right. The man who told Mo's husband, Jon, that she "drank too much of the devil's buttermilk (whiskey)" is obviously a comic genius.

Mo is naturally happy to recall the historic all-night session of talks which led to the signing of the Good Friday Agreement in 1998, but, at the time, it was just too much – and too big – to take in: "We were all incredibly tired. Everyone clapped and cheered and it was an incredible moment, but we were so exhausted it took a couple of days to sink in. I got on the plane afterwards, had a whiskey and fell asleep."

But looking at the future and the chances of a truly long-term solution, she stresses; "I am not naive. It will take years. Violence may well continue. Sectarian bigotry will take generations to get rid of. But if we can keep making progress in the Assembly, the violence on the edge will decline."

"I thought Eric Heffer was going to punch me on the stage at THAT party conference," September 26, 2005

To coincide with the 20th anniversary of his famous/ infamous (delete according to your views) attack on Liverpool's Labour council, I went to London to interview former Labour leader Neil Kinnock, now Lord Kinnock and Baron Kinnock of Bedwellty.

***

Many of his supporters believed Neil Kinnock's speech at the Labour Party conference in Bournemouth on October 1, 1985, would represent a big step in winning the support of Middle England's *Daily Mail* readers (though it would be another 12 long years before Labour came to power).

He had considered making an attack on Liverpool's Militant-dominated council in 1984, but decided to hold his fire due to the miners' strike.

It was on Preston railway station, as he was making his way back to London from the TUC conference in Blackpool in September 1985, that he decided the time was nigh: "I saw the local newspaper, which carried a story about the issuing of redundancy notices to Liverpool city council workers and I said to (current Home Secretary) Charles Clarke, who then worked in my office, 'I've got 'em. I know exactly what to do.'"

But what of their defence that this was a tactic to buy them time – and the fact that nobody was made redundant?

My Lord isn't buying it.

"If it was a tactic, it had not been communicated to the workers and, in the short term, the Militants enjoyed the publicity and notoriety. It was a very dramatic, revolutionary gesture. Also, if it was a tactic, it was so ill-conceived, so arrogant and so ruthless that it deserved to be smashed to smithereens. But I don't think it was a tactic. I think it was a gamble of their own fervour, of their excessive melodrama – and it was unforgivable."

Kinnock told Liverpool City Council and the world: "I'll tell you what happens with impossible promises. You start with far-fetched resolutions. They are then pickled into a rigid dogma, a code, and you go through the years sticking to that – outdated, misplaced, irrelevant to the real needs – and you end in the grotesque chaos of a Labour council – a Labour council – hiring taxis to scuttle around a city handing out redundancy notices to its own workers.

"I'm telling you, no matter how entertaining, how fulfilling to short-term egos – I'm telling you and you'll listen – you can't play politics with people's jobs and with people's services or with their homes."

The images surrounding the speech which remain are of Eric Heffer, the late Labour MP for Walton, walking off the platform in protest, and Derek Hatton, the then deputy leader of Liverpool City Council, shouting in the hall.

The Red Baron remembers it with relish: "Eric walking off the platform could not have been choreographed by the most brilliant director. It added to the drama and was an absolute gift to me. It did go through my mind that Eric was going to try and throw a punch at me. I remember thinking, as I caught him out of the corner of my eye, 'Good, he's coming from my left,' which meant my right would be free to use. But he just walked off.

"Actually, and I've always been sorry about this, he stalked off and that added to the drama and, very quickly, the tragi-comedy, when he went down to the floor and started looking for his wife. One of the newspapers said the next day he walked off the stage into political oblivion and that's about what happened." (After this interview appeared, Eric Heffer's widow, Doris, wrote to the *Echo* to take issue with Kinnock's remarks about his belief that a punch might be thrown – stressing that her late husband would never have considered taking such violent action).

Kinnock adds: "As soon as the shouting began, they were putting the ball right at my feet. I was inside the six-yard box and it was just a matter of putting the ball in the net. I didn't have to answer Hatton – I couldn't even hear what he was saying. I just had to deal with the nature of it and I did that with the line 'I'm telling you and you'll listen' – that was unscripted. And after the line about 'playing politics' you see my eyes go back down, because I was determined to get back to the script. So I didn't do what I may have done nine times out of 10 and that was go for Hatton."

But those you were attacking still point out that, between 1983 and 1987, they continued to be re-elected, during an era, unlike today, of high turnouts.

"I've heard all that before. People who live in their own assumptions don't like coming out and breathing oxygen. If you only win pyrrhic victories where the casualty list is higher than the number of yards gained, then it's difficult to give credit to the generals in such circumstances."

Kinnock on... John Hamilton, former leader of Liverpool City Council: "John is a decent man whose decency was systematically abused, particularly by Hatton and his closest associates."

Kinnock on... Derek Hatton, former deputy leader of the council: "Hatton's theatrical approach demonstrated that he either didn't understand the territory in which he was fighting or he didn't care... people like that, who are intent upon their own pre-eminence, will fight to the last drop of everybody else's blood."

Kinnock on... Tony Mulhearn, former president of the District Labour Party: "Mulhearn was totally misguided, but sincere. I've always distinguished between him and Hatton because Mulhearn came to the (expulsion) hearings, represented himself, took his medicine and went back to work."

Rebels With A Cause, September 27, 2005

The day after my Neil Kinnock interview was published, the *Echo* ran a report on my meeting in the Casa on Hope Street with a dozen of the 47 Liverpool Labour councillors who were surcharged and suspended from holding public office for five years by the district auditor for failing to set a legal budget.

***

We had got together to talk about the pulsating political events of 20 years ago, but it was as if it had all happened the previous week.

Joining Paul Astbury, Eddie Burke, Jimmy Dillon, Peter Ferguson, Alan Fogg, Roy Gladden, Jimmy Hackett, Frank Mills, Tony Mulhearn, Terry Prout, Harry Smith and Franny Wiles were former Broadgreen Labour MP Terry Fields, famously jailed for refusing to pay his poll tax, and John Kennedy, who raised funds for the surcharged councillors.

All spoke with feeling and, while there isn't the space to quote everybody, the men shared a common bond – and their words covered common themes.

Eddie Burke said of Neil Kinnock's 1985 speech, which talked of the "grotesque chaos" of a Labour council handing out redundancy notices to its own workers via hired taxis: "What was grotesque was that the Labour Party should attack Labour councillors because they were doing their duty, at a time when the Party in Liverpool was so vibrant."

Roy Gladden points out: "We were never going to and we never did make any redundancies. At that time, the council employed around 31,000 people – now it doesn't employ anywhere near that figure."

Terry Prout stresses: "The redundancy notices issue was a tactic to buy us time. Everyone involved knew what was going on. I'm proud of what we did. We built houses and protected jobs."

Perhaps Mr Kinnock was an imposter. Jimmy Dillon says: "Myself and my friends always thought Kinnock was a plant, sent in to destroy the Labour Party."

If he wasn't an imposter, says Terry Fields, he had certainly changed: "He had been a young firebrand, with socialism spewing out of every orifice – but he finished up with something else spewing out of every orifice." Alan Fogg adds: "We were looking at ways of improving the quality of people's lives. We built 5,000 homes and did tremendous work in this city. What did Neil Kinnock do? He insulted us and then sent (the future Labour MP for Walton) Peter Kilfoyle round to witch-hunt all the socialists out of the Party."

For his part, Jimmy Hackett says: "That speech was a defining moment for us – and for Neil Kinnock. It ensured he would never be elected." Remembering the Liverpool of the mid-1980s, Paul Astbury claims: "What we created in this city was debate. There was a council meeting taking place in every pub in Liverpool." And John Kennedy looked around the Casa and told me: "Everyone in this room has stayed true to their colours."

Something tells me they don't believe Lord Kinnock has done the same.

But perhaps the most telling line came from Frank Mills, who recalled: "Some people said of us 'These people are trying to implement socialism... don't they realise they're in the Labour Party?'!"

***

John Hamilton on Neil Kinnock's speech: "I didn't know what he was going to say, nor was I informed that people were going around in taxis giving out redundancy notices. Militant supporters, despite their influence, were in a minority in the Labour group – roughly speaking, there were about 10 of them – but we all agreed that things were bad in Liverpool and the government was not helping at all.

"All we wanted was £30m which, incidentally, they deducted off our rate fund to spend on the 1984 International Garden Festival.

"I firmly believe we wouldn't have all the investment we have today, together with Capital of Culture status, if we hadn't made our principled stand."

Derek Hatton on Neil Kinnock's speech: "It was nothing short of treachery and a gift to the government. The word you can see me shouting on TV is 'Liar.' Yes, he managed to expel a lot of people from the Labour Party in Liverpool and change the way it was governed, but it wasn't the people of Liverpool who got rid of us, it was the House of Lords.

"Kinnock then went on to get battered. He was a total failure; a loser. He never won an election and we never lost one. I'm very proud of what we achieved, but Kinnock has got to dismiss the positive Militant legacy because he knows it is fact."

Tony Mulhearn on Neil Kinnock's speech: "The consensus among delegates was that the speech would live in infamy. It followed his refusal to back the miners, and, in response to pressure from the Press, the Tories and their supporters, he launched his premeditated attack on the 47.

"Eric Heffer's dramatic exit from the platform underlined the enormity of Kinnock's treachery. 'Malevolent', 'traitor' and 'cowardly' were just some of the words used to describe his action.

"A right-wing Labour MP told me Kinnock's speech had destroyed any ongoing efforts at a negotiated settlement with the Tory government."

Tony Mulhearn and Derek Hatton

I interviewed Tony, who died in 2019, and Derek on many occasions.

My time in the features department began five years after the pair had been booted out of office, and I came across Tony first – when he was a private hire driver for Davy Liver Cabs, which then had a contract with the *Echo*. The former politician was, at the same time, studying for his combined Social Sciences degree at Liverpool John Moores University, incorporating history, economics… and politics. He graduated in 1996 with a 2.1 Honours degree, having achieved a first-class pass for his dissertation (on Trotsky, which reaffirmed his socialist beliefs) and been acclaimed as the "most meritorious mature student."

Meanwhile, the book he wrote with Peter Taaffe, Liverpool: A City That Dared To Fight, was on the course reading list! Tony and Derek both loved appearing in the *Echo*.

Tony, as well as featuring in the news and features pages,

was one of the most frequent contributors to our letters pages.

Derek was very keen on getting one of the opinion columns – which ran alongside the letters – and, before he was unleashed on those pages, was a regular contributor to the My City column on Page 2. My City was written by different people each day – sometimes staff members like myself, and on other occasions people from outside the company.

Tony was always keen to talk about, discuss and debate the three Ps – politics, politics and politics – and was a brilliant campaigner and organiser. He was a lifelong activist and, in his later years, vice-chair of, and the media and publicity officer for, the Merseyside Pensioners' Association.

Despite the slings and arrows each had faced over the years, I would describe both men as optimistic and positive individuals. Both were good company, although things didn't always run smoothly with Derek. There were occasions when I found he could be volatile and quick to temper – but, then again, equally quick to cool down.

The My City column had a strict 280 word count. That was the template. It couldn't be changed. I would occasionally have to call Derek to explain that we would have to lose 20 or 30 of his submitted words, or that a certain paragraph would have to be delicately rewritten. He would start shouting, insisting that his words had to stay in – but would then quickly return to his previously calm and friendly self after I had explained that he had either broken the word count or that some of his words, as they stood, were libellous.

But occasional eruptions aside, Derek is a charming and generous man – he helped me out when I was struggling to get a ticket to watch Everton in Nuremberg, and twice invited me to be his guest at Goodison Park (duly declared!) He is a brilliant networker – and I wish I had just 20 per cent of his confidence and self-belief.

And he doesn't hold grudges – even against Neil Kinnock! Tony's relationship with the *Echo*, and myself, lasted until his death. I was so privileged to be able to see and speak to him shortly before he died, at 2.30am on Monday October 7, 2019. I had been in touch with Lynn Mulhearn, one of Tony's seven children, the previous Friday. Tony was desperately ill and being cared for by his beloved family at his home of more than 50 years in Childwall. It was arranged that I would call Lynn on Sunday morning to see if Tony would be well enough to welcome me that afternoon. Thankfully, he was – and our last meeting was profoundly moving.

Tony, due to the effects of his devastating lung condition, had found it frustratingly difficult to speak. But, sitting with two of his children – Lynn and Joe – I heard one of the very first things he said to me heartbreakingly clearly: "Will you please write my obituary?"

It was, as I told him it would be, a privilege to do so.

Later, I held his hand and planted a kiss on his forehead as we exchanged our fond farewells.

***

I first met Derek in 1998, when I brought him and Tony together for a series of features – 15 years after the start of their tumultuous reign of power, which ultimately changed the face of the city and British politics.

Mark Davies – someone with a keen interest in politics – was my then features editor, and he was delighted with the idea, and delighted when the first of several pieces was filed.

The first few paragraphs read…

They were comrades-in-arms, two high-profile figures at the forefront of a pulsating political scene when Militant sensationally stormed Liverpool Town Hall in the 1983 local elections. Derek Hatton and Tony Mulhearn.

"Jobs! Services! Houses!" was the three-word Militant mantra during a turbulent time in local – and national – politics. A time when everyone had an opinion.

***

Mark shouted something to the effect of, "Yes! This is the stuff!"

Not everyone was as happy.

The series had been promoted in the lead-up to its publication, and Mark had taken calls – but only a couple, I think – from readers who wanted to double-check which days the articles would be in, so they could avoid buying the paper on those days.

The series ended with a small comment piece by myself, which reflected on my meeting with the pair.

Looking back at it now, it seems clear that the mobile phone (at least in my mind) was still a revolutionary new thing!

Dream team at the double, November 27, 1998

Perhaps I shouldn't have been but, when Derek Hatton started shouting and then reached across the table to switch off my tape recorder while I was asking Tony Mulhearn a question, I was a touch taken aback.

So, it transpired, was Tony Mulhearn (I think I was asking Tony how he felt about Derek saying that he would approach things differently in 1998 because life was now different to how it was in 1983 – and that Derek misunderstood me and perhaps thought I was trying to suggest he no longer believed that what they did together was right).

Whatever your views on the deadly double act, I would defy anyone who has any kind of interest in Liverpool life – or life, in general – to deny that they are interesting. They're not bland. Not vague. Not wishy-washy. They know where they stand and what they stand for. Like it or lump it. Take it or leave it. And you won't get any embarrassing silences. An interviewer's dream, then. Almost.

Despite having worked at the *Echo* for 11 years, I had never spoken to Derek Hatton before. But after introducing myself on the phone ahead of our meeting, he said: "Alright Paddy mate, how are ya?"

It was as if we'd known each other for years.

I had met Tony Mulhearn before – another man who is easy to talk to and who has a good sense of humour (although, it has to be said, he is a little less voluble than Mr Hatton).

We did the interview at the Crowne Plaza Hotel – Derek's

choice – and despite Degsy's reputation for being the smartest man in the Militant Tendency, it was Mr Mulhearn who wore the tie. If the choice of hotel seemed incongruous (after all, I'd previously interviewed Tony in Frank's Café on the Dock Road), so did seeing both men place mobile phones on the table. I don't know why, but it did.

***

And some examples of what they said…

November 26 and 27, 1998

Derek Hatton and Tony Mulhearn believe everything they did during their period in office has since been vindicated, though they are at odds over whether a similar movement would be as effective today.

Hatton says: "If it was May 3, 1983, I wouldn't do a single thing differently because there was a passion and belief and we were all committed to what we did. But the fundamental difference was we believed then we could do it.

"If it was May 3, 1998, I don't think I'd do a single thing the same because life's different, politics is different, society is different, certainly Derek Hatton's different, and, to a degree, Tony Mulhearn is different."

Mulhearn is convinced that, in time, people disillusioned by New Labour will look back on the '80s and decide that Liverpool got it right: "I think that process will take place again because, within society, if a substantial section of the population feels excluded and deprived, there will be

t beats working for a living: Writing about Liverpool people has been a joy

low tickled I am: It was a privilege getting to know Sir Ken Dodd so well

Undercover reporter... stopped in my tracks by the famous Wonderbra advert in 1994 and (right) behind the scenes at Ann Summers

Telly people: Presenting Leon from Gogglebox with a special *Echo* page on his 80th birthday and (right) surprising Michael Aspel with a few 'antique' photos

The right stuff: The inspirational Alan Bleasdale and (right) me on Scotland Road, at the spot where Cilla Black's home used to stand

Life's Grand: At Aintree and no sign of the obnoxious John McCririck

Fab times: On the famous Abbey Road before interviewing Geoff Baker and (left) at St Peter's Church Hall, Woolton, where John Lennon and Paul McCartney first met

Rickymania: A Royle walkabout in Liverpool city centre wasn't such a good idea

All in a day's work: I was given some colourful assignments over the years! (Clockwise from top left) asking a Liverpool cabbie for his opinion on the *Echo*; enjoying a fish and chip taste test; en route to the capital for a feature on the London train link; escaping from a Dalek; welcoming the iconic Superlambanana to the city and in the world-famous Philharmonic pub loos

Fantastic, actually!
Holding a Frank
Sidebottom double
album from 1988
and part of my varied
record collection

Ideal world:
'I'd rather play
Thornton Hough
Village Club than
Wembley Arena' –
Henry Priestman
(right) and
(below) with Mary
McCartney in the
Lowry, Salford

Labour of love: Ready for a day's work at Everton's former training ground, Bellefield

Blue remembered thrills: (Above) getting my hands on some silverware with legend Neville Southall in 2009; (above right) true Blues Eileen, Collette and Tony Snell – and Reds' fan Sonny Ellison, grandson of Eileen's next-door neighbour, Mim Ellison. (Right) behind the scenes with long-serving Everton kitman Jimmy Martin

Rebels with a cause: Talking politics with Tony Mulhearn and Derek Hatton. Tony would ask me to write his obituary

Boy blunder: Boris Johnson in the city and (right) in Asda with Michael Portillo, 2003

Inspirational mums: Gee Walker and Doreen Lawrence meet at the Crowne Plaza in Liverpool. (Right) on election duty

Never forget: The best thing I ever did during my 33 years working on the *Liverpool Echo*. (Top) With Andy Burnham

Favourite photo: With Tom and Sandra, in Oxford, on my 50th birthday

payback time – and your spin doctors won't be able to spin those problems away. And so my major difference with Derek's position is that I can see that kind of movement and party beginning to emerge."

On Margaret Thatcher:

Hatton: "I think she's fundamentally changed society in a way that nobody else has in peacetime.

"The whole thing about greed, competitiveness, all the nationalism verging on almost fascism – that side of things emerged through the Thatcher government. You might hate and despise what she did, but you can't but admire her ability."

Mulhearn: "Her determination was unquestionable. She set out to transfer wealth from the poor to the rich.

"I personally have neither respect nor admiration for the woman. Without a doubt she was successful, but successful in what? After 10 years of Thatcherism, attacks on the unions, cutbacks on local authority spending, hiring the butcher Ian MacGregor to smash the coal-mining industry, the state of the British economy not improving at all – what we have seen is a massive shift in wealth. That's her legacy.

"I've heard Labour movement representatives saying they admire her, but I've got absolutely no admiration for the woman."

Hatton: "I'm not saying I admired her for what she did, I admired her ability in being able to say 'I'm going to start here and I'm going to finish there.'"

On the public's reaction to them:

Mulhearn: "There is very little hostility. Those who do say something are usually very congratulatory – and ask 'How are you doing? What are you doing this job for?'" (Tony was a private hire taxi driver at the time).

Hatton: "In the '80s, it was real love or hate. People either wanted to kiss the face off you or put a knife in your back – although the vast majority, of course, wanted to kiss the faces off us, and that's why we never lost an election. These days all the people who say anything only say good things."

***

"I'll never retire...but I'd have a facelift," January 16, 2008

I remember that this interview with Derek Hatton – on the eve of his 60th birthday and in which he talked about Botox, pills, property developing and politics – raised a few eyebrows. Here are some lines from it…

***

"I probably take about 20 odd vitamin pills every morning. My kids say it's psychological but, even if it is, it's working."

The former deputy leader of Liverpool City Council, who has always taken an enormous pride in his appearance – his health and, ahem, beauty regime involves four or five 6.30am visits to the gym a week, and twice-yearly Botox treatments on a line on his forehead – has long raised many people's hackles. Now he's raising eyebrows. As in: "Hatton turns 60 on Thursday? You could knock me down with a redundancy notice!"

***

Post-politics, Hatton has done panto, radio, motivational speaking and been involved in various businesses. He is currently chairman of his son Ben's online agency, Ripplef-fect, and spends time in Cyprus as a property developer for Morpheus Investments.

Have you sold out, then?

"It's a different world to the '80s and I make no apologies whatsoever for doing this now. It's property developers that have transformed Liverpool.

"Don't forget, this city is now a much better place despite the council – it's because of outside developers and the private sector." You read it here first, folks: Derek Hatton is helping to lead the capitalist revolution! What about politics – your politics?

"There's no point in being involved at the moment because they're all the same. I mean, seeing Gordon Brown outside No. 10 with Margaret Thatcher – how can anyone claim to be a credible Labour leader when they are hugging someone who, in my opinion, did more to destroy life as we know it in the last century than any other peacetime leader?"

Anyway, you'll be retiring soon, won't you?

"That's not f****** funny. I'll never retire."

But he would consider plastic surgery: "The line on my forehead is the only thing that niggles me but if, in five or

10 years' time, I hated my face and wanted something done I'd have plastic surgery. I wouldn't think twice."

You were the Peter Pan of Militant, weren't you?

"Well, I'd prefer to be compared to Peter Pan than Cliff Richard."

That, then, was the Cliff Richard of Militant, very nearly having the last word.

"I must have been doing something right to upset Margaret Thatcher," May 13, 2019

Tony and Derek gave me so many great interviews containing so many great quotes. Here are some from the last interview Tony gave me, ahead of the publication of his memoir – Tony Mulhearn: The Making of a Liverpool Militant.

***

"My biggest political disappointment was being expelled from the Labour Party by (then Labour leader Neil) Kinnock and his cohorts in 1986. Around the same time, my trade (I was a printing man – a time-served hot metal compositor) also disappeared. This also meant an end to my trade union activities. The death knell for the industry came when (Rupert) Murdoch moved his printing and publishing works to Wapping.

"It was traumatic to be thrown out of office by (Margaret) Thatcher and the district auditor, out of the Party by

Kinnock and out of my job by Murdoch. But to upset Thatcher, Kinnock and Murdoch – I must have been doing something right!"

***

"Today we have a neo-liberal government in office driven by the objective of transferring public wealth into the pockets of a tiny minority.

"And, sadly, the opposition, both from the TUC and Labour, has been pathetic. There has been no real organised response. Locally, we have a Labour council – a Labour council – which is just passing on every single cut demanded by the Tories without a flicker of opposition."

Solidarity is writ large! October 14, 2019 – a report on the previous day's tribute to the late Tony Mulhearn

Just days after his death, hundreds of people packed out the Casa in Hope Street for the official launch of Tony's memoir.

His son Joe told them: "My dad always spoke about 'terminal velocity' – the maximum velocity attainable by an object – and going out with a bang.

"Almost to the hour, this time one week ago, me dad had his last interview on the book with the *Echo's* Paddy Shennan. It was probably his last lucid conversation, he chatted with Paddy, lamented the ongoing cuts, spoke about this event and, sadly, asked him to write his obituary.

"After they'd finished, my sisters took Paddy in to see my

dad's office. And I said to him, 'Terminal velocity – going out with a bang.' He nodded his head and gave me a smile. And, looking around at all the people here today, and at the amazing film (a short film about Tony's life had been shown earlier), I'm sure you'll agree that Tony Mulhearn has certainly gone out with a bang!"

In his tribute, Derek Hatton revealed how Tony had urged him to "keep telling our story," and he ended his heartfelt and emotional speech by saying: "He was my comrade, and he was my best mate as well – and I miss him so much."

Chapter Ten

Laughing matters

TWO OF the comedians I interviewed most could not have been more different – Sir Ken Dodd, Squire of Knotty Ash, and Alexei Sayle, Squire of Anfield.

I always enjoyed interviewing comedians who were, at times, very serious – there are some who simply fire gags at you for the duration of your time together, and, believe me, that can be tiresome.

***

I met and interviewed Sir Ken (as there was such a long-standing campaign to get him knighted, and he was 89 when it finally happened, I feel I ought to use the title whenever I can) on many occasions in the later years of his incredible life, and was privileged to be the only journalist to be invited to his bedside as he lay extremely ill in the Liverpool Heart and Chest Hospital just weeks before his death.

The great man, who I had previously only ever seen when he was totally in charge of whichever room he happened to be in, suddenly seemed so vulnerable as he took my hand and thanked me for coming. It was an honour to be there.

And at 1.20am on Monday, March 12, 2018, I was also honoured to be the first journalist his press agent Robert Holmes called with the sad news that the veteran entertainer had passed away late the previous night. Robert, himself, had just received the news in a call from a distraught Lady Anne Dodd. He was 90 and died in the house on Thomas Lane, Knotty Ash, where he was born and lived his whole life.

Sir Ken had married Anne Jones, his partner of 40 years, at their home just two days before his death.

Following his death, it was a pleasure to interview Lady Anne on several occasions – and tell the world about the good causes in and around Merseyside that would benefit from her husband's £27m legacy of happiness.

And, perhaps fittingly, one of the last stories I went out on before leaving the *Echo* was the unveiling of two Doddy murals on the wall of Liverpool's Royal Court Theatre, which he had helped save many years earlier.

September 15, 2014

Doddy, then 86 and still plain old Ken, was about to mark 60 years as a professional entertainer – and there was no sign of him slowing down. He visited me in the *Liverpool Echo* offices in Old Hall Street (I think he was only a couple of hours late) to reflect on his past, but also look ahead.

***

Ken's work ethic – he performs shows up and down the

country throughout the year – would put many younger comedians to shame. And the word "retirement" just doesn't apply to him. He explains: "I am stage-struck. I adore being an entertainer. My idea of a great night is to be slaving over a hot audience. And you must keep your brain going. The secret of happiness is to keep doing what you love, keep active and to feel that you are necessary – to feel that people still want to hear and see you.

"I've never contemplated retirement. The thing is I'm not working – I don't go to work. I used to, but that was when I was learning my trade. Show business is a wonderful profession and anyone in it will tell you we are very blessed. So while I can do it and they still want me, I'll be there."

★★★

Though a famously guarded and private individual, I asked him if he was tempted to write his autobiography – and found his answer intriguing…

"I will write my life story, but not yet… I don't know. I thought, I've read life stories and biographies and it's like people rummaging in your laundry. But then I listened to the inner man and this is what I've decided – for the greater part of my life I've been an entertainer, so it's got to be an entertaining book. I'd like to have some of the true life anecdotes and stories that have been told to me and have brought me a lot of laughter and happiness."

★★★

This was typical Doddy. He was a driven man – driven to

entertain and spread the gospel of happiness. Even when he was in hospital, and less than a couple of months before his death, he wanted to keep things light – so he arranged for Anne to email me a collection of hospital-related jokes, to amuse *Echo* readers. And this was less than 24 hours after sick individuals had posted a fake news report online claiming Sir Ken had died. The irresponsible and distressing lie was then spread across the world via social media, and Doddy told me: "These monstrous evil trolls – people – should go back to the hell they came from. I wish them a reverse curse."

Doddy's jokes included the following: "When I arrived, a man in a white coat came in to see me... I said: 'What can you do for me?' He said: 'I can do you a couple of undercoats and a nice gloss finish... I'm not a doctor, I'm a painter and decorator'." And: "I asked the doctor to take a look at me – he said: 'Do I have to?'"

***

Back to the interview celebrating his 60 years in show business, and Doddy was keen to set the record straight about his stage shows: "I don't do long shows, I give good value! And the doors aren't locked. If the audience is enjoying it and I'm enjoying it and we're on a roll, it seems a shame to stop."

***

Doddy, of course, was an old school comedian from the music hall tradition, while at the other end of the comedy spectrum, Alexei Sayle virtually invented alternative comedy single-handedly. Sir Ken was fond of talking about the "rainbow of laughter." He would explain that at the top of the rainbow is the white laughter you hear when you pass a school playground where little children are jumping up and down with the sheer joy of being alive, while yellow laughter was traditionally the laughter of clowns and the red and the pink represent the laughter of love and romance. Finally, at the bottom of the rainbow, are the dark colours which, said Doddy, represented the "dark forces" of sarcasm, irony and cynicism.

Sir Ken said that, as an entertainer, he didn't go there because his role was to make people feel good. We had a fascinating discussion about this once. I asked him about sensitive people – perhaps on the front rows of an audience – who may have feared being the butt of one of his jokes or one-liners. There was also the time Doddy walked past a colleague of mine after arriving at the *Echo*, pointed at his generous stomach and immediately said to me, "I wouldn't fancy keeping him in chips for a week."

I later asked him about this type of humour, and also explained that, being a shy and sensitive type, I would always seek to sit well away from the stage, for fear of a comedian targeting my physical appearance, or just targeting me in general. But Doddy couldn't really see it, and told me: "It's just banter!"

There was a happy ending for a female colleague who had, years earlier, been likened to a Hovis loaf at one of his shows. She told me she thought Doddy had been referring to her weight – but then I saw him use that line on someone, and was able to tell her he had been referring to her suntan. It was a little delayed, but she now felt flattered!

Liverpool Heart and Chest Hospital, January 26, 2018

When I visited Sir Ken in hospital, tears welled up in his eyes and he told me: "I've been to a very dark place."

But, again typically, he wanted to divert attention from his serious plight, which he did by praising the hospital and its staff, the NHS in general, and thanking all those who had sent him 'get well soon' messages. While he wanted to make it clear that he had firmly set his sights not just on a return to his Knotty Ash home, but to his spiritual home – the stage. The Lord Mayor of Liverpool, Cllr Malcolm Kennedy, had also been invited to visit him, and Doddy told him he wanted to put on a big show for the Lord Mayor's charities that April or May – stressing: "I will be there! I shall return!"

***

He told the *Echo*: "The first and most important thing I want to say is 'Thank you.' I want to thank everyone for being so wonderfully kind and caring. The NHS is marvellous. The nurses here are absolutely wonderful and the doctors are excellent… But I also want to say there are lots of other people apart from me being cared for in this way. The medical attention is superb and the staff do their very best for everybody – it all makes me cry with gratitude."

Sir Ken was at his most emotional and tearful as he

thanked people – including those *Echo* readers who have sent him cards and their best wishes, and the children of Knotty Ash Primary School who made him a giant "Get Well" card.

He was also delighted to be given a special *Echo* front page, created by my colleague Mike Price, which said "Get well soon, Sir Doddy."

Doddy's home, February 28, 2018

It was a pleasure to be able to report on Doddy's discharge from hospital, although nobody was to know that he would pass away less than two weeks later.

This time I presented him with two front pages, one saying "Welcome home, Sir Doddy!" and the other "How tickled we all are – Sir Doddy is going home!"

***

The King of Comedy was cheered on by his famous Diddymen as he left Liverpool Heart and Chest Hospital in Broadgreen, where he had spent more than six weeks recovering from a severe chest infection.

And as he looked forward to being taken on the very short drive home, the 90-year-old entertainer told the *Echo*: "I'm most looking forward to being reunited with my poodle, Rufus – and having a nice cup of Knotty Ash tea!"

Doddy left hospital to a soundtrack of one of his big hits – Happiness – and said: "I wanted to make coming out of hospital a celebration, because this is a happy day. I still have a long way to go, but I'm doing OK." He added: "I have had a lot of time to think and, because this is a place which cares for people and makes them better, a wonderful thought came to me – 'an ounce of help is worth a ton of pity.'"

Sir Ken said he would have to build his strength up and teach his legs how to walk again, before "going back to the only job I've ever had."

But he insisted: "I will carry on!"

"This was a funeral fit for a King... the King of Comedy," March 29, 2018

Supreme showman Sir Ken Dodd always attracted appreciative and adoring audiences throughout his long and wonderful life of laughter.

And an army of devoted fans and admirers made sure they were there for his final curtain call, joining family and friends at one of his favourite venues of all – Liverpool Cathedral. This was more than a funeral fit for the Squire of Knotty Ash, this was a funeral fit for a King – the King of Comedy.

You could almost sense the great man looking down and saying: "What a wonderful day, and what a wonderful and kind tribute – thank you all so, so much!"

***

Later in the report of the funeral, I revealed that Lady Anne, ahead of it, had told me: "I have been overwhelmed by people's kindness and I would like to thank them all. It's love that has come out of this – and it's been incredible. Every letter is about love and so many people have told me they met Ken. That's because he had time for everybody."

And it was love that was all around Liverpool Cathedral.

This may have been a heartfelt send-off. This may have been a funeral service which gave people the chance to say "Thank you" and "Goodbye." But this wasn't the end. Sir Ken Dodd left millions of happy memories and, courtesy of all those priceless television performances, a powerful and poignant legacy that will live on forever.

It was a life devoted to comedy. It was a life devoted to spreading happiness and making people laugh. It was a life devoted to Knotty Ash, Liverpool and Merseyside.

And it was a life like no other.

How tickled we all were – and will remain.

***

And as well as those millions of memories, Doddy left millions of pounds to good causes.

The incredible Christmas gifts Ken Dodd keeps leaving for his beloved Merseyside, December 24, 2019

Big-hearted Sir Ken Dodd's multi-million pound legacy will continue to benefit his beloved Merseyside for many Christmases to come, his widow told the *Echo*.

On behalf of the Ken Dodd Charitable Foundation, set up by the comedian several years ago, Lady Anne continues to make a series of gifts courtesy of his £27.7m estate. St John the Evangelist's church hall in Knotty Ash has received a "substantial sum" for ongoing renovation and extension work, and is set to be renamed The Ken Dodd Happiness Hall for Church and Community, while the Shakespeare North Playhouse project in Prescot has received an initial £250,000 gift. This was announced by Lady Anne in September.

***

Some of the many other beneficiaries, which had either already received donations, or were set to, included the Liverpool Heart and Chest Hospital, Clatterbridge Hospital and Clatterbridge Cancer Centre, Alder Hey Children's Hospital, Strawberry Field, Liverpool Central Library and the Young Everyman Playhouse.

"This could be student flats or a Wetherspoons if it hadn't been for Doddy," March 12, 2020

This story was published just five days before I left the *Echo* offices for the last time, after 33 years with the paper – not that I realised I wouldn't be returning!

It was the first Covid lockdown, and the beginning of working from home (which, for me, led into furlough and then voluntary redundancy later in the year).

I thought it was fitting that my last Doddy story should be such a positive and uplifting one.

***

How tickled and discomknockerated he would have been!

Exactly two years after his death, two magnificent murals were unveiled in memory of the great Sir Ken Dodd – on the wall of the theatre he helped to save.

They adorn the Liverpool Royal Court, and Lady Anne Dodd – who performed the emotional ceremony – told the *Echo*: "They are just amazing, absolutely amazing. I'm humbled. I'm thrilled to bits. I woke up sad this morning, because it's a sad day in one way, but this just shows he brought happiness.

"Ken would have felt humbled – he would have said it was tattyfilarious, plumptious and 'I'm totally discomknockerated!'"

The bright and colourful murals were commissioned by The Comedy Trust and created by the artist Paul Curtis, best-known for his Liver Bird wings mural in Jamaica Street. Sir Ken, who performed at the Royal Court across several decades, starting in the 1950s, played a huge part in keeping the theatre open in the 1970s. In 1974, he entered the Guinness Book of Records thanks to his "marathon Mirthquake" at the theatre – it lasted three hours, 30 minutes and six seconds, and included 1,500 jokes! Later, he became part of the Royal Court Theatre and Arts Trust – and even sold the first tickets at the box office for The Ken Dodd Laughter Show, which reopened the theatre in 1978.

Comedian Sam Avery, artistic director of The Comedy Trust, said: "This could be student flats or a Wetherspoons if it hadn't been for Ken Dodd – no disrespect to student flats or Wetherspoons, but there's a time and a place for everything, and I'd rather have the Royal Court here!"

Alexei Sayle, February 28, 2006

I also always enjoyed being in the company of a very different comedian – Alexei Sayle – and wish I was as confident and self-assured. At times, I would read what he had written or listen to what he said and think – "The cocky, arrogant get!"

But the more I've thought about it – and the more I think about the laughter which often followed his various proclamations – the more I have viewed it as refreshing honesty. Some examples...

I asked Alexei if he now called himself a "novelist" on his passport, having first found fame as a stand-up comedian and then actor.

"Yes, I try to pass myself off as a writer. It was a very conscious decision to do that. You get treated differently by people as an author. When you're an actor on a set, people treat you like you've got brain damage – they try to help you down steps. And when you're a comic, even if your material is about Proust, they tend to treat you as if you're Freddie Starr."

I have to ask Alexei about a recent interview in which he said: "I've been compared to Stendhal, Maupassant and Waugh and, I think, rightly so. I've got a talent."

Have you always been so self-assured, Alexei? "I think so. Often, people don't mean it when they're being self-effacing. I'm just trying to be honest!"

And later in the interview, he admits: "Success does offer you the chance to disappear up your own arse."

August 9, 2018

He was brought up at 5 Valley Road, Anfield – and explains: "That house is where modern comedy was born! It should be a shrine!" This may come across differently in black and white, but when he says things like this it is always accompanied by laughter. Cue Alexei talking about his recent Radio 4 show, Alexei Sayle's Imaginary Sandwich Bar: "I remember thinking, after recording show one of Season Two, they should stop comedy now because it's been done! That was the night comedy reached its apotheosis!"

Cue more laughter. But will there be more stand-up?

"I should do more. Linda (his wife) hates me doing it. She hates the way stand-up has gone – she thinks sometimes it's kind of casting pearls before swine. There should be a different name for me."

Alexei ponders his wife's viewpoint and, with a big smile, says: "I am trying to think of somebody... who can I insult? Jack Whitehall! We are different. We shouldn't both be called comedians. He should be called something inferior."

He adds: "You don't want to be a crotchety old man and there is some good stuff out there, like Stewart Lee... There is a lot of me in Stewart. He's not imitating me, but I'm a massive influence on him and that's something to be proud of. He's such a great comic and getting better."

February 28, 2020

In a contender for the funniest press release quote of the

year, our Alexei says: "This tour won't be another a******* comic talking about his girlfriend or the funny things his kids do, or the funny things cats do or how he doesn't understand the internet or bleeding Brexit... This is ALEXEI F****** SAYLE you'll be seeing."

February 28, 2006

Alexei was never bland or, even worse, discreet...

***

And is the new Alexei still in touch with any of the old Alexei's work colleagues – the likes of (from The Young Ones) Rik Mayall, Adrian Edmondson and Ben Elton?

"Not really, Lenny (Henry) and Dawn (French) are the only ones I see regularly. We were all very close for a long time and I think we went through something very profound, but I suppose it's a bit like being in the same regiment in the army. Afterwards, there was nothing to keep us together."

I'm intrigued to find out what he makes of Ben Elton's major commercial successes – and major critical maulings. And he's happy to tell me...

"I think we all felt with Ben that what motivated him primarily was popularity and power. He wanted to be as popular as he could be, while I was more concerned with shouting mad stuff. But the problem with pursuing that popularity, I think, for him, is that it can never make you happy. It's like trying to fill an emptiness in yourself. That's why he's started to make mistakes, I think."

June 2, 2008

The *Echo* carried a two-part interview of mine with Alexei ahead of the screening of his three-part BBC2 series *Alexei Sayle's Liverpool.*

I asked if I could interview him in The Philharmonic pub – as a nod to the scene in his *Comic Roots* documentary, broadcast on BBC2 in 1983. It showed Alexei crawling into The Phil, before revealing this was the first pub he ever went to – when he was 14.

I had visions of myself enjoying a few pints with the great man. In the end, we did have a couple of pints each – though mine were pints of bitter and his pints of lime and soda. Disappointing. As was the fact that I paid for both rounds.

At one point, Alexei left the pub to make a phone call. One of the blokes who had been sitting on a nearby table and was on his way out had also recognised me as being from the *Echo* – and told me: "Don't forget to write 'Alexei Sayle wears shit trainees.'" As if I would pass on such a potentially hurtful comment – actually, I did (though I might not have done if he had got his round in!)

After the interview, we walked down Hardman Street – and a *Big Issue* seller attached himself to Alexei, saying: "I know you! You're a comedian! Don't tell me, I'll get it" – and so on.

This went on for a good while, or at least it seemed to. Alexei claimed he was Lenny Henry, but I don't think his forgetful fan was convinced.

Anyway, it was another entertaining chat…

***

Alexei Sayle knows home is where the heart is, and he now realises – despite moving to London, when he was 18, in 1971 – his heart belongs to Liverpool. There are two Alexei Sayles and I met the pretty sensible, serious and thoughtful version in the first pub he ever set foot in – The Philharmonic on Hope Street – for a leisurely couple of drinks (pints of Cains bitter for me and, disappointingly, pints of lime and soda for Alexei). So, you think Scousers are touchy, don't you?

"Yes, I think Liverpool people are really touchy. But if people are a certain way, it's for valid, psychological reasons. I think the city has had an extraordinary arc in that people so loved it because of The Beatles and football – and then it was so reviled. The city was traumatised by these extremes. That's why, I think, people can be kind of quick to take offence. A confident person would let it go. And the more confident Liverpool becomes the more it will let these kind of insults go by. It's only someone who is not confident who lashes out."

And regarding the Liverpool psyche, he says: "There is that thing about being 'The most exceptional whatever,' and 'The people are unbelievable' and so on. It is an interesting city, but the people here are not magic! A lot of their thoughts and feelings are the same as people's anywhere else."

***

Part one of my interview ended with one of my favourite

quotes of Alexei's when talking about his home city: "It feels like real life here, while being in London doesn't. You feel more connected and more alive when you are here. You feel comfortable as well."

June 3, 2008

Alexei, who was born in Anfield, told me he likes football but has no allegiance to Everton or Liverpool – he also has an interesting explanation regarding his lack of tribalism: "I never got that thing about Everton or Liverpool. It's that thing about being proud of other people's achievements… I'm not saying it's wrong. I just don't understand it."

At the end of the series, the comedian concluded: "I've learned things that I didn't think were important to me, about the sense of community, friendliness on the street and being among my own people."

***

But how did Alexei take that comment from that fellow drinker in the Phil, who wasn't at all impressed with his trainers?

Not very well!

February 28, 2020

Ahead of playing a run of five nights at the Epstein Theatre in Liverpool, I was again talking to Alexei about this and that. I asked for his thoughts about the BBC in general, including the accusations by many that it was anti-Labour during the recent General Election campaign.

***

He said: "It's not the comedy department and it's not the drama department that's done this shit – it's news and current affairs who, in my opinion, have been all Tory."

Alexei then points out that Radio 4's influential Today programme is edited by Sarah Sands (ex-deputy editor of the *Daily Telegraph*, ex-editor of the *Sunday Telegraph* and ex-consultant editor of the *Daily Mail*), while Nick Robinson (ex-president of Oxford University Conservative Association and founder member of Macclesfield Young Conservatives) is one of its presenters. It's important to stress, as ever, that Alexei's quotes are often punctuated by bursts of laughter – including when he says: "If they (the BBC) could just sack Nick Robinson and close down current affairs!"

***

And let's end on Alexei with another of my favourite quotes of his – from this same article – relating to his home city…

***

"When I was making the Tate Liverpool programme (Tate Liverpool at 30, for BBC1 in 2018), I was staying at the Hope Street Hotel. One day I came out and this bloke who was cycling past just shouted 'Victory for Palestine!' I thought, 'I'm in Liverpool now!'"

***

Heard the one about the brand-new Scouse comic who is up for a top award? August, 2001

I thought there was something familiar about the 34-year-old aspiring comedian who came to meet me in the hope of getting into the *Echo* – and this was aside from the fact he looked like Liverpool FC player Jamie Carragher.

The truth was soon revealed – John Bishop had appeared in the *Echo* several times in 1992-93, when the paper had supported him as he carried out a nine-month sponsored bike ride from Sydney to Liverpool to raise £30,000 for the NSPCC.

Now he was hoping for a little more exposure, ahead of appearing in the final of the prestigious So You Think You're Funny? competition, sponsored by Channel 4 (John wasn't placed – the competition was won that year by Miles Jupp, while Alan Carr was joint third. Steve Coogan was among the judges).

Looking back at that first article on John, the comedian, it's interesting to note his modesty and how he wasn't taking anything for granted.

***

Past winners of the competition include Peter Kay, Dylan Moran, Rhona Cameron and Phil Kay, who all went on to be given their own TV series. Others who have taken part and went onto great success, despite not winning, include Ardal

O'Hanlon, Johnny Vegas and Ed Byrne. And last night, John was a runner-up in the final of an open mic competition organised by a national newspaper.

"It's an important week for getting exposure, but I don't mind not winning," says father-of-three John, who's a sales and marketing manager for a London-based company which produces anti-rejection drugs for kidney and liver transplant patients.

And why should he when he only began doing stand-up 10 months ago?

***

Later in the interview, he told me: "My feet are on the ground. Leaving my job has crossed my mind, but I've got a different life to a lot of other people starting off. I'm not a 23-year-old ex-student with no commitments. I've got to balance things."

Despite only taking to the stage in his early-30s, John says the idea of doing stand-up has always been there: "It's something I've always been interested in and, when I did the sponsored bike ride, I found myself doing some after-dinner speaking, which I enjoyed. I think you reach a time in your life when a lot of your inhibitions go and you think 'It's now or never.' I went to a couple of comedy clubs and watched Merseyside comic Brendan Riley. I realised it wasn't all about pressure because he was enjoying himself so much."

Being a Liverpool fan, John was happy to walk on stage one night and hear an audience member shout "It's Jamie Carragher!" He explains: "I have a good laugh with that. I've walked into pubs in Liverpool with three medals I bought for £1 in a sports shop, casually put them down on the bar and then ordered a drink. Some people have done a double-take."

***

The article ended with John saying: "Cycling from Sydney to Liverpool was an adventure. Getting married and having kids was an adventure. I see this as an adventure as well. We'll just have to wait and see what comes after it."

***

That ended up being a fair bit – though it wasn't an "overnight success" story. He didn't leave his job until 2006, five years after that interview. In 2008, I enjoyed watching him do a short spot at Liverpool Cathedral, during a special dinner to mark the launch weekend for Liverpool's year as European Capital of Culture.

John was basically getting more and more experienced, and more and more well-known. I later asked him what it was like performing in front of Ken Dodd that night at the cathedral: "It was like trying to make love to your wife in front of a porn star – 'I'm doing my best here! I know you can probably do it better, but don't look at me like that!'"

"It's been mad… I still pinch myself," May 28, 2012

It's tempting to look back and think John Bishop became an

overnight success story after he belatedly took to the stage (at the Frog and Bucket in Manchester, in October 2000). Tempting, but wrong.

He finally packed in the day job in 2006, though his "breakthrough" year didn't arrive until 2009. Over a period of several months, from the middle of that year, came three key TV appearances – on the Michael McIntyre Comedy Roadshow, Live at The Apollo and Friday Night with Jonathan Ross: "That's when it all happened," says John. "Before that I couldn't get much telly. I was told people didn't like my accent and thought I was too northern or too Scouse." But once things started – the TV stand-up, chat shows, panel shows, acting roles, two runs of John Bishop's Britain, a record-breaking DVD and, above all, record-breaking tours – they didn't stop.

John says: "It has been mad and I'm always pinching myself when I think about everything that's happened."

***

I was reminded of something very important when I rang John once – always think about the last thing you wrote about the person you are set to speak to before you make the call. There was a long pause after I rang him out of the blue about something or other.

"Hello," I said, for a second time, "are you there, John? It's Paddy from the *Echo*." There was another long pause, before he said, "Cheap and cheerful."

I didn't quite follow. And then John helpfully – and not too happily – reminded me of a TV review I had written about the first episode of John Bishop's Britain, a few months earlier. The review, from July 31, 2010, stated:

It's good to see the charming and eminently-likeable John Bishop becoming a big fish in the comedy mainstream – but does John Bishop's Britain (BBC1, Saturday) provide the best showcase for his undoubted talents?

I'm not sure it does.

There is always talk about "finding the right vehicle" for someone who is suddenly considered worthy of being given their own prime-time series. The problem here is that Liverpool man of the moment Bishop has been given a mediocre Mini Metro, as opposed to a smooth and super-sleek sports car. So let's bash the BBC, not the Bish.

There's nothing wrong with cheap and cheerful – as long as there isn't too much emphasis on the cheap, and I reckon Bishop has been sold short here (and not just because James Corden was one of the celebrity talking heads interspersed with Joe Public talking heads). And for many viewers, the first show wasn't helped by the fact that the host re-told the (admittedly very funny) tale of how he got back with his wife, Melanie – as recently featured on Friday Night with Jonathan Ross.

There were a tricky couple of minutes during which I wasn't sure if the phone call and our ongoing professional relationship were about to be cut short. John was in a right grump with me, and I later wished I had the review to hand, as I would have said "Hey! What about the 'charming and eminently-likeable' bit?" I tried to explain my point again and, thankfully, though he clearly didn't agree with it, the atmosphere improved and the conversation carried on – as did our professional relationship.

Eddie Braben, January 18, 1997

Eddie Braben was the modest, magnificent Merseysider who made countless people laugh by putting countless funny words into the mouths of Morecambe and Wise.

He crafted those words in a back bedroom at his home in South Drive, Sandfield Park, West Derby, Liverpool.

I had the pleasure of interviewing Eddie on a couple of occasions, but was shocked to hear how much of a "nightmare" writing had been for him.

***

"The tension was incredible while I was working on Morecambe and Wise. I knew that 20 million people were waiting to see something which would make them laugh. I'd be pacing up and down at home on the night a show was on TV. I'd be thinking 'This isn't how I remember it. It's nowhere near as good as I thought it would be.' It'd be another three or four months before I could sit down, watch it properly and enjoy it."

But millions of people were able to enjoy it from the moment Eric and Ernie appeared on the screen – and we were oblivious to the blood, sweat and tears that had gone into creating the masterpieces.

The writer adds: "There's no reason why the ordinary viewer should think 'Eddie Braben worked 18 hours a day, seven days a week to bring us this programme. He almost had a nervous breakdown – he was sent to bed with nervous exhaustion and an ulcer.' But that is what it was like.

"I never enjoyed writing. It was a nightmare. I would go into my little upstairs room every morning and there would be a pile of paper waiting for me. And I had to fill it – every day. I used to describe it as 'fighting the dragon.'" He didn't have a choice. It was just something he had to do: "I was given a little bit of a gift, like we all are. Mine was to make people laugh and I think sometimes 'Wow! What a gift to have' – especially these days. I can't explain how it works. If you asked Constable how he painted The Hay Wain, he wouldn't have been able to tell you."

Is Xmas telly a turn-off?, December 8, 2003

In a feature looking at the state of Christmas television, Eddie, who moved to North Wales in his late 50s, told me: "I'm not very religious, I simply live by a set of rules and treat people like I'd like them to treat me. But in the 1970s, I began to realise that the Morecambe and Wise Show, for a lot of viewers, was Christmas.

"They were forgetting what Christmas was really all about. We got 28 million viewers for the 1977 show, half the population at the time. How many people go to church? People would stop me in the street in Liverpool and ask 'Who's going to be on this year?' There was an incredible amount of interest, but it was always the worst time of the year for me because there was so much pressure.

"And I never enjoyed the Christmas shows when they went out. I used to sit there, tensing my fists, watching, wondering and thinking 'This is the moment of truth.' But once it had finished, once all that tension and stress had been removed, then I was able to start enjoying Christmas. Now it's different. Now I can watch them with a nice, warm smile.

"What is gratifying is that I can watch the shows now and think 'That's still good.' Some of it hasn't stood the test of time, but the majority of it has. I'm pleased by that – and astonished."

***

Johnny: I lost myself in Vegas, November 30, 2009

Like many people, I've often found it difficult to separate the comedian from the persona he or she has created. That has probably been the case, at times, when I looked at Michael Pennington, aka Johnny Vegas.

In this interview, he was quite candid about the problems that can arise when these two worlds collide.

***

Thoughtful and a little reserved, Johnny Vegas is no longer 18 Stone of Idiot – in fact, the unofficial Champion Slimmer of St Helens isn't even 12 Stone of Idiot.

Few people can have embraced their public personas

more enthusiastically than Michael Pennington, aka Johnny Vegas.

Some might say Johnny – it's such a powerful character, it has to be "Johnny" – created a monster with his ranting, Guinness-guzzling performer who caused chaos wherever he went. But despite revelling in the launch of a new monthly comedy night in his beloved home town, there are signs that the pride of St Helens is shrinking the previously larger-than-life Vegas brand – spiritually, as well as physically. He explains: "I think the big challenge for me now is writing more of my own things. I find I'm getting to enjoy it more and more and I wouldn't be that fussed about being in front of a camera."

***

We spoke later in the interview about one of the funniest things I thought he had done – the "Pub Lock-in" sequences on 18 Stone of Idiot on Channel 4 (Johnny's successful attempt at making a series that wouldn't be recommissioned), when he and a group of fellow drinkers allowed the cameras to roll as they got rolling drunk.

"I'm very disappointed that bit didn't get made into its own series!" he jokes, adding; "I've realised I can't be around drunk people without having a drink. It makes my skin crawl to think of the times I thought I was fascinating company – suddenly your opinion becomes the most important opinion in the world!"

Johnny adds: "I obviously wasn't mentally in the best place I could have been! Because of the idea behind it –

shamelessly getting drunk very quickly – it was bound to be messy." Proof that his persona is all-powerful came recently when one national newspaper journalist described the actor/writer/stand-up as being "more intellectual than you expect." So is "Johnny" just too convincing?

Johnny (Michael!) says: "The whole point was to make him convincing, but then you get to a point where you say 'Are you now allowing yourself to be like that to get away with things in the guise of this character when you are not on stage?' You've got to be careful with that. I took it as a huge compliment whenever people couldn't separate fact from fiction – then, later on, I lost myself in this character."

Have you got through that now and found yourself again?

"I hope so. There's something to be said for going back to do stand-up because I know where the line is drawn now."

***

Busy Neil Fitzmaurice: a man for all seasons, November 25, 2009

Neil Fitzmaurice was a great friend to the *Echo* and I interviewed the actor, writer, broadcaster, stand-up and film-maker on several occasions – from his hilarious appearances as the hopeless DJ Ray Von on Peter Kay's Phoenix Nights to the time when he was MC and a judge for the relaunched *Echo* Stand-up of the Year (a competition he won in 1996).

***

I finally get Neil on the phone and within seconds he is proving my point.

My point being he is one of the most versatile and hard-working people in show business. Neil, who last night starred in the first episode of new BBC drama Paradox, alongside Tamzin Outhwaite, and also features in new British comedy film Nativity, is in a cab on his way to Euston.

Having appeared on a programme for the sports channel ESPN the night before, he is heading back home to Liverpool for a meeting about a sitcom he is developing.

Never mind air miles, Neil must have racked up millions of rail miles over the years. As well as making frequent trips to Manchester, Neil's career – which has included roles in the likes of Peter Kay's Phoenix Nights (which he co-wrote), The Office, Peep Show, Eyes Down, Mobile, Buried, Moving On and The Bill – has often seen him travelling from Liverpool to London three times a week.

And since February, Neil, who is still battling to secure a distribution deal for his second feature film, Charlie Noades RIP (his debut was Going Off Big Time – and yes, he secured that distribution deal), which he took to the Cannes Film Festival in May, has been presenting his weekday drivetime show for Radio City and a Saturday morning show on City Talk. Also, every other Friday and Saturday, he's the compere at the Laughterhouse comedy nights at The Slaughter House pub in city centre Fenwick Street. Oh, and the Liverpool FC fan also took on the role of Reds' boss Rafa Benitez in the recently-released film 15 Minutes That Shook The World.

Asked about his varied and lengthy CV, Neil says: "I don't know about being the hardest-working man in show business, but my career has always been about chasing jobs – nothing has ever fallen into my lap and I've never been hired for a long run in a soap or anything like that. It's always been about finding the next job.

"Sometimes, there are a flurry of things – it's either feast or famine. And when there's a famine of acting work, that's when I work on my own things."

With all the hard yards (and miles) he continues to put in, has he ever felt like following in the footsteps of others and relocating down South? Er, what do you think?

He says: "It has never, ever crossed my mind. I love where I'm from and I've always felt Liverpool inspires me in my work. The city has such a vibrancy to it and, in recent years, I think it's got its confidence back."

***

Meet Top Joe, winner of the *Echo's* Stand-up of The Year competition, September 23, 2016

I had good fun working with Neil on the *Echo's* relaunched Stand-up of The Year contest, which took place at Laughter-house Comedy at The Slaughter House in 2016.

It was won by Top Joe (rumoured to be Chris Jenkins from Aigburth) and it was a joy seeing him go on to claim his prize of an appearance on stage at The Philharmonic Hall (where Chris worked as a steward), and then go on to appear at the Edinburgh Fringe Festival.

Wearing his trademark hi-vis jacket and proudly clutching his *Echo* trophy, our winner, a very enigmatic, engaging and entertaining man, said: "I will celebrate with a pint of really strong tap water, a Pot Noodle and by doing some Vipassana meditation." He added, possibly half-seriously: "I've been doing this since January 2015 and my ambition is to do it full-time – going around doing these conferences in front of captive audiences and keeping art alive, spreading positivity and introducing philosophical concepts."

***

At the end of 2016, Top Joe went down a storm when he shared a stage with a host of TV favourites at the Philharmonic Hall. His five-minute spot at Laughterhouse Comedy's Christmas Laughterhouse Live Show, saw him appear on the same bill as Stewart Francis, Joe Lycett, The Boy With Tape On His Face, Tanyalee Davis, Terry Alderton and MC Chris Cairns.

Joe Lycett was full of praise for the newcomer, saying: "I think he's really solid. I really enjoyed watching his act. I thought he was great."

Paula Harrington, director of Laughterhouse Comedy, said: "I think Top Joe did brilliantly and I was so proud of him. I loved him from the first time I saw his act...He has definitely got a talent for character comedy and I've not seen someone stay in character like Top Joe does since Frank Sidebottom."

Towards the end of his act, Top Joe told the audience: "My father used to say 'Anything is possible in a hi-vis jacket.

No-one asks you any questions.' It's just like tonight. I'm not supposed to be here, but I got in."

And the following August, it was a further delight to see Top Joe playing the Edinburgh Fringe Festival – at one of my favourite venues in the city, the famous Waverley bar on St Mary's Street. That hi-vis jacket was working its magic again!

***

Jimmy Carr, July 7, 2006

Myself and my colleagues in the *Echo's* features department would often interview out-of-town comedians who were heading to Liverpool – and, though not a massive fan of his comedy, I really enjoyed interviewing Jimmy Carr ahead of one of his appearances in the city. Here's just a snippet…

***

There's a simple reason why Jimmy Carr loves playing to sharp-witted and sharply-dressed Liverpool audiences…

They remind him of himself.

"You always get good heckles in Liverpool," says the posh, prefectorial comic with the potent put-downs. And he adds: "The other thing I love about Liverpool is that people really dress up when they go for a night out. Girls wear beautiful dresses and guys wear suits and shine their shoes. It feels more like Vegas – there's a real sense of occasion."

Carr is known for being dapper himself. And he reveals: "I always dress up – maybe I should have been born in

Liverpool. There's just something about dressing up to go out. I want to look nice and I wouldn't feel right going on stage in a pair of jeans and a T-shirt, especially when people have paid £17, or whatever (this was 2006, don't forget!) to see me."

People hardly heckle Jimmy these days, but he still loves the idea of a good heckle: "If someone heckles and it's funny then that's great, because sometimes you're not the funniest person in the room. And you have to remember the heckles are the only bits I haven't heard before!"

Chapter Eleven

James Bulger

JAMES BULGER was abducted from the New Strand Shopping Centre in Bootle on the afternoon of Friday February 12, 1993.

Ten-year-olds Robert Thompson and Jon Venables eventually led the terrified two-year-old to a railway line behind Walton Lane police station. James's body was discovered there – just over two miles away from where he had been snatched – two days later. By complete coincidence, I had earlier that week arranged to join officers on their night shift at Walton Lane, reporting at 10.30pm that Friday, for a behind-the-scenes feature about policing. This went ahead as planned.

The *Echo* carried a story in one of its later Saturday editions which included a grainy CCTV image of James being led away from the Strand by two boys. This was when I first became aware of the news.

Despite its close proximity to Bootle, I had heard no mention of James having been reported missing while I was with the police in Walton Lane. Of course, the totally unrelated and now totally meaningless feature I had been working on was ditched. I worked on a couple of features relating to the murder – including a defence of the city and its people, after various national newspaper writers had basically waged all-out war on Liverpool. But the vast majority of the *Echo's* excellent coverage was provided by the news reporters, not least my good friend Caroline Storah. Such huge and shocking stories, of course, never go away, and I was involved in many anniversary pieces. Here are extracts from a couple of them.

January 22 and 23, 2018

Ahead of the 25th anniversary of James's death, I interviewed his mum, Denise Fergus, who had just written her powerful and poignant book I Let Him Go.

She talked about how that haunting CCTV image once had a different meaning: "When I saw James with two young lads, I honestly thought they had taken him, not meaning to, but – they enticed him out of the shop but I didn't know that at the time – I just thought he went off with them to play because James loved kids and he trusted them. What child wouldn't trust another child?"

Responding to rumours, gossip and labels: In her book, Denise talks about the "unforgivable rumours" that she had been shoplifting in The Strand, and points out that "my whole shopping trip was captured and examined frame by frame once the police went through the edited CCTV coverage." And she tells the *Echo*: "I've never shoplifted in my entire life. And I certainly wouldn't take a child if I was shoplifting. I'm just not that way inclined. I wouldn't shoplift. I'd go without before I did anything like that and the way my luck runs I'd be locked up for it if I tried. I'd be caught straight away. And people have accused me of leaving James outside the shop, but I would never dream of doing that. Why would I?"

Denise has also been accused of organising vigilante groups to track down Thompson and Venables: "I would never do that because I wouldn't want blood on my hands. Give them enough rope and they'll hang themselves, that's the way I think. Let them live looking over their shoulders."

On being labelled "hard-faced": "It was hard in the beginning, but I've had to move on and deal with everything I've dealt with in life, and if people want to judge me that's entirely up to themselves. I don't judge people by a smile on their face or a frown. But, once you do get judged, that name will stick with you forever."

The trial of Robert Thompson and Jon Venables – "You're laughing over taking my child": "They had their backs to me but they were moving and I thought 'Oh, they're crying, finally they've realised what they've done.' But they were actually laughing, and that image will stay with me forever because I thought 'You're laughing over taking my child. I've had to bury him and you two are sitting there thinking it's hilarious.'"

More supporters than detractors: "There are only a couple of people who have tried to pull me down, and there is more positivity than negativity. The amount of messages I get on social media from people saying they are supporting me – I get them to this day."

My pride in the James Bulger Memorial Trust and my pride in my family: "The charity keeps us going and I am proud of what it does. And I couldn't be any more proud of the lads than I am (Denise has three other sons). I tell them all the time. I absolutely idolise and love them. Although my lads never met their brother, I wanted them to know him, so James is always getting spoken about."

***

Five years earlier, I interviewed the two men who acted as solicitors for Robert Thompson and Jon Venables.

February 13, 2013: "I still see Thompson... who else could he drop this bomb on?"

Solicitor Dominic Lloyd makes a frank confession when asked about the challenges of representing Robert Thompson. He says: "I have no regrets about taking on the work. But I was shit-scared about dealing with you guys. I didn't know what to say to the media. I clammed up. It was such a unique set of circumstances.

"I was in the eye of a media storm – and I became part of the focus of some people's obsession. A lot of people were angling for information and wanted to know details about the offence – small details that wouldn't increase people's understanding."

Mr Lloyd is still in contact with Robert Thompson today, even though he hasn't formally represented him since 2001. He explains: "Yes, I still see Robert from time to time. There is no legal work going on but we are in contact. We review matters from time to time. If he needs some advice on something or other, what is he going to do? He's not going to go to someone he doesn't know and drop that bomb on them."

Has he ever wished the family had contacted another firm?

"Not at all. It presented a lot of challenges to me as a lawyer. I would never have sought them out but I'm glad I faced them. You don't say 'Yes, great – I'm delighted I've got this case' but you respect the challenges." Though he adds: "I didn't want the publicity and the case didn't help me in any way."

Recalling the atmosphere of the time he says: "It was difficult for people who were angry. And people were very angry. A very young boy had been needlessly and violently taken… but it was difficult for people to find a target for their anger. There wasn't a focus – they just had those CCTV images and 'Child A' and 'Child B'."

***

"Nazi war criminals have to be represented – and so do child killers."

Laurence Lee, who represented Jon Venables from February

1993 until the end of 1994, describes it as the phone call of fate.

He explains: "Every kid that had truanted in Liverpool had been called in by the police and every solicitor pal of mine had told me they had represented a truant.

"I'd just won a case in the magistrates' court on Dale Street and decided to have a skive. As I walked towards the solicitors' room to have a coffee with my mates, I could hear the phone on the wall – it was always ringing and no one ever answered it.

"God knows what possessed me but I picked it up – the first time I'd ever done so.

"A voice said 'You've not seen Laurence Lee, have you?' It was a Sgt Bond at Lower Lane police station and he said 'I've got a young lad here.' I replied 'Yippee, I've got a truant!' He said 'I think it might be a little bit more than that' – the understatement of the century. And if I hadn't taken that call, they would have sought out another solicitor because time was of the essence." He adds: "At Lower Lane I was greeted by Jon Venables, a 10-year-old boy who looked no more than eight. I'd been told why he had been arrested but thought there was a nought per cent chance of him being involved.

"But then, when the interviews began and he was told that Robert Thompson had admitted being in The Strand, Venables – having first denied being there – said: 'OK, we were in The Strand but we never grabbed a kid.' That was when the walls of the dam broke and I thought 'Jesus Christ! What am I in? What am I doing here?'

"I was in my 30s. I needed a mentor to bounce off, someone older than me. I spoke to my solicitor friend Alan Berg the next day and he said 'Pull yourself together. Get real. You're a professional. You're a solicitor.'

"I was scared of reprisals. The police searched under my car because they feared for my safety. I was spooked. Then we had the reconstruction on the Saturday, when we took Venables along the route they had taken poor James.

"Talk about fate – his father, Neil, had been out looking for him and just missed him in the Walton area. He was seconds away from bumping into him, Thompson and James. It's absolutely incredible. He could have stopped it all, as so many others could have done. The fates were against poor James...

"I would love to meet Denise Fergus and show her I am not a cold, callous lawyer. I didn't choose to represent Jon Venables, but even Nazi war criminals have to be represented – and so do child killers. I represented the interests of this boy, but I never defended him. If I had been asked to prosecute him, I would have done so as professionally as I represented him."

Chapter Twelve

A Blues medley

i) Mike Walker is a genuinely funny man.
ii) Joe Royle: "Pat Shennon (sic) is a quarterwit."
iii) I kissed Barry Horne – and I liked it!
iv) Introducing Wayne Rooney (long before Clive Tyldesley shouted "Remember the name!")

LET'S BRIEFLY revisit the Mike Walker era at Everton and re-evaluate him – as a human being, if not a football manager.

No, he wasn't at all successful, while many have added several words to his previously plain name – no longer is he merely "Mike Walker" but "Mike Walker, the most unsuccessful manager in the history of Everton Football Club."

Maybe, however, we can now afford to show a little generosity of spirit in considering a previously overlooked plus point.

I travelled to Norwich to interview the much-maligned man for a two-part series about his understandably short spell as Everton manager, which had ended a year earlier. The headline – Nowhere man! – was cruel, but reasonable, while, all these years on, many Evertonians still forcibly put the boot in whenever his name comes up. This is under-standable when looking at his pitiful record – but I'll always have a soft spot for the man, simply because he took the trouble to call me at home soon after I had got back from deepest Norwich, to provide me with an extra line which was so funny (and proved he could be so wonderfully self-deprecating) I used it to begin my two-part series…

Nowhere man! October 31, 1995

And you thought the laid-back, grey-haired man had no sense of humour… A couple of hours after arriving back in civilisation from Norwich, the city which always sleeps, the phone rang.

"Hi, it's Mike Walker. I forgot to tell you something funny. When I was at Goodison, I received an anonymous Christmas card – in October. The person who sent it wrote 'I'm sending it to you now, because you won't be here at Christmas.'"

He or she was right. Mike Walker was sacked in November.

"I thought it was hilarious!" he told me.

***

You've got to laugh – and I was pleased Mike did.

***

Although it has been a good story for the pub over the years, I remain saddened about how things turned out regarding one of my childhood Everton heroes – Joe Royle. I greeted his arrival in the managerial hot seat at Goodison Park in 1994 with great joy – even marking the occasion by interviewing his lovely dad, Joe senior (a man with his own fascinating story to tell), for a truly affectionate feature. This was published on November 21 – hours ahead of Joe junior's first match in charge of the Blues, a 2-0 triumph over Liverpool at Goodison, on the night Duncan Ferguson scored his first goal for Everton.

My piece on jazz pianist Joe senior revealed how he had been entertaining audiences since long before his only child was born. As a member of the Royal Engineers Band, he played in front of thousands of troops during the war. Later, he formed The Joe Royle Showband, though the name was soon changed to The Saturated Seven – a tongue-in-cheek response to The Temperance Seven.

They were a big name on the Liverpool club circuit, released their own record and can be seen performing at the Broadway club in Norris Green in the 1971 film Gumshoe, which starred Albert Finney and Billie Whitelaw. There were also many TV appearances, including Opportunity Knocks in 1971 – The Saturated Seven finishing second in the viewers' vote after winning on the studio "clapometer."

And thanks to Everton reporter Dave Prentice (who went on to become a great friend of his) my piece also included some nice words about his dad from Joe junior.

***

Vic Gibson, the football reporter on the *Echo's* less well-resourced sister paper, the *Daily Post*, needed some freelance match-reporting help in the 1994-1995 season. My *Echo* colleague Brian Reade was invited to write some reports – as he had done before – but his transfer to the *Daily Mirror* led to the ball falling at my feet.

I ended up writing occasional match reports between September '94 and October '96 – under the pseudonym Tom Roberts (in tribute to my young son, Thomas Robert) – though all but the first one were Everton games. I explained to Vic and his sports editor, Len Capeling, that I'd found reporting on Liverpool far too challenging! Or words to that effect.

For that one game at Anfield on September 10, '94 – a goalless draw against West Ham – I spent much of my time silently willing the Cockneys to hold on for their point (a task which became trickier for them when former Blue Tony Cottee was sent off on his second debut for the Hammers).

Shortly after a pompous Main Stand season ticket holder turned to him to ask "How are our poor relations doing today?" (Everton were on their way to getting beaten 3-0 at Blackburn), I told my *Echo* colleague, Liverpool reporter Ric George: "I don't know how you do this every week!" Ric supported Everton – what a professional!

In the end, I decided to knock the occasional moon-lighting on the head for two reasons. One was that it took up too much of my time on Sundays (writing a reflective match report and an accompanying news/quotes piece). But the main factor was that I longed to return to the stands full-time – the idea of once again always being able to shout, swear and relax (well, sometimes) as an ordinary fan, sitting with other ordinary fans, seemed much preferable to being paid to sit in relative silence and solemnity in the Press box (even with the free pre-match and half-time hospitality).

My last match report was arranged to be Everton v West Ham on October 12, 1996. I remember it well – including the theatrical shout of "Resign!" which rang out when Joe Royle entered the technical area early in the game. One or two fans in the Main Stand looked a little bemused – because the cry actually came from a writer who was sitting behind me in the Press box! Everton won 2-1, but it had been a dismal display – and perhaps my subconscious mind was telling me to enjoy myself in my final report.

It began…

How much longer can we go on putting up with days like these? Isn't it now time for heads – or, at least one head – to roll?

Surely we can't be expected to continue swallowing the drivel we are fed week in, week out. It's driving good, honest people clean round the bend – and it's time their voices were heard. It's time… for action.

Quite simply, it's high time we were spared that awful Spice Girls song at half-time. Sadly, it's the same old song on the pitch as well.

It also included the following paragraphs…

Joe Royle deserves undying praise for saving this great club from near-certain relegation, winning the FA Cup and then finishing sixth last season.

But, as he suggested himself after the second watershed that was York City (the second division side dumped the Blues out of the Coca Cola Cup 4-3 over two legs, in September '96 – first division Port Vale having knocked them out of the FA Cup in February that year), things appear to have come full circle.

Progress is no longer being made. The team is going backwards.

No one likes criticism and Joe Royle appears to absolutely hate it but, then again, no one likes to pay good money to watch sub-standard fare.

Oh yes. Saturday's game. Dire, dreary, desperate, depressing. No. None of those words adequately sum up a terrible match.

***

But back to that introduction to the match report – and me taking to task the person who chose the half-time music. Now, I ask you, how on earth could that have been mischievously misconstrued as a call for Joe Royle's head?

Joe, though, wasn't happy. He made his feelings abundantly clear – including in a letter to Len Capeling. I've not seen it, but I do have a copy of Joe's subsequent reply to Len – who was a great fan of my reports.

It read…

Dear Len,
What a load of whitewash.
You write the letter as though you have no knowledge that the report from Tom Roberts 'Pat Shennon' (sic) was going

into the Daily Post on Monday morning, but we both know that is not the case.

What is nearer the truth is that your one and only sports reporter Vic Gibson had gone to see the Manchester United v Liverpool game and you then allotted our game to a quarterwit by the name of Pat Shennon (sic), who duly went to Goodison Park with a fully sharpened pencil. The report was a total disgrace and has been judged so by everyone who has seen it, a report of such like that you would never dare enter into your paper about Liverpool. By allowing the 'dross' (sic) to enter onto your back page you have put yourself firmly behind Shennon's (sic) views, and for me to further support the Daily Post would be akin to turkeys supporting Christmas.

I shall continue to deal with Vic Gibson on a day-to-day basis and that is all.

Yours sincerely,

Joe Royle.

P.S. I see that your one and only reporter was at Liverpool away from home on Saturday, leaving us with no identifiable journalist, yet again.

***

He may have got both my names wrong – and also been wrong about other things, including his claim that my report had been judged a total disgrace by everyone who had read it – but I did like "quarterwit"!

Joe always had a way with words. I was told he came out with another classic after Everton had earned a 1-1 draw at Anfield through a late Gary Speed equaliser on the night of

Wednesday November 20, 1996 – several weeks after my final match report.

Standing outside the Press room, Joe was apparently asked if he was entering – "Not if that spiky-haired twat is in there," he allegedly said.

Brilliant! But I was actually on my way to the pub, having cheered on the Blues from the Main Stand – after paying my way that evening, rather than being paid to write about the game. Things got worse for Joe, who banned all the Press from Everton's Bellefield training ground following a piece about the manager in the *Daily Express*.

Len Capeling's column of February 5, 1997 was headlined: "The day the dummies flew out of the Everton pram." This was a reference to a previous winning one-liner from Joe – "Sounds like a few dummies have come out of the pram" – after he had heard that Roy Evans believed his Liverpool side had been kicked off the park in a dull 0-0 derby on January 24, 1995. As Len wrote: "Banning is always a sign of weakness."

The then *Echo* writer Phil McNulty returned to this theme after Joe left the club the following month. His Friday column, on March 28, began: "Joe Royle – if he runs true to form – will have left Everton believing he was witch-hunted out of Goodison Park by his enemies. It is a theory which is, of course, a total nonsense. The reality for Royle is that he has been defeated by the only enemies he ever truly had. Everton results and Everton tradition."

Later in the piece, Phil wrote: "He showed weaknesses in his armoury when he turned on his critics – myself included

– who rightly criticised Everton's pathetic demise at York City and a run of awful results matched by dreadful performances."

***

It may not please the egos of some working in the media, but I believe managers should rise above – and essentially ignore – what is said about them by journalists, not least in smart-arsed, mickey-taking match reports.

Joe Royle, it seems, just couldn't do that. And he couldn't let things lie.

Don't get me wrong. On a human level, I did have some sympathy with him. After all, I've always had a thin skin and been far too sensitive.

But, then again, I wouldn't go into football management.

***

I kissed Barry Horne – and I liked it!

I remember it like it was yesterday – just like I remember his wonder goal which helped secure Everton's top flight status on May 7, 1994.

The venue was the Beluga Bar on Wood Street, Liverpool city centre. The date was Saturday, January 24, 1998. The occasion was a birthday celebration for a friend and then colleague, Jane Wolstenholme.

I was drinking with my wife Sandra, Jane and the rest of our happy gang when I suddenly saw him across the crowded room. Barry Horne was in the house! I remember being impressed that he had made it into town that night

– after all, earlier that day he had been playing for Huddersfield Town against Wimbledon in the FA Cup fourth round. Sadly, Huddersfield had lost 0-1.

Wimbledon, of course, had been the team which seemed set to kick Everton out of the Premier League back on that incredible May day in 1994, after they took a 0-2 lead, courtesy of a penalty and an own goal. But a Graham Stuart penalty got the Blues back in the game, before Barry Horne's spectacular 25-yard drive brought us level – before Stuart's second goal sent Evertonians berserk (one person fell arse over tit after running on the pitch – but I have no regrets!)

That scruffy third goal was the vital one, but the game, along with the Premier League, seemed to be drifting away from us before Horne scored the goal of his life. Fast forward nearly four years (by which time my Barry Horne memory bank also contained an FA Cup Final victory and countless other brilliant performances by the midfielder, as one of Joe Royle's "Dogs of War") and here he was – just feet away from our drinking party.

As I looked across, I saw my moment was fast approaching. Barry and his friends were leaving the bar – and would have to walk past us to get to the door.

We – or, rather, I – may have been a little happy and, perhaps, loud, as I recall seeing a little fear and anxiety in the footballer's eyes. It was understandable – perhaps he thought we were all Liverpool supporters, and were about to take the piss rather than praise him.

Actually, I think I was the only one of us who was interested in approaching the great man – and I duly did so, telling him: "I love you, and I always will" before planting a smacker on his right cheek.

As I kissed him, I could hear my Liverpool-supporting wife behind me delivering the sneering commentary: "Bloody sad Evertonians."

She will never understand.

But what did Barry say? He told me: "You have no idea how much that means." Now, being a cynical man, I have since reflected on this and feared it was his sarcastic way of saying it meant absolutely f*** all. But, having replayed the magical moment in my mind again and again, and thought about his expression on the night, as well as how he has come across in interviews since, when asked about his time at Everton, I'm pretty sure his words were genuine and heartfelt.

Yes, that was a great night.

I kissed Barry Horne – and I liked it!

Introducing Wayne Rooney (long before Clive Tyldesley shouted: "Remember the name!")

It wasn't an easy assignment – write the life story of a 16-year-old who you're not allowed to talk to (oh, and we're not quite sure where his parents live). But, somehow, I got three parts out of The Wayne Rooney Life Story. Everybody was happy!

Well, not quite.

I was later told that Rooney's new agent, Paul Stretford, wasn't at all pleased that Wayne's parents had allowed *Echo* photographer Martin Birchall to copy all those precious photographs of Wayne at various ages, and posing with various people – including Everton stars Duncan Ferguson and, when a mascot in a Merseyside derby, Dave Watson.

And one of my *Echo* colleagues was definitely aggrieved – because she proudly told me in the pub that week after work that she wouldn't be reading a single word of the series. Her point was that it shouldn't have been written as it would heap undue pressure on the teenager. Bill Kenwright, on the other hand, had told me Wayne's story was a wonderful one – and he was happy for it to be told.

He said this to me on the phone, just minutes before Martin Birchall and I arrived at the Rooney family home. He had actually rung up to have a go at me – which he did – for the "snotty" column I had written in the previous day's *Echo*.

I had been justifiably unkind about the single – No Other Team (sung to the tune of Home On The Range), backed by Oh Come All Ye Faithful (an operatic arrangement of the hymn) – which was being released by Everton in celebration of the club's 100 seasons of top flight football.

I wrote: "I could be mischievous and just quote the first sentence uttered by manager David Moyes: 'I asked Bill Kenwright to help build on the atmosphere at Goodison Park and this is what he has come up with.' Quite.

"But the man of the People's Club did add: 'They are great songs, although I'm sure the fans will find their own words for them.' Oh yes."

Snotty? Well, yes. But it could have been much worse!

Luckily, Bill rose above his initial irritation – and I was able to tell Wayne's mum and dad: "I've just been speaking to Bill Kenwright and he thinks you have a wonderful story to tell about young Wayne!"

And, once we got inside the house, there was the boy wonder himself. I introduced myself and explained that I knew I wasn't allowed to speak to him, but was delighted to be able to shake his hand – sadly, I was already committed to the act when I realised he had just removed his hand from down his trackie bottoms.

Ah well, it was Wayne Rooney's hand, wherever it had been!

August 15 to 17, 2002

He's just 16 years and 294 days old, but Wayne Rooney is Everton Football Club's Great Blue Hope. The hottest young property in Merseyside football – in English football – has already been compared to Michael Owen, Kenny Dalglish, Alan Shearer and Ryan Giggs. And yet the kid from Croxteth hasn't even kicked a ball in the Premiership. Blues fans have seen too many promising young members of their flock come and go – often to Liverpool Football Club. Michael Owen. Robbie Fowler. Steve McManaman.

And Jamie Carragher. All once supported Everton. All, for one reason or another, decided to desert and ply their trade at Anfield. While young, potential-packed players who have emerged at Everton in recent years have also fallen by the Goodison wayside. Danny Cadamarteri and Michael

Branch promised much, but delivered less. Francis Jeffers still promises much, but is now an Arsenal player. Michael Ball is also still young and gifted, but is now a Rangers player. Everton, then, need a hero. A young hero. Step forward Wayne Mark Rooney.

Echo writer Paddy Shennan brings us the boy wonder's story so far…

***

Three Everton pennants and an Everton car registration plate are on show in the front bedroom window. And, inside the Croxteth council house, live three Everton-mad boys aged 16, 14 and 11 – together with their Everton-mad parents.

It could be one of any number of Blue-blooded families on Merseyside. But this is a very special house. This is the house where Goodison Park wonder kid Wayne Rooney lives. "Young Wayne" shares it with his proud-as-Punch parents, Wayne senior, 39, and Jeanette, 35, together with younger brothers Graham, 14, and John, 11. If you adopted Loyd Grossman's voice and asked a Blue "Who'd live in a house like this?"… they'd tell you in about three seconds. All they'd have to do is look at the framed pictures on the wall and the trophies on top of the TV. And this is before mum and dad dig out more photographs from the growing Rooney scrapbook.

One framed picture stands out. An 11-year-old Wayne is standing in the Anfield centre circle alongside then Everton captain Dave Watson and former Reds' skipper John Barnes

– the youngster was the Blues' mascot for the derby, which took place on November 20, 1996. The game ended 1-1 (Robbie Fowler scored for Liverpool and Gary Speed for Everton).

Another photo from that night, of a smiling Stan Collymore and unsmiling Wayne Rooney, is kept on the floor behind a chair. Meanwhile, Duncan Ferguson, a second-half substitute in that game, is pictured with his arms around Wayne and his brothers at the Blues' Bellefield training ground the following season. It's probably fair to say Big Dunc wouldn't have predicted that he'd be playing alongside young Wayne just a few years later.

As we arrived at the Rooney home, Dad was reading the *Echo* – while the *Echo's* well-thumbed pre-season special was on the coffee table. This was the second time *Echo* photographer Martin Birchall had met Wayne senior – Martin having taken the first Press picture of young Wayne and his two brothers in March, 1998, when all three were at the Everton Academy.

Knowing that Everton, quite rightly, wish to protect Wayne as much as possible, the *Echo* first approached manager David Moyes to ask if we could speak to him – "Yes... when he's 37," came the reply. Fair enough. But there is also a story to tell about the people who have helped him get to where he is today – the brink of the big time at sweet 16.

"A wonderful story," as Everton owner and deputy chairman Bill Kenwright told me on the phone on the day we called at the Rooney home (he wanted to berate me for my "snotty" column about the new club song – and then play it to me over the phone. My ears are still stinging – from both Kenwright and the song).

Wayne's unassuming mum and dad were kindness itself, as they dismantled various photograph frames for us and recalled facts and figures about their three talented lads. Graham, a pupil at De La Salle, is now concentrating on his boxing. John, who is about to start at the secondary school, is still at the Everton Academy – a promising midfielder in its under 12s team.

Recalling the *Echo's* 1998 photograph, when Wayne was 12, Graham was 10 and John was seven, and his hopes that one or more of them may one day play for the Blues, dad says: "You don't really think it's going to happen at the time." While about Wayne, he says: "He began to kick a ball as soon as he could walk. And, like me, he has always been an Evertonian."

His first game at Goodison? "I can't remember, but he was probably about six-months-old!"

Now Wayne senior and the rest of the family (Main Stand season ticket-holders) are looking forward to watching young Wayne play at Goodison Park – in the Premiership. Jeanette says: "We're really excited about seeing all the games Wayne plays in – home and away."

Sadly, all requests to see – and print in the *Echo* – pictures of Wayne as a toddler kicking a ball were politely declined: "He'd go berserk!" says his mum, who, herself, was too shy to be photographed: "Tell the *Echo* readers I was out!" she jokes.

But she was more forthcoming when recalling Wayne's exploits on the football field: "They didn't play football at his primary school, Our Lady and St Swithin's, and he played his first proper game when he was seven. It was for an under 11s or under 12s team from the Western Approaches pub in Storrington Avenue. Despite only being seven, he came on as a sub and scored!"

And the goals just kept on coming. Jeanette adds: "He also played for the Copplehouse pub team in Fazakerley when he was nine and other teams, including East Villa and Pye FC. He won the Golden Boot for them, after scoring the most goals in the BT Challenge Cup competition. He also scored loads of goals in his first year at De La Salle – he won a league and cup double with them – but then stopped to concentrate on playing for the Everton Academy. He actually scored 99 goals in one season for the Academy's under 10s. And he broke the goalscoring record for Liverpool Schools' FA under 11s, which he still holds." Jeanette thinks he scored 80 odd goals, although Wayne's then manager, Tim O'Keeffe, thinks it was 72 from a total of 158. Whatever, he's a record-breaker!

Wayne's brother, Graham, 14, is equally proud, saying: "I knew Wayne would do it. And I think John could follow in his footsteps as well."

As for himself, he explains: "Although I'm doing boxing now and don't play for the Everton Academy any more, I still have a team – Crosby Stuart in the Maghull and District League." If the Wayne Rooney bandwagon continues to roll, his family could soon be under siege. But the idea of seeking sanctuary in a more anonymous part of Merseyside doesn't seem to have crossed his down-to-earth parents' minds: "I think we'll try and stay here," says Wayne senior. At home with the Rooneys, things seem pretty ordinary – but you sense that once Wayne starts scoring goals in the Premiership, things will never be the same again.

Reds wanted him, but Wayne's a True Blue

Wayne Rooney turned his back on Liverpool FC – at the age of nine. The born and bred Blue trained with the Reds – in his Everton kit – but was soon signing a registration form to enable him to play for Everton Academy's under-nines side. Bob Pendleton, the scout who recommended him to the Goodison Park club, told the *Echo*: "He only ever wanted to do one thing and that was play for Everton." The *Echo* understands Liverpool made a big play for the youngster, but his True Blue resolve held firm.

Bob, from West Derby, adds: "It doesn't matter what they would have said to him, he wouldn't have gone there. His dad also said he wasn't going anywhere else. And he was also adamant he wasn't going to Liverpool."

The 63-year-old retired train driver, who has been scouting for the Blues for 12 years, first spotted Wayne playing for Copplehouse under 10s in the Walton and Kirkdale Junior Football League around the time of his ninth birthday in the autumn of 1994. He recalls: "It was on a Sunday morning at the Merseyside Youth Association's Jeffrey Humble playing fields in Long Lane. Copplehouse's manager, a guy called

'Big Nev,' told me about Wayne. I watched him play – and when you see someone special, which he was, you just know.

"But Liverpool had already seen him playing in a Saturday league in the Bootle area. He had one or two training sessions at Melwood, but within days I took him down with his dad to meet Ray Hall, Everton's academy director. Ray saw him training and backed me 100 per cent, signing him there and then. And now he's looking forward to playing in the Premiership for the team he's always supported, at the age of 16. It's a real Roy of The Rovers story."

Bob, who also tipped off the Blues about young defender Tony Hibbert, adds: "I've kept in regular touch with Wayne and his family and they're smashing, down-to-earth people. If Wayne continues to listen to the right people I'm sure he'll have a great future. Colin Harvey, the youth team coach, has been his mentor. He loves Colin and thinks the world of him."

Coaching a star of the future

The season was 1996-97 and Wayne Rooney was a quadruple-trophy-winning, record goalscorer for the Liverpool Schools' Football Association Under 11s city team, which then played at Penny Lane.

His old manager, Tim O'Keeffe, says Wayne, who was 10 at the start of the successful campaign, scored 72 goals (out of a team total of 158), breaking a record set in the late 1970s by Steve Redmond, who later made a name for himself, as a defender, at Manchester City. The record still stands.

It was also the season Wayne won his first European trophy, after the team competed in an international tournament in Holland.

Tim recalls: "Wayne had strength, aggression, pace and a great ability to finish – with his right or left foot, or his head. I would rate him alongside former Liverpool schoolboy players Robbie Fowler and Steve McManaman at that age. They all had that bit of magic which helped them stand out from the others. Wayne was a very quiet boy, but popular with the other lads and the staff. A lot of lads are quiet off the pitch but different on it. But with Wayne, it was a case of controlled aggression when he was playing. At times he could be annoying, because he would go against everything in the coaching manuals. You'd think 'He can't do anything from there' – and then you'd see him put the ball in the net. Yet he was a good listener and did take things on board."

But there was a famous occasion when Wayne ignored everyone and everything – except his own goalscoring instinct. His dad, Wayne senior, was shouting encouraging words from the touchline, as were manager Tim O'Keeffe and his assistant, Jim Milne. Wayne was in a central position heading deep into the opponents' half: "Take him on, take him on," shouted his dad. "Pass it wide, pass it wide," shouted the coaches. The youngster did neither. He simply let fly an unstoppable shot from 30 yards or more. Another Wayne Rooney goal.

Jim Milne says: "He took no prisoners on the pitch. It was obvious to us he was destined for greater things. He was a strong, powerful boy, but he was also sensible." Tim, a Blue, and Jim, a Red, who are no longer involved in the Liverpool Schools' FA set-up, are now looking forward to seeing their former star striker going on a teenage rampage through the Premiership.

Jim says: "I hope he does well, as long as he doesn't score in two games during the season!"

All those who have helped Wayne get to where he is today can feel proud, and Tim says: "It was always satisfying for us to see players go on and do well. Wayne had so much natural ability he was always going to succeed. I think he will eventually play for England."

(Although Wayne did, of course, return for a second spell at Goodison, Evertonians may need to steel themselves before reading Tim's final quote from 2002)...

"And the good news for Evertonians is that he has always been a strong Blue – and his family are all Blues. I think he will want to stay at Everton for as long as they want him to stay."

Wayne's world

Teacher John Hennigan was Wayne Rooney's head of year last season... this season he'll be cheering him on from his seat in Goodison's Park End, starting today against Tottenham.

"It'll be a little bit special watching someone I know – an ex-pupil – playing for the team I support," says the Everton season ticket-holder.

"Let's hope it's a good season for Wayne and Everton. We

don't want to go overboard, but he has certainly got a lot of potential."

John adds: "Wayne's not an academic lad; he does his talking with his boots. I have never coached him but he's undoubtedly a great athlete – the sort of lad who, apart from being a great footballer, could win the high jump and the 100 metres." His former teacher says Wayne's world is about to change beyond all recognition, explaining: "Like any other 16-year-old, he has been used to mixing with his peers. But now he'll be spending a lot of time with people who are quite a bit older than him. He's going to need a lot of luck along the way and it was comforting to hear Everton manager David Moyes say he is going to look after him."

John's colleague, Graham North, was Wayne's head of year in his second, third and fourth years at De La Salle, and says: "Wayne has been good for the school and the school has been good for Wayne, supporting him whenever it could. He was never any problem. He came in and got on with his work. He was a rather quiet lad who took things in his stride – nothing seemed to bother him too much."

So will Graham be joining John Hennigan at Goodison to cheer on Wayne in the Royal Blue of Everton?

"Er, no... I'm a Red!"

Mother's Pride, October 21, 2002

I spoke to Wayne's mum on the Monday morning after the Saturday he scored that goal – his first for Everton – against Arsenal.

Looking back at her quotes, and remembering the raw excitement that surrounded this raw, brilliant young player, makes me feel quite sad.

Still, it was great while it lasted. Heady days!

I even remember Wayne's mum looking bemused (and amused) to find herself being treated like a superstar at a Hall of Fame dinner at the Adelphi Hotel. At one point, there was a long queue of Evertonians waiting patiently to get her autograph – I know this because I was the first person to get one (Wayne wasn't in attendance, but Jeanette was on the top table so she was the next best thing – and ended up signing my copy of Virgin Blues by David France and Dave Prentice).

I think there was even a chant that night of "Rooney's mum! Rooney's mum! Rooney's mum!"

***

Wayne Rooney's overjoyed mum Jeanette today reflected on her son's glory goal – and told the *Echo*: "We've been celebrating ever since the final whistle!"

And amid frenzied speculation linking her 16-year-old son with an immediate move away from Goodison Park, she promised: "He's going nowhere!"

Jeanette watched Saturday's game from the Main Stand, together with Wayne's dad, Wayne senior, and Wayne's brothers, Graham, 14, and John, 11.

And it was to his family that Wayne ran when he scored in the last minute to open his Premiership account and end Arsenal's 30-game unbeaten run.

At the family home in Croxteth, Jeanette said: "It was a very emotional day. I had tears in my eyes when Wayne scored – and we've been celebrating ever since. That's why I've almost lost my voice!"

And then she uttered the four words all Evertonians will be delighted to hear. Asked if her son is leaving Goodison Park, she said: "No, he is not!"

***

I was also delighted to speak to Bob Pendleton for this piece – and the scout who had recommended Wayne to the Blues told me: "Wayne has set the city on fire. And the good news is this is just the start – there's so much more to come from him. He was born to score goals. As soon as he took the ball down and faced the goal I knew he was going to hit it. I'm not afraid to admit it – like Wayne's mum, I had tears in my eyes. And the crowd's reaction to the goal just made it even more emotional – they went berserk!

"Like everybody else I found myself chanting 'ROONEY! ROONEY! ROONEY!'" He added: "I know there's already been talk about Wayne going to another club, perhaps Manchester United, Arsenal or even Liverpool, but I honestly can't see it happening." Wayne turned down the chance of joining Liverpool as a nine-year-old, and Bob added: "I can't see him going anywhere. Wayne and all his family are Everton, Everton, Everton."

Ah, Wayne Rooney... Whatever happened to him?

Chapter Thirteen

Voices of peace in the face of hatred

October 4, 2006

SOMETIMES, IT'S better to keep your voice out of things and simply allow your subject or subjects to do most, if not all, of the talking. And when I went to interview two brilliant and inspiring women, I knew exactly what to present to readers – a straightforward conversation between them.

Gee Walker and Doreen Lawrence were brought together by harrowing heartbreak – but also by hope. Each lost a son in the most vicious and violent of circumstances, and for the most shameful and sickening of reasons.

Stephen Lawrence was murdered in Eltham, south east London, on April 22, 1993 – because he was black.

Anthony Walker was the victim of a murderous attack in Huyton, Merseyside, on July 29, 2005 (he died in the early hours of the next day) – because he was black.

Both were 18. Both were targeted at bus stops. Both were intelligent and ambitious young men with bright futures ahead of them. On the day after her son's murder, Gee Walker said: "This is on a level with the Stephen Lawrence case. My son was killed purely because of the colour of his skin." Doreen Lawrence, meanwhile, felt compelled to travel to Huyton to lend Gee her support. At the shrine created at McGoldrick Park, the scene of Anthony's murder, she asked: "How many young people have to die before society sees and makes changes?"

And on the first anniversary of her son's death, Gee revealed: "Doreen and I have kept in touch. She has been very supportive."

And now the two mums were together again, renewing their strong bond and friendship at the Be Inspired 2006 event, organised by Merseyside Expanding Horizons in partnership with Merseyside Disability Federation and held at the Crowne Plaza hotel in Liverpool.

***

Gee: "It was so refreshing to meet you, Doreen. We were from the same backgrounds and our sons had many things in common. I'd always thought about you, even though we had never met. You were in my thoughts and prayers."

Doreen: "I had just come back from holiday. My son picked me up and said 'Someone has been killed in Liverpool' – and my heart sank. I thought 'Not again.' I didn't hesitate in coming up to Huyton."

Gee: "That was so important to me because when people say 'I understand,' unless they have been through the same thing they don't understand at all. Remember, Doreen, I asked you 'Does it get any easier?' And you said 'No.' I just slumped. You were right, but you somehow learn to get through each day."

Doreen: "I couldn't give you any answers. And, for me, it was like reliving everything again. Here was another young man being killed for no other reason than he was black. I was thinking 'What's changed?'"

Gee: "We've bumped into each other at a couple of conferences now, haven't we? But living in Liverpool and London, it's not easy to keep in regular contact, is it?"

Doreen: "Remember the last time you tried to ring me, Gee? I was in America."

Gee: "That's right. I was just ringing to say 'Hello.'"

Doreen: "Yes, you called me on my mobile – it was a very expensive 'Hello'!"

Gee: "But we have a mutual understanding, don't we? We have shared a lot of pain, but the main difference is that two men are behind bars for Anthony's murder. My heart goes out to you, because Stephen's killers are still free."

Doreen: "I'd like something new to happen in Stephen's murder investigation, but I don't think anything will. As for me, I'm Stephen's voice and I feel I have to keep speaking out."

Gee: "I feel like I have been catapulted into this situation. But I'll shout tolerance, peace and forgiveness from the rooftops as long as people ask me to."

Doreen: "If I was sitting in a room with racists, I'd try to educate them, make them see a different viewpoint – and ask 'If we took the lives of your children, how would you like it?'"

Gee: "It's about ignorance – if people here knew the history of Liverpool, there would be no racism. The boys who killed Anthony went to school with him. I need to find out from them, when I'm ready, what went wrong."

Doreen: "I have no desire to talk to Stephen's killers. I know there is no regret in their hearts."

Gee: "How do we carry on, Doreen? I draw strength from Christ – and the thought that if I can reach one person, that person may be able to change a family and, by a domino effect, a community might change."

Doreen: "Yes, I get my strength from the hope I can change or help save just one life – and help make things safer for my other children."

"They say time is a healer... how long is time?" July 24, 2006

I had interviewed Gee Walker earlier that year, to mark the first anniversary of her son's brutal murder.

Here is a heartbreaking extract.

***

The sound of basketball on pavement was always the sign that Anthony had returned home – and it's a sound that still haunts his mum today.

She explains: "I get up and look out when I hear a basketball bounce outside – and then I sit down again, deflated."

And the mum-of-six can still hear Anthony, himself.

We're sitting in the Grace Family Church in Aigburth,

where Anthony was a youth worker, and there is both laughter and tears during our meeting.

The tears, naturally, are brought on by what happened to her popular and beautifully brought up boy – and the laughter by the things he said and did and the things he would be saying and doing today.

I ask Gee what her son would have made of Mrs Gee Walker, The Stateswoman-like Public Figure who has addressed thousands of people at vigils and race crime conferences. And a woman whose strength and dignity has seen her being embraced by the nation. He'd be as proud as Punch, wouldn't he?

"I hope so," says Gee, quietly. "I imagine his little face smiling at me and him saying 'Go for it, ma!'

"Yes, he'd have a sheepish grin and say 'That's my mum!' And if I see a spider running across the floor I still shout 'Anthony!'"

One year on, Gee still catches herself preparing meals for her dead son, explaining: "I'll do it subconsciously but, if I stop and think about it, I won't put it on the table, like I used to." Anthony used to wash the dishes on Tuesdays and mow the lawn and put the bins out on Thursdays – and his mum says: "I do those jobs now and, I'm telling you, that's hard. There's always a pang there when I do them.

"When people say 'move on' that's when it's difficult – it's like an elasticated bungee rope, it's always there pulling you back. They say time is a great healer, but how long is time?"

***

On December 1, 2005, Paul Taylor, who admitted murdering Anthony Walker; and Michael Barton, who was found guilty of his murder, were jailed for life. Taylor was to serve a minimum of 23 years and eight months and Barton a minimum of 17 years and eight months. In 2016, Barton's sentence was reduced by a year.

On January 3, 2012, Gary Dobson and David Norris were found guilty of Stephen Lawrence's murder and the next day jailed for life. Dobson was to serve a minimum term of 15 years and two months and Norris at least 14 years and three months (it was explained that they were sentenced under guidelines in place at the time of the attack, and as juveniles, because both had then been under 18).

Chapter Fourteen

In search of Madeleine

"No news is better than terrible news" – the Madeleine McCann interviews

I MET and interviewed the Liverpool-based grandparents of Madeleine McCann – Susan and Brian Healy, the parents of Madeleine's mum, Kate McCann – on many occasions during the first year after Madeleine was abducted in Praia da Luz in Portugal.

Kate, meanwhile, as well as a "thank you" letter written two months after her daughter's disappearance, wrote a lengthy article for the *Echo* as the third anniversary approached. Eventually, my links with Susan and Brian, who were always so welcoming to me and generous with their time, were restricted to brief news pieces about the anniversary services held in their parish church after Kate and Gerry's spokesman, Clarence Mitchell, asked me to no longer contact them for interviews.

Below are major extracts from most of the interviews I carried out with Brian and Susan – two kind and lovely people who did so much to support their daughter and keep

Madeleine in the public eye – and the two powerful pieces penned by Kate.

Brian died, aged 80, on January 20, 2020.

In June 2020, German national Christian B was identified as a murder suspect in the Madeleine investigation by German prosecutors. Suspects' surnames are not usually revealed in Germany for privacy reasons. In April 2022, the same man was reportedly declared an "arguido" – formal suspect – by Portuguese prosecutors. A statement issued by the Portimao section of the Faro department of criminal investigation and prosecution did not name him, but said the person was made an "arguido" by German authorities at the request of Portugal's public prosecution service.

My first interview with Brian and Susan Healy – published on Madeleine's fourth birthday, nine days after her abduction, May 12, 2007

You can almost reach out and touch the heartache, fear and frustration – but it's impossible to fully comprehend it.

Outside, under blue suburban skies in this tree-lined street in the shadow of busy Allerton Road, there is precious normality. Birds are singing. People are shopping. It's a blissfully ordinary day. Brian and Susan Healy, the grandparents of abducted four-year-old Madeleine McCann, would give anything for ordinary.

For an extraordinary and horrifying drama – one they have absolutely no control over – is being played out behind the doors of their comfortable and well-kept semi-detached home. Hope is keeping body and soul together, but their hearts are slowly breaking. It is now nine days since their first grandchild was taken from her bed – and today is her fourth birthday.

They should be with Madeleine, together with their daughter, Kate, her husband, Gerry, and the couple's two-year-old twins, Sean and Amelie, celebrating the youngster's birthday at the family home in Leicestershire. Instead, they are in Allerton… willing the phone to ring with good news.

Susan said: "We are praying for the best possible birthday present for Madeleine – her safe return to her family. If that happened, it would be a perfect day.

"I just believe we are going to get Madeleine back – if we don't get Madeleine back, I think none of our lives will ever be the same again."

We are sitting in Brian and Susan's front room. Their ordinary front room, with its lovely, ordinary family photographs on the walls and window-sill.

Later, just before we leave, Susan and Brian show us a much-cherished Easter present from Madeleine – a heart-shaped plate featuring her handprints and inscribed with the words "I love you grandma and grandad. From Madeleine, 2007." Beautiful and, in today's painfully sad circumstances, devastating.

Kate and Gerry's children were born thanks to the wonders of IVF, and Susan explained: "The same church I am praying in now – our parish church of Our Lady of the Annunciation, Bishop Eton – is where I prayed before Madeleine was born, because Kate was so desperate to have children. It's also the church where Kate and Gerry got married in December 1998.

"Madeleine was such a gift. Kate loves all her children, but Madeleine was her first child and she had waited so long for her."

The grandparents are keen to thank the people of Merseyside – and beyond – for their support, their offers of help and their prayers: "The response has been fantastic and absolutely overwhelming," said Brian. "It really does help us and we really appreciate it. But it still feels like it's all happening to another family – we feel as if we're in a movie."

Regarding her daughter's daily torment, Susan explained: "I think her worst time is around 10.30 to 11 at night, at the end of another day – another day that Madeleine has not been found. Kate is normally a very placid person but I have seen her kick furniture and do things she has never done before in her life. Gerry has had to go into automatic pilot mode to cope, but I heard him howling the first night we were out there. They are so concerned about what Madeleine is going to be feeling."

Susan, a proud mum and grandmum, fought back tears on several occasions as we spoke, but, like her husband, she is determined to keep this heartbreaking story in the news – and determined to tell the world about an ordinary, loving family.

A family which, God willing, will soon be back together.

A heartfelt letter of thanks from Kate McCann – while Madeleine's grandparents say: "We'd rather our suffering

go on than have an ending that's just too hard for us to think of," July 27, 2007

Kate provided the following letter to the *Echo*, as she and Gerry wanted to thank the people of Merseyside for their continuing support.

***

I would like to say a huge 'thank you' to all the people in Liverpool and Merseyside who have supported Gerry and I, in different ways, over the past few months. Our family as a whole has gained a great deal of strength from such kindness, and it has been particularly important to me that my mum and dad have experienced such solidarity and support.

It is through such goodwill that we have been able to keep on going, even through our darkest moments we continue to hope and pray that our beautiful little Madeleine will be back with us soon and able to continue bringing such joy into many people's lives.

***

Twelve painfully long weeks. Eighty-five heartbreaking days. And an aching, anguish and agony which shows no sign of ending.

Life may have moved on for others, but the world stopped turning for the family of missing youngster Madeleine McCann, including her Liverpool grandparents Brian and Susan Healy, on the nightmare night of Thursday May 3.

When I first visited Brian and Susan's Allerton home, it seemed as if the entire world's media was covering their horror story. But recently, it's felt as if almost the entire world's media has been looking the other way.

"Time has stood still for us," Susan tells me. "The longer it goes on the worse, I think, it becomes. At first you get swept along by all the support, but now I'm thinking 'How long will this go on?' and 'How long can you put your life on hold?' Doubts creep in, because we are only human.

"And the big question is 'How are we going to get Madeleine back?' And we can't answer that." At this point, Brian says softly: "We're just hoping for a miracle now."

He adds: "I have thought it gets a bit easier, but not completely. I will go out and see something in a shop and think 'I'll get that for Madeleine' – and I'm stopped short. It's a horrible feeling." And don't let anyone tell these remarkable people that what they need is news of any description.

Susan stresses: "We'd rather go on suffering in the way we are than have an ending that is too hard to even contemplate. No news is better than terrible news."

"My Kate would never hurt Madeleine – how can they think she is a suspect?" September 8, 2007

The investigation into Madeleine's disappearance took an incredible turn when Kate and Gerry McCann were named as suspects (this suspect – or arguido – status was officially lifted in July 2008, as it was for a man called Robert Murat, who had also been falsely suspected). Regarding what follows, it's merely a style point – and the difference between the news and features operations at the *Echo* – but you may notice my "Susan said" and "Brian said" as used in previous interviews became "Mrs Healy said" and "Mr Healy said".

***

It's a nightmare which becomes more horrific by the day – and the drained, distraught and devastated grandparents of missing four-year-old Madeleine McCann wonder if they will ever wake up from it.

Friends and family members fill every downstairs room in Susan and Brian Healy's smart suburban semi off Allerton Road in south Liverpool, while TV crews and reporters pace the pavements.

At 8am yesterday, Mrs Healy thought it best not to speak publicly – but by lunchtime, when it emerged that Kate McCann, her only child, was now being treated as a suspect over the disappearance of Madeleine, she believed she could keep quiet no longer.

Justine McGuinness, the family's campaign manager, revealed that police believed that traces of Madeleine's blood were in the couple's car, hired 25 days after she went missing. Mrs Healy said: "If the forensic results are right and there's some DNA that links Madeleine to the hire car – that evidence must have been planted. There is no other explanation." She added: "It doesn't add up unless you believe she killed Madeleine, hid the body and then put it in a hire car several weeks later. This is a couple who have spent all their time looking for Madeleine and raising awareness about

Madeleine while the whole world has been watching them. But the hurtful thing is that the Portuguese police, who have worked with Kate and Gerry so closely, could possibly go along with the theory that Kate could be involved. They can't be any judges of character." Mr Healy went even further: "I think Charlie Cairoli the clown must be in charge of the investigation."

Among the speculation is that Madeleine may have been sedated. Mrs Healy said: "If Madeleine was sedated, we believe the person who came for Madeleine did this. Kate and Gerry use Calpol very occasionally and never give their children any kind of drugs. In fact, they don't use Calpol unless they really have to."

Mrs Healy spoke to Kate yesterday morning, and revealed: "She said 'I'm all right, mum.' She is worried about the twins, Sean and Amelie, and what's going to happen to them. I told her we were going to the papers now, we are not going to sit back any longer."

"Insult upon injury for Madeleine's grandparents," September 12, 2007

In my weekly column, I said that Brian and Susan Healy's "pain and anguish is magnified by the fact that this is a drama being played out on the world stage – with complete strangers in far-from-supporting roles."

***

I went on: "Everything is going on all around them – 24

hours a day – and, at times, they must feel as if they don't exist, as the world and his wife natter away about their family. And you just have to look at various internet forums – where cowardly, know-nothing fools and friendless geeks and goons hide behind pseudonyms – or listen to the 'expert' analysis of amateur detectives, all of whom have zero access to the evidence, to know that many people have already made up their tiny minds.

"Their knowledge may only be based on what they've seen on Sky News – er, remember the incredible fuss, broadcast live into our living rooms, when Robert Murat first came under suspicion after he was "shopped" by a Sunday newspaper reporter? – and read in the *Daily Mail*, but they don't have doubts, they have 'cast-iron certainties.'

"I would say let's ignore the amateurs who speak out so confidently before anyone has been charged, let alone tried, and leave things to the professional authorities – but they've hardly covered themselves in glory so far, have they?

"Through it all, though, surely everyone can agree that we shouldn't be overlooking a missing four-year-old girl called Madeleine – or her heartbroken grandparents."

"If I weighed two stone more, had a big bosom and looked maternal, people would have more sympathy" – what Kate McCann told her mum, October 16, 2007

Kate McCann's parents today hit out at the "scurrilous rubbish" being printed about their daughter – and said she is being persecuted because of her appearance.

"She said last night 'If I weighed another two stone, had a bigger bosom and looked more maternal, people would be more sympathetic,'" Madeleine's grandmother, Susan Healy, told the *Echo*.

"I think it's terrible that she's having to think like that. She does feel persecuted, not by the general public, who have been extremely supportive, but by some sections of the media, and I just feel it's important I let people know she is not this person who is in control all the time. Kate is a very sensitive, caring person and one of the most maternal people I know – she puts me to shame. Her life revolves around her children but now she's got to the point where she feels she is being persecuted, in her mind, if her twins, Sean and Amelie, cry in public – it's absolutely crazy."

She adds: "All this stuff is going on inside my poor daughter who's not done anything wrong. She and Gerry went to a restaurant which was just metres away from their apartment and part of the holiday complex – it was a terrible mistake but they did it out of naivety."

It's now 166 days since Madeleine was last seen alive and Susan and Brian admit that the enormous strain is telling on all the family. Kate's health and well-being has given particular cause for concern, and her mum reveals: "She and Gerry do have counselling – Kate saw a counsellor at the end of last week. It's the same person they saw in Portugal and I know it does help them. But I think they continually go back to the feeling that they can't afford to go to pieces because they have to keep trying to get their daughter back – that overrides everything else they are feeling."

There have been concerns about Kate's appearance and apparent weight loss, and Susan says: "She's always had that kind of build and has never carried any weight. But she does look very traumatised. It must be unbearable for her to think about the possibility of never seeing Madeleine again, or that it's going to be another six months before she sees her again."

She adds: "We've no idea when Kate and Gerry may have their suspect status lifted, but we hope it will be soon. Until it is, they are not allowed to defend themselves in public – and that is dreadful.

"They need to be exonerated as soon as possible and there are people who will then need to apologise to them – but whether that happens in the real world, I don't know."

Susan says she has had difficulty sleeping, while Brian reveals: "Anger keeps me going, so I'm doing pretty well because there has been a lot to be angry about."

But despite all the agony and anguish, Susan says: "We need people to realise that nothing has changed since day one. Madeleine is still missing and the police haven't found anything to indicate she isn't alive, so we have got to go on looking. Kate and Gerry are as innocent as you or I, or anyone reading this. The perpetrator or perpetrators are still out there. We still pray that someone will open a door and say 'Here she is – it's all been a terrible mistake.'

"In my heart of hearts I still feel we will get Madeleine back, although I naturally get scared when I hear about the police carrying out searches."

Brian adds: "I've heard nothing yet to convince me that

Madeleine isn't alive and I am clinging onto the hope that we will get her back."

But he and Susan are realistic enough to accept that some people are not only convinced that their granddaughter is dead, but that Madeleine's own parents were responsible. Susan says: "Strangers are still coming up to us and saying 'We don't believe a word of what we're reading, you know' – that happens again and again and it's important for us to hear that. I also know that if you throw enough muck at people, some of it can stick. But you've got to credit people with having the intelligence to work out that there has been a lot of scurrilous rubbish written."

"There have been so many lies; people will have to hang their heads in shame," January 11, 2008

Madeleine McCann's grandfather today makes a heartfelt plea for the police, public and media to refocus their attention on "the most important story"... the search for the missing four-year-old. Brian Healy believes his beloved grandchild, who has not been seen for 253 days, is in danger of being overlooked amid the daily torrent of spurious stories, speculation and wild rumours. He also tells the *Echo* there is so much he is looking forward to doing with his first grandchild, like running through the water fountains in Liverpool's Williamson Square. And he pays tribute to the warmhearted people of Liverpool and thanks them for their constant support and good wishes.

Brian says: "There has been so much that has been said and

written, much of it untrue and hurtful, but so often it seems to me as if the only really important person in all this has been forgotten – and that's Madeleine. Finding Madeleine should be at the forefront of everyone's minds – everything else takes the attention away from this and wastes so much time."

He adds: "There have been some good, positive and helpful stories written about the search for Madeleine, but it seems to be the more sensational and negative stories which get the main headlines. And there have been so many lies written. People say not to read the papers, but you can't avoid seeing them. A lot of people will end up having to hang their heads in shame. I have got so mad reading some of the lies about Kate that I've rung up the newspapers concerned, but it doesn't seem to do any good."

Later in the interview, Brian told me: "As Madeleine's grandfather, there are so many things I long to do – for example, I'd love to be able to run through the water fountains with her in Williamson Square."

Desperate for a breakthrough in the search for Madeleine, but frustrated at the lack of any positive news from Portugal, Brian says: "I've never felt so helpless in my life." Despite the negativity from various quarters, Brian, and Kate's mum, Susan, have been bowled over by the response from strangers on the streets of their and Kate's home city. Brian says: "We want to thank everyone in Liverpool for their fantastic support and their good wishes – they have been great. We have had so many hugs from people who approach us when we're out shopping. Sue was in town on Saturday and she was getting hugged all the time. These people care about Madeleine and they know what the real story is – that Madeleine has been taken and needs to be found and brought back to her family as quickly as possible."

"If it was any other child, I would think 'She's gone' – but it's Madeleine, so we have hope," April 28, 2008

It's a tough question to ask and an almost impossible one to answer.

As they approach the anniversary of Madeleine's disappearance, her grandparents Brian and Susan Healy bravely face up to the horrendous possibility of their worst nightmare coming heartbreakingly true.

So do they now, after all this time, believe little Madeleine is dead and, if she is, would they rather face this devastating fact – or continue living in ignorance, with only their daily turmoil and torment for company?

Susan takes a deep breath, and says: "I think Kate feels she needs to know what's happened to Madeleine, because her imagination…"

Her voice trails away as the enormity of what she is saying hits home, before she adds, softly and sadly: "Kate said 'If Madeleine is dead I need to know.' That goes for us as well."

But explaining the trap they fear falling into, Brian says: "If you say 'We want a resolution' you are tempting fate… If I was talking about any other child, I would probably think 'She's gone.' But it's Madeleine, and so we have hope."

Susan, as if grasping hold of that most powerful of four-letter words, stresses: "We still have a lot of hope, because we have no reason not to have. Sometimes when I'm having a bad time – which has been most of the time recently – I would be quite fearful of the chances of Madeleine being found alive. Then I'll read something or speak to someone who will say 'You will get her back, you know.' That makes me feel a bit ashamed, so I pull myself together."

And Kate? Is she, as some newspapers have suggested, on the verge of falling apart? "I can't believe how strong Kate is," says Susan. "I just don't know where she gets this strength from. Prayer does give you strength. If nothing else, it is something that has kept us going… prayer and the support of other people.

"I do fear for the future, of course I do. But as for her appearance now, Kate's always been thin and I don't think she's any thinner than before. I've looked at pictures in the early days when people said how cool she looks and, to me, she looks in anguish. I think, if people can't see the anguish in her face, they are blind, they really are. No one takes less time on themselves than Kate. She's not into make-up. She comes across in pictures quite well. She looks very attractive, though she wouldn't think that. But some people want to write anything at all to make her appear less caring about her children and more caring for herself.

"I am absolutely amazed at the strength she has shown. I know she feels she let Madeleine down. The only way she can cope is by trying 100 per cent to get Madeleine back. She can't possibly give up because the twins deserve everything they had before."

This mention of three-year-olds Sean and Amelie, as with so many things the grandparents say during the course of our conversation – a conversation punctuated by the tears which occasionally fall down Susan's face and the unutterable sadness in Brian's eyes – prompts memories of happier times.

"When you see the two of them laughing together now," says Brian, the proudest of grandads, "it's always in your mind that there should be three of them laughing."

So much has happened in this past year from hell – and yet, so little has happened. Nothing, essentially, has changed since Thursday, May 3, 2007 – Madeleine went missing that night in the Portuguese resort of Praia da Luz, and she is still missing.

Susan says: "It's quite frightening to think that 12 months has almost gone by – 12 months since we were sitting in this room and just expecting the phone to go, and hearing they had found Madeleine."

"I'm so proud of Kate on this saddest of anniversaries," May 3, 2008

Madeleine's McCann's grandmother today spoke of her pride in daughter Kate as they faced this evening's first anniversary of the youngster's disappearance.

It was the milestone no one wanted but, in a bid to keep their four-year-old daughter in the headlines, Liverpool-born Kate McCann and husband Gerry put themselves back in the glare of publicity with a series of TV interviews.

And Kate's mother, Susan Healy from Allerton, told the *Echo*: "I know the person Kate is. I know how self-effacing and shy she is as a person. She's been thrust into this public role, but she has carried it out admirably. I was very pleased that Kate and Gerry were given the platform to say what they wanted to say.

"I am just so very, very proud of Kate."

***

As the third anniversary of her daughter's abduction approached, Kate McCann kindly wrote an article for the *Echo*. The following extracts are, inevitably, powerful, poignant… and heartbreaking.

"My Liverpool and why we're closer to finding Madeleine," April 28, 2010

"Every time I'm back home at my mum and dad's and I head off for a run, it fills me with a great sense of warmth and hope to see the green and yellow 'Madeleine rosettes' tied to the railings along Allerton Road. It makes me very proud of my Liverpool roots.

"Liverpool has been a bedrock of support for all our family. We frequently receive positive comments, reassuring hand squeezes and pats on the back with general hopeful encouragement from passers-by when we're here.

"My mum and dad have had so many comforting hugs

from friendly strangers and I know my dad's had a fair few pints bought for him over the past three years! It makes us feel that we are not alone in this relentless battle. And that helps!

"It's incredibly painful to think that three years have gone by since we last saw Madeleine. Just the thought of it makes me panic. Strangely though, it sometimes feels like it all happened yesterday, but then reading my journals reminds me very clearly of just how much has happened and how much we've done during this time. It's suddenly very apparent how three years have passed!

"Although our lives are very different now (I often refer to my life pre-May 2007 as 'my previous life'), we have reached a new kind of normality.

"Gerry works full-time at the hospital and concentrates on 'Madeleine-work' in the evening when the children have gone to sleep. I have not returned to medical work but spend my 'working day' dealing with the campaign to find Madeleine.

"This set-up also gives me the flexibility to support Sean and Amelie as much as I can. As for the twins – they are just fantastic. They are enjoying school and are incredibly happy children – and really funny! They play together constantly, a little like having your best friend with you all the time.

"I honestly don't know where we'd be without them. They bring us that vital bit of joy, laughter and warmth that makes you want to get out of bed in the morning.

"Their understanding of what has happened and what we are all trying to achieve is quite remarkable.

"Madeleine remains a hugely significant person in their life. She appears in their role-play, in their conversations and in their prayers at night. I've heard them on many occasions talking to other children in the park saying 'our big sister's six-and-a-half... blah, blah, blah'. It makes me very proud of them and even more determined to bring their big sister back home. Madeleine is certainly not forgotten in Sean and Amelie's life.

"It's difficult to talk of 'success' when we still haven't found Madeleine but this year has certainly enhanced our chances of doing so.

"The court case in Portugal over the past 10 months, which led to the injunction against (ex-detective) Goncalo Amaral's book and DVD, has been a significant step forward. The damage caused in Portugal, by this book and 'documentary', to our efforts to find Madeleine may not have been apparent in the UK but we believe it has been highly detrimental...

"The injunction has brought us great relief, as we can hopefully start moving forward with the search, in the places where it really matters. At least now, all our efforts stand a chance of being successful."

***

"There is much that can still be done to find Madeleine... It's very hard to feel that the key piece of information, which would unravel this whole nightmare and bring Madeleine home, could be sitting on someone's desk.

"We will continue to request a review of all the information held and hope that in the coming months, the governments and law enforcement agencies will work together to achieve this.

"In the meantime, we will continue with our work, knowing that there's somebody out there who knows what's happened to Madeleine and where she is.

"And of course, it will not just be the person who took Madeleine that could help to give us this breakthrough...(it could be) their mother, father, brother, sister, aunt, uncle, cousin, grandmother, grandfather, partner, colleague, neighbour or friend.

"Everybody is known to someone. Everybody confides in someone.

"All we need to do is reach one of these people or hope that one day, they will find the courage and compassion to come forward and tell us.

"As long a period as three years sounds, it's incredibly small when compared to a lifetime. It's those many, many years ahead with Madeleine that we long for and aim towards. The effort of perseverance pales into insignificance compared to a reward so precious.

"Madeleine is a real little girl and she is still missing. We will not be going away and will never stop looking.

"We will press on with the same commitment and tenacity, for as long as it takes.

"A very special 'thank you' to everybody in Liverpool who has helped us and continues to support us in the search for our little Madeleine."

Chapter Fifteen

This Is My City

IN 2010, I launched a series called This Is My City, in which I asked well-known people for their views on Liverpool. Here are brief extracts from some of those revealing interviews.

John Bishop, February 26, 2010

"I automatically feel at home in Liverpool, which is really odd considering how little I've lived there," says the Liverpool-born comedian, who was raised in Winsford, Cheshire. "Liverpool and Dublin are the two cities where I feel most at home – where I can walk into any pub and not think about it.

"There's an edge to Liverpool and there's an openness and friendliness about the people. And I think Liverpool people have a much more enhanced sense of identity and feel a greater sense of pride than people from many other cities.

"One thing I'd say about Manchester is that possibly because it lacks its own strong identity, it also lacks what Liverpool has been guilty of – an insularity. In the past, when people have come up with new ideas for Manchester, the city has been willing to embrace them – often, people in

Liverpool, unless those with the ideas are born and bred in Liverpool, won't listen." But he adds: "If there was one word I would use to describe Liverpool it would be 'optimistic' – and optimism drives everything else."

Pete Wylie, March 5, 2010

"Liverpool One means nothing to me. I prefer other places which, I think, have more atmosphere. I was in the Midland pub opposite Central Station recently and there was this barmaid – Lynne, I think – who was funny, fantastic and clever. She had an answer for everything and now I'm going to make the Midland one of my pubs. This is what happens in Liverpool. It's like the women who work in Tesco on Aigburth Road – they're my best mates. Another pub I like is The Liffey on Renshaw Street – you could be in Ireland.

"I don't think we realise what a great thing the river is – I always go to Otterspool if I feel a bit down or confused, which is quite often! I go down there and just find it breath-taking. I'd also take people up to Crosby to see Antony Gormley's Iron Men. No matter how many times I go, it's always different because of the weather or the tide."

Pauline Daniels, March 12, 2010

Some people reckon a particular breed of Liverpool women are head cases – and actress, comedienne and broadcaster Pauline Daniels certainly has a bee in her bonnet about them. She says: "I'd love to stop women walking around in public with big rollers in their hair. I think it's atrocious. These girls should be banned from shops because they are dragging down the city – and don't get me started on people who wear their pyjamas in public!

"You wouldn't see any of this in Paris or New York – and I think we have better-looking girls. My message to them is 'Get rid of the rollers and pyjamas – and stop painting yourselves orange!' Haven't they got mirrors? Can't they see what they look like? People shouldn't have that attitude of 'We can do what we want.' It's like those kids who ride their bikes and skateboards around people who are shopping."

Marina Dalglish, March 19, 2010

Her soft, Glaswegian tones may reveal her roots, but Marina Dalglish doesn't hesitate when asked where her heart lies.

"We've still got family up in Scotland, but this will always be our home. And when Kenny and I go on holiday and people ask, we say we live in Liverpool. Yes, it's Southport but everyone around the world has heard of Liverpool.

"Glasgow and Liverpool are very similar. It's the people – they are so friendly in both cities. So it was very, very easy for us to settle here.

"When we first came down we lived in the old Holiday Inn on Paradise Street, where Liverpool One is now. We stayed there for nine months, because Kenny was always in his bed and wouldn't come and look at houses! We had a great time in the hotel and had everything we could possibly want – three rooms and a swimming pool downstairs!"

Roger Phillips, April 2, 2010

Radio Merseyside's Roger Phillips, everyone's favourite Mancunian, says: "I once did a debate for Radio Three called 'Is Liverpool an English city?' and the conclusion was it's not. We are different. I think it's the massive amount of immigration, while Liverpool and the likes of Marseilles and Naples have been classed as 'cities on the edge' which don't have a hinterland beyond them. I think it makes a difference. You are never travelling through Liverpool, you are going to Liverpool.

"There's a great generosity about Liverpool people which isn't just parochial – and there's a great sympathy which can be seen as being mawkish but isn't. When James Bulger died, there were all these flowers laid in Walton and I remember the reporters from London saying this was a bit over-sentimental – a few years later, Princess Diana dies and everyone picks it up! It suddenly becomes the norm and it's OK."

Margi Clarke, April 23, 2010

"We are different because Scousers still own their city. We can still make our voices heard and we can still tell our stories.

"Liverpool is a good example of what my mother (the late Frances Clarke, former Kirkby Labour councillor and Mayor of Knowsley) used to say to me: 'An individual is only as strong as the group he or she comes from.'

"Liverpool is full of big families, unions and communities

– and yet we have got loads of mad, crazy individuals, too, and that twain ain't supposed to meet!

"In Liverpool, everything starts with the river – which is the lifeforce and heartbeat of the city, pumping energy that comes from the banks at Birkenhead over to Liverpool, itself.

"We shouldn't ask 'What time is it?' but 'What tide is it?' That's a line from a great book called Edgy Cities, by Steve Higginson and Tony Wailey."

Keith Carter, May 14, 2010

He's the comedian whose alter ego, scally Nige, famously impressed Capital of Culture judges – telling them "We've got culture coming out of our arse!"

Keith, himself, says: "I'm always taking people around Liverpool because a lot of comics come and visit. I take them down to the docks and to the museum in William Brown Street and into the Central Library.

"I also show them where The Beatles played and take them to Sefton Park… Everyone who visits is really impressed, not least by the architecture, and people from London are especially taken with it – they say the capital is the only other place that offers as much.

"I always take people to the Philharmonic and, of course, to the greatest pub in Liverpool – the Cracke, which captures everything I love about the city. It has an edge to it and is full of characters – you can always learn something about someone's life."

Ian McCulloch, May 21, 2010

"It's the funniest place in the world – and I've been everywhere. People here take the mickey out of each other, are quick-thinking and their glasses are always half full. I couldn't live anywhere else – because of the humour more than anything. But it's also the cloud formations, the sky and the sunset.

"There's always a confidence about Liverpool people. It's self-assurance – we know who we are. And while the media may look at us in a negative light, most people who come here say Liverpool people are so friendly and they'll do anything for you.

"I do get homesick (on tour) – just things like missing a pint in a Liverpool pub. I like the Gardeners in Woolton, this place (the Monro) and the Blackburne Arms. I also like the Roscoe Head, but I tend to stick to the ones I know because I don't like walking into a gaff if I don't know it – because I'm quite shy. Oh, and the Bear and Staff in Gateacre – that's really nice."

Liz McClarnon, June 4, 2010

"In the past I've had to champion the city and defend it, but I've noticed it's not like that anymore. I don't think it's because of Capital of Culture. I just think people are travelling around more and the word has spread because of that. People used to assume a lot of things about Liverpool but now most people seem to know what it's really like –

and that's a great relief. I don't know why we had to defend it so much because I don't think it's changed that much over the years – yes, a lot of money has been injected into the city and we've got a new shopping development but the people are the same and the city is essentially the same.

"The first place I'd take people to is where I'm from – Garston. It's got such a strong community and there's such a good feeling about it. I can walk around without a hint of make-up on and without a brush having been through my hair for 12 hours and people will just say 'Hiya babe, how are you?' I just feel so comfortable there."

Michael Starke, June 11, 2010

"I think we are a little pocket of originality and that our achievements have helped define the city. We're also defined by the fact that so many people like to knock us, although I know we can be our own worst enemies – because we are touchy (I certainly am. If I have a chip on my shoulder, I'll bear it gladly!)" And one thing the actor is touchy about is the use of the term "Scousers" to describe Liverpool people. "I don't like the word 'Scouser' because I feel it's often used in a slightly derogatory way. I'm trying to use it less."

Regarding the city's architecture, he says: "The Liver Building is my favourite building in the world. I've got a model of it and my kids bought me a painting of it – yes, I'm slightly obsessed! I love the new museum at the Pier Head. I think we needed something like that – something that stands out."

Billy Butler, June 25, 2010

"What I've always said about Liverpool is we're the quickest to laugh and the quickest to cry. We've got the warmest hearts and the quickest ability to be funny. We've always been targeted by the Press but it's about believing in yourself. We're not ashamed to show our joy and we're not ashamed to show our grief.

"First, I'd take people to The Beatles' Story exhibition, which has recreated the Cavern to a remarkable degree. I'd also probably take them on a tour of where the old clubs were – like the Mardi and the Downbeat – and you'd have to take people to the Blue Angel and the Jacaranda. Because of our maritime history I'd have to show people the Merseyside Maritime Museum, so they could see our rich heritage. Today, there are so many more places to take people – when I was young it was the Walker Art Gallery and that was it!"

Jake Abraham, July 9, 2010

There are two Liverpools, according to actor Jake Abraham, who grew up in Toxteth and Kensington.

He says: "I'd take visitors to all the nice places, but I'd also show them places that people aren't normally taken to. I had a conversation about this with someone who had taken a friend around the city – to Liverpool One, the football grounds and all the usual sorts of places. But I asked 'Did you take him to Granby Street? Did you show him where the riots took place? Did you take him to Kensington?'

"I'd take people to all the great places – to the docks, Sefton Park and to Oggy (Oglet) Shore near Hale village – but I'd also give them the full history of Liverpool. One of my grandfathers was African – the other side of the family is Irish – and I'd talk to people about the city's links with the slave trade."

Eithne Browne, July 23, 2010

Proud Liverpudlian Eithne Browne looks up in wonder at the city's beautifully crafted, awe-inspiring architecture – and in sadness at some of the new buildings on the block. And she has a pertinent question: "Who does Liverpool belong to now?

"Our unique city is disappearing. The docks have gone and tourism is supposed to be the future but people won't want to travel to see Lego buildings.

"I always urge people to look up in areas like Castle Street, Dale Street and Tithebarn Street – look up at the wonderful decorations and designs that were simply put there to make us happy.

"They serve no practical purpose but give our eyes something to catch on to.

"But compare that to the cold, cynical, square and aggressive buildings that have been put up recently. I don't care if they're nice inside – because many of us won't be going inside them.

Some of the buildings on the waterfront look like bad dentistry – they're not in harmony with each other."

Bill Kenwright, July 30, 2010

"My Liverpool is geographically divided by where all the city's cinemas used to be. I knew every cinema in Liverpool when I was a kid. I was an addict. In those days you would open up the old broadsheet *Echo* and see two full pages of classified ads because there were so many cinemas.

"I drive up every other week with my best mate, Laurie Mansfield, and he now knows my Liverpool off by heart. Whatever route I take, I point out the locations of all the old Liverpool cinemas. I went to the pictures every Saturday night with my gran (Lil Jones), who lived at 31 Vallance Road in Anfield.

"I went to a psychotherapist for a couple of years regarding my love life. It was after my divorce (Bill was briefly married to former actress Anouska Hempel in the late 1970s) and he said he'd never come across a man with such an affinity for the past. I told him my past was what moulded me. And the reason why my gran, Vallance Road and Everton FC are so precious to me is because I don't think I had an easy childhood. I was very shy, nervous and timid and we weren't rich."

Neil Fitzmaurice, August 27, 2010

"I just think Liverpool is an amazing place," says the actor, comedian, broadcaster, writer and film-maker.

"I love the history and character of it – and its vibrancy. Back in the day, I went all over the country doing stand-up – each city brings something to the table but it was never long before I was pining to come back. That's why I never left.

"For many years, through the Merseybeat era especially, we were known as having a bit of a swagger, but then, through the Thatcher years and various things, our confidence went and it was a city that people knocked. Since 2008, however, our cockiness and swagger has returned – it's not a bad cockiness, it's more saying 'Take a look at us.' The difference between having a swagger and being cocky is a matter of opinion and that's the problem. People see different things in that. But Liverpool has always had to retain a little bit of confidence because it was constantly being knocked."

Les Dennis, September 10, 2010

"Many people have out-of-date ideas about Liverpool but they change their minds when they see what we have. Friends have been absolutely gobsmacked by our waterfront, while Liverpool is a melting pot of cultures and there's a warmth among the people – although there's also a mardiness, because we love a good moan! But since 2008 we've got our mojo back. I think there is a resilience among Liverpool people that has helped them get through very difficult times.

"I take people to the Walker Art Gallery because of its eclectic and brilliant collection of art. Then we have the Anglican Cathedral (I also love Paddy's Wigwam), which is a stunning building. And when I come back, I always have The Beatles song In My Life in my head. I was born in Garston, moved to Speke, then Childwall and went to Quarry Bank School. Today, I'll drive people to Strawberry

Field and Penny Lane – and many of them are amazed because they didn't realise these places existed!"

Tony Snell, October 8, 2010

Radio Merseyside presenter Tony (Snelly) Snell has some interesting theories about Liverpool and its people.

He says: "I always see Liverpool as a bit of a planet – all the other cities are planets and go clockwise, but we go anti-clockwise. That's not to say we go backwards; I just think we like to be different. I could see how that could wind the rest of the country up – but it's not saying 'We are the special ones,' just 'We're a bit different.' We can be contrary – if someone says 'black' we will say 'white,' just to get a reaction. It's not even to be abrasive, it's just a trait of ours as we try and weigh people up. And if I'm waiting at a train station, I find it very difficult to stand there in silence. I'll have to make some comments, even if it's just clichéd ones about the weather – anything to break the silence. I don't think Scousers do loneliness very well."

P.S. I once interviewed Snelly's wonderful mum, Eileen (she had featured in a German football magazine about what it's like to live in the shadows of Anfield and Goodison Park – the True Blue's house backs onto the car park in front of Anfield's Centenary Stand). *Echo* photographer Colin Lane and I arrived between breakfast and lunch and the last thing we were expecting was for Mrs S to have laid on a gargantuan spread. Or any spread at all. It was so generous – and I don't think we were able to eat for the next fortnight as a result!

Chapter Sixteen

Jim Beglin is not amused

"THEY SHOULD just brick Jim Beglin up, with the Gok Wan acolytes… brick him up!"

A line from Fix It So She Dreams of Me, from the album 90 Bisodol (Crimond) by Half Man Half Biscuit.

***

Ridiculing the ridiculous and taking the piss out of the pompous was always very enjoyable.

And the pleasure intensified if you ever found out your target was wound up by your mickey-taking remarks.

While it was always lovely to receive "thank you" cards and letters from people I interviewed and wrote about, there was also something richly satisfying about receiving hate mail.

Sadly, I hardly kept any mail – good or bad – but I'm glad I've still got my letter from former Liverpool player Jim Beglin, who, to my mind, went on to become a preposterous pundit and co-commentator.

On my TV review page of April 4, 1998, I had written the following…

Football is going through a torrid time: inept referees, cheating players, out-of-touch chairmen and directors, and over-excitable (and, in some cases, violent) fans.

And then there's Elton Welsby and Jim Beglin (Granada Tonight, Monday). The pompous pundits should be put forward for a Best Comedy BAFTA for their hilarious weekend footy review slot.

Elt gravely ran through the action from Oakwell – Liverpool's 3-2 victory over eight-man Barnsley – as if he was charged with the solemn duty of announcing that the end of the world is nigh. But it was his equally ridiculous sidekick who stole the show by appointing himself judge and jury, before delivering the verdict that would cure all soccer's ills at a stroke. Joker Jim decreed that any fan who encroached on a football pitch should automatically be given a Deirdre Rachid… left to rot in the choky.

"But not for life," added the man of reason. "A week or two should do it."

The governors of our overcrowded prisons must have breathed a sigh of relief. Fans, let's get this straight, should not be running onto football pitches.

But let's get things in perspective. Is Beglin really suggesting that the dozens of Liverpool fans who mobbed Steve McManaman after he scored the winning goal should be jailed for a fortnight?

And perhaps they could be joined by all those footballers who get such a thrill out of inciting thousands of frustrated, highly-charged fans.

Let's bring back public floggings, stonings and executions.

Better still, let's physically gag those precious know-alls who get paid to pontificate – rather than pay to watch a game of football. Crazy? Well, you started it.

***

Jim addressed his peeved prose to "Mr Paddy Shennan, TV Cynic." Nice one!

And he wrote:

Dear Paddy,

Your pathetic attempt to ridicule my comments regarding crowd encroachment was brought to my attention.

You know only too well my remarks were directed at those who invade the playing surface with real menace on their minds and not those who wish to leave their seats for celebratory purposes.

Having been struck by an opposition supporter in my own playing days and considering a linesman was recently knocked unconscious, along with an attack on a Rugby League referee, I stand by my suggestion of a small custodial sentence for fans (who have no business being on any pitch) encroaching with malicious intent.

After witnessing Hillsborough's tragic events at first hand, I would hate to see the return of perimeter fencing but clearly a deterrent needs to be implemented to prevent would-be offenders from causing even more serious harm.

Your trivialisation of this whole issue is frankly very sad. Perhaps you've got a better solution. Please write and let me know, otherwise why don't you just stick to programmes you appear to know a lot about, like Coronation Street!

Here's hoping I've lived up to your pompous impression of me.

Yours unfortunately,
Jim Beglin

***

Oh yes, Jim, most definitely!

Chapter Seventeen

Never listen to a PR person

"NEVER LISTEN to a PR person" would be great advice to give to any young journalist about to embark on a career interviewing famous people.

That is unfair, of course. Many members of the ever-growing public relations army are extremely good at their jobs and don't just provide a brilliant service for their clients, but also the journalists who are looking for access to them. And yet there are those who just seem to be obstructive, and who aren't always – as many naive journalists may assume – speaking on behalf of the people on their books.

I had been looking forward to interviewing Mick Jones, of The Clash fame, ahead of the gig he was to play with his then band, Carbon/Silicon, in Liverpool in 2004. As an old fan, I was particularly looking forward to hearing if he remembered The Clash gig I saw as a 14-year-old – at Blackburn's King George's Hall in 1978.

But sadly, I listened to the PR – who told me that Mick would put the phone down if I dared to mention The Clash during my allotted 15 minutes.

The conversation went well enough and Mick was an easy

and engaging interviewee. But I felt something was missing – and took what I thought was a big gamble. It wasn't, as I explained in the subsequent article for Debbie Johnson's music page, part of which read…

A public relations person had warned me earnestly that Mick wouldn't talk about The Clash – even though he and former bassist Paul Simonon happily plugged the 25th anniversary reissue of London Calling on Friday's Later With Jools Holland on BBC2.

But sounding totally taken aback, the affable, softly-spoken hero to so many says: "I'm happy to talk about anything you want to talk about – it's not a problem."

And with obvious honesty and humility, he adds: "I'd never thought we'd be talking about all those times again now – it constantly surprises me. The great thing about being in a group is travelling to a lot of different places, and we'd meet so many people who liked us and could relate to it.

"It happened in Liverpool (a place we always loved playing), with that famous gig at Eric's in May, 1977, when the audience included people like Pete Wylie, Ian McCulloch and Julian Cope. I've been back many times since, and I'm really looking forward to Saturday's gig."

***

Sadly, there was no time for Mick to share his memories of that Blackburn gig, because his next phone interviewer was waiting. I should have known better.

***

Similarly, the PR apparently speaking on behalf of actress Liza Tarbuck, for an article of mine which appeared on Peter Grant's TV page on May 2, 1995, had given me a very clear warning. My piece began...

"DON'T MENTION HER FAMILY!" pleaded the BBC woman. But it was too late. Liza (daughter of Tarby) Tarbuck had overheard.

"There's no reason to say that," she said cheerfully. "He knows the score." Indeed, I do. And I had no intention of mentioning her famous golfing father – until I was asked not to.

Chapter Eighteen

Banned by
The La's

I REALLY don't think I need to add anything regarding the following stroppy behaviour I wrote about in my weekly column, which involved Lee Mavers of The La's. The episode still makes me chuckle, all these years on.

To misquote Lee Mavers: There he goes, off on one again, June 22, 2005

Banned by The La's!

Or, at least, by Lee Mavers, the born-again band's predictably unpredictable, mercurial and maverick front man.

What a story. Good enough – well, odd enough – to be telling in the pub for years to come.

Last week, I was hoping to report from Sheffield on the long-lost Liverpool group's first English gig in a decade.

Despite hearing that Mavers was refusing all interview requests and had blocked the taking of a single, up-to-date publicity pic, I still harboured the slightest of hopes that he may want to speak to his hometown paper.

The gig promoters directed me to a public relations

company, which confirmed that Mavers was keeping mum – at least for the time being.

But he's not the only Mavers known to the *Echo*, so I tried his brother, actor Gary, of Casualty and Peak Practice fame. He told me: "Neither of us are that into doing interviews or talking about ourselves." Gary, though, said he'd be happy to be quoted in my review/feature article. He said: "Lee's a genius – he's the talented one of the family! I'm absolutely delighted that The La's are back together. They've given people so much pleasure."

He also said he had enjoyed talking to me. And then...

A few days later, the PR man called. Had the gig been cancelled? No, but I had. And my "guilt" had been decided without a hearing, fair or otherwise.

My "crime"? Apparently, the angry singer felt I'd been hassling his family. That's right, I had the nerve to ring his brother! So, along with the *Echo* photographer, I was to be removed from the guest list of the sold-out gig.

I wasn't sure exactly how loudly I should laugh. Could this be for real?

But on reflection, I wasn't that surprised. One Liverpool musician had suggested to me the comeback could be aborted "if a member of an audience looked at Mavers in the 'wrong' way" while, back in 1990, the peeved perfectionist "promoted" the band's only album by declaring it to be "shit."

Harsh. I love seven of the 12 tracks on The La's album, with only one or two sounding, to these ears, like a poor man's Rutles.

So was it worth the long wait for the man, the myth and his music? No point asking me, but the reviewer on Sheffield paper *The Star* confirmed that the songs Mavers is said to have stockpiled over the years are being kept under wraps: "The set was very similar to the one they were doing 15 years ago, but even in those days most of their songs sounded like oldies from the mid-60s' Merseybeat days... The La's: still slightly above average after all these years."

A former *Echo* colleague, however, who saw the band in Manchester the next night, thought they were "fantastic," while I've heard very mixed reports about the London gig which followed. It's a shame I haven't been able to share in your long-awaited return but welcome back, Lee. And don't worry – I won't be asking your brother how it's going.

***

You could describe it as childish, cowardly and unkind – cruel, even – but, at times, it was very difficult to resist having a go at certain people (as with the Rutles comment). It was me having the last word – like I did on November 18, 1993, when I started a piece for Peter Grant's TV page: "The minute she walked in the joint... I could tell she was a presenter from The Word. She was standing in the foyer of a Liverpool hotel, it was pouring with rain outside, there wasn't a sunbeam in sight – and Dani Behr was wearing shades."

Shame on me. There was really no need for that, was there?

Chapter Nineteen

Nerys Hughes 1 Geoffrey Hughes 0

YOUR PRECONCEPTIONS can often be challenged during an interview with someone you had either previously admired or had no time for.

In December 2007, I had phone interviews lined up on the same day with actors Geoffrey Hughes and Nerys Hughes – ahead of the screening of BBC Three's live musical extravaganza Liverpool Nativity, in which they would play the Angel Gabriel and Betty (a kindly figure who befriends Mary and Joseph) respectively.

My favourite Coronation Street characters had always been Stan and Hilda Ogden, and I also loved their lodger, Eddie Yeats, who was played by Geoffrey Hughes.

I still had my Stan, Hilda and Eddie keyring on the day I interviewed Geoffrey – though I didn't keep it much longer.

Sadly, it wasn't the easiest of interviews. The actor gave me the impression he wasn't at all fond of journalists.

Unfortunately, when some people have a bad experience with one journalist (or maybe a few of them), they dismiss them all as being a pain in the arse.

Nerys was up next.

I didn't really have any strong feelings about her, though I wasn't enamoured with the Rhyl-born actress's soft and soppy Scouse accent in The Liver Birds, while I had laughed along many times to Half Man Half Biscuit's song, I Hate Nerys Hughes.

I wasn't really looking forward to our chat.

But she was delightful – so delightful, in fact, that I almost asked her if there were any Nerys Hughes keyrings on the market.

Never assume, as young journalists are always told.

Chapter Twenty

'Take your Echo and shove it up your arse!'

THE ART of abusive letter-writing is, sadly, dying out.

These days, angry readers rarely seem to bother going to the time, trouble and expense of sending letters.

This is not at all surprising when you consider the price of stamps, and the fact that it is so easy to make your displeasure felt digitally, via, say, Twitter, Facebook or the paper's website – and these avenues of complaint are free, too.

But thankfully, there are still some people out there who have not given up on sticking it to journalists the good old-fashioned way!

The following beauty was sent to me by Steve Best, from Bootle, who was angered by the fact that *Echo* page designer and sub-editor Gary Bainbridge had decided that the following words should appear beneath my name every week for my Wednesday column. "Likes: Pubs, Everton and Half Man Half Biscuit. Hates: Everything else."

***

2.57pm, May 30th, 2018

Paddy Shennan,

Who is the c*** responsible for printing 'Hates: Everything else' under your photograph? It is simply not true.

Does everything else include chairs, desks, laptops, spectacles, trousers, shirts, shoes, books, newspapers, cars, Coronation Park, Victoria Park, socks, food, haircuts, beer, Crosby beach, the River Mersey, the Irish Sea, television, radio, coats and money?

I detest the media. Who was the c*** who wrote that Niasse would go down as one of the worst signings by Everton Football Club? Was it Jones in August 2017?

How many years has Prentice been writing shite for the Echo? Jones is not good enough to lace the boots of Niasse. He is not worthy.

An apology is in order. Take your Echo and shove it up your arse!

Steve Best,
Bootle.

***

With the permission of *Echo* editor Ali Machray, I replied in the following way...

Dear Mr Best,
Many thanks for your letter of May 30.

My colleague Gary Bainbridge is the 'c***' responsible for printing 'Hates: Everything else' underneath my photo.

I don't recall which 'c***' wrote that about Niasse.

Neil Jones, incidentally, has now left the Echo.

Dave Prentice and myself have been writing for the Echo for around 30 years – but hopefully it's not all been 'shite'!

Best wishes,
Paddy Shennan

Chapter Twenty-One

There was fan mail, too – honestly!

IT WASN'T all hate mail, bad feeling and argy-bargy with PRs.

I got plenty of lovely letters and cards over the years – I just wish I'd kept more of them, too. I interviewed the wonderful Frankie Vaughan on a couple of occasions, in 1992 and 1998, and he wrote to me after each piece had been published.

In the first letter, he asked for my forgiveness for taking so long to thank me, and said, "I hope we meet again one day soon." In the second, he told me he would treasure my article, and signed off "Looking forward to seeing you many times in the near future."

Alan Bleasdale sent a card, which I also still cherish: "Just a brief note of many thanks for the generous and gentle piece in tonight's *Echo* about The Boys. And me. You did us proud. And you got all the names right! Now that is a first, as our daughter – 'Pamela, Tiffany, Tamara and Tasmin' – will testify. Anyway, I'm very glad you twisted my arm, and the next time we meet, let's make sure the sun is down and the bars are open. Please thank Frank (Loughlin, the photographer) too, for being so fast and flattering.

Best, Alan."

***

My interview with Alan (see Chapter Four) had mentioned that his children – Timothy, Tamana and Jamie – played Yosser's children in Boys From The Blackstuff. His daughter Tamana's name had been spelt incorrectly by other journalists – in several different ways – and I was glad I had got it right!

And finally, there was the thoughtful card from Keith Chegwin's parents, Margaret and Colin, following one of my articles on him. The card said: "Thank you for the write up on our son, Keith. It was very nice and much appreciated."

Chapter Twenty-Two

Hillsborough

I WROTE about Hillsborough more than I wrote about any other subject during my 33 years at the *Liverpool Echo*.

In this chapter, there is so much else I could write about the disaster and its aftermath – but mostly, I want to concentrate on the fantastic successes achieved by the families, survivors and each and every campaigner.

I want to focus largely on events in 2012 and 2016 – the publication of the Hillsborough Independent Panel report and the findings of the second inquests – not the shocking and disgraceful facts that not one police officer has been held responsible for the disaster and no one has lost a day's pay or freedom.

I don't even want to mention the names of those who were dragged to court – or those who should have been. God bless the 97 – and God bless all the families, survivors and campaigners.

Please note: all the articles have been reproduced in their original state, and so there are mentions of "the 96", which were made prior to the death of the 97th victim, Andrew Devine.

***

"I walked through the door after arriving home from the other semi-final at Villa Park and my fiancée, a dyed-in-the-wool Red, threw her arms around me and said 'Thank God you don't support Liverpool – those poor families.'"

November 21, 1992

For this day's pink *Echo*, I had been invited to fill the paper's new FanScene column ("A highly personal viewpoint from the terraces.")

My main piece was headlined Lest We Forget On Derby Day – and, to be honest, it included a line which was soon proved to be utter bollocks.

It began well enough…

***

Derby day is looming. History will be made on Monday. December 7, when the classic Everton-Liverpool league encounter at Goodison Park will be broadcast live by BSkyB. Of course, the majority of those without tickets will be watching the satellite dish of the day in the pub. The beer will flow and rival fans will rub shoulders, shake hands and embrace each other – whatever the result.

Back in the real world…

I've been to too many Merseyside derbies to believe the myth that all Everton and Liverpool fans live side by side in perfect harmony. We don't!

And the bitching and bitterness is quite understandable

when, for better or worse, our teams mean so much to us. The rivalry could be a little healthier though.

I used to describe May 10, 1986, as the worst day of my life. I had been in a Blue Heaven, just half an hour away from achieving my life's ambition of seeing Everton rubbing the Reds' noses in it at Wembley on FA Cup Final day.

Then three heartbreaking goals went past Bobby Mimms and I had to share a mixed coach home, with a load of gloating Liverpudlians in among the way-beyond-blue Blues. I even put on the video of the game (briefly) when I got home, to make sure I hadn't been dreaming. No, it was an utter, real-life nightmare.

This is what football can do to reasonably sane people.

Hillsborough changed, or should have changed, everything. I remember arriving home from Villa Park on that fateful day after watching Everton v Norwich and being greeted by my relieved fiancée (now wife) – a dyed-in-the-wool Red – who threw her arms around me and said, 'Thank God you don't support Liverpool – those poor families.' Other partners were not so lucky.

I cheered on the Blues in the 1989 final, but there was no misery in defeat. The result was irrelevant.

Few things matter much and most things don't matter at all – and that includes any football result.

Fanatical football fans, however, are only human and old habits die hard. But as the big game approaches, the hype begins and the tension mounts, I will be doing my best to stay calm and keep things in perspective.

Let's continue to enjoy the great derby tradition, but

remember that football is not more important than life or death. And let us never forget those people who are no longer here to watch the games.

***

And then came the well-meaning, but embarrassing, line which I have failed miserably to live up to…

***

I will never again experience the negative emotions of May 10, 1986. They have been consigned to the dustbin of history. Where they belong!

***

There were no negative emotions associated with derby defeat for me on December 7, 1992, because a Billy Kenny-inspired Everton came from behind to beat Liverpool 2-1, thanks to goals from Mo Johnston and former Red Peter Beardsley.

It wasn't all sweetness and light in the ground, but my own verbal clash with a perfect stranger – a Red who had been sitting near me – was more complex than the usual sort of heated exchanges that had previously taken place between Blues and Reds.

The evening had started in almost serene fashion – I remember telling Peter Harvey, the Liverpool-supporting friend who accompanied me to Goodison, that I now cared so little about derby day I would be happy for my then nine-month-old son, Tom, to grow up supporting whichever team won that night. By the end of the night, of course, I was almost delirious with derby victory joy – though a joy tainted by a toxic exchange with a Liverpool fan who was, quite clearly, a decent bloke.

In April of that year, on the third anniversary of the Hillsborough disaster, there had been a furious reaction to Liverpool manager Graeme Souness, who was recovering from his triple heart bypass surgery, doing an exclusive interview with *The Sun*. Souness rode out the story, and at some point, during that game at Goodison, a song which included his name was sung by a sizeable group of Reds in the Park End. My derby day emotions got the better of me and I shouted, "Bloody *Sun* readers!" The Red in front of me angrily replied: "I'm not a bloody *Sun* reader!" Harvey moved in to calm us down, as, pointing to the Park End minority who had upset me, I asked: "What about them?"

Looking back, it seems astonishing that Souness was still in charge. Today, in the social media age? I think it would have been a different story.

The headline on the *Echo's* front page story on April 16, 1992 – the day after the third anniversary of the Hillsborough disaster, of course – was STORM OVER SOUNESS. Reds issue statement as fans' fury mounts.

It was written by Ric George and myself. At the time, I was still the *Echo's* district reporter for Knowsley and the previous day's *Echo* had included a story I had written about a play, Our Game, which had been written by John Eile to counter criticism of Liverpool supporters in the wake of the disaster. It was being staged by Kirkby Response Theatre, on April 15 only, at the Central Hall in Renshaw Street, Liverpool. Donna Carlile, whose brother, Paul, 19, died at Hillsborough, and the Hillsborough Family Support Group (HFSG) were backing the play.

Donna was quoted in the article, while I also asked her about Souness and his exclusive deal with *The Sun* newspaper. The following day's story included these paragraphs: "Donna Carlile, who lost her 19-year-old brother Paul in the disaster, wants the Reds' manager to explain WHY he collaborated with *The Sun*.

"Donna, 25, from Kirkby, told the *Echo*: 'I still have to defend Paul, and others who died at Hillsborough – because of *The Sun*.

'I would just like Graeme Souness to explain why he chose to speak to *The Sun* – of all newspapers'."

Calls for Souness to go, meanwhile, came from two fathers – Les Steele, whose son, Philip, 15, died at Hillsborough, and Barry Devonside, who lost his 18-year-old son, Christopher, in the disaster.

A statement issued by Liverpool FC chief executive Peter Robinson assured supporters that the issue would be discussed: "The Board has noted all comments and complaints and will be discussing them at the first appropriate time. It also proposes to discuss the matter with Graeme Souness as soon as he is fully fit."

But the article ended: "Club chairman David Moores refused to comment on the articles in *The Sun*." He told that day's *Echo*: "That's between *The Sun* and Mr Souness."

I interviewed Souness at the Crowne Plaza Hotel in Liverpool in June 2002, for a feature article about his support for a health campaign called Caring For Your Heart, and I took the opportunity to ask him about his comments 10 years earlier. I wrote that, as *Echo* readers were well aware, "Souness did himself no favours when he gave an exclusive interview to *The Sun* – which, three years earlier, was burned on the streets of Merseyside and then boycotted after the lies it told about Liverpool fans at Hillsborough."

Souness told me: "It was a very difficult time for me – and I know I'll always be remembered for giving my exclusive interview about the heart surgery to *The Sun*. That's something I can only apologise for."

He went on to say that Liverpool would always be a special place to him: "I had a great time there as a player, but not so great as a manager. But you can't turn the clock back. I have made mistakes and I apologise for them – that's all I can do."

***

It is sometimes easy to forget that the story of Hillsborough has by no means always been to the forefront of the news agenda. Writer Jimmy McGovern deserves enormous credit for his blistering and brilliant drama-documentary Hillsborough, which was first screened on December 5, 1996. Brian Reade ensured it was treated to blanket coverage in the *Mirror*, while the *Echo* also comprehensively covered it.

I had the privilege of watching the film with the legendary campaigner Anne Williams – who lost her 15-year-old son, Kevin, at Hillsborough – at her home in Formby.

***

"I feel angry seeing it all again. You can see what SHOULD have happened..." December 6, 1996

Paddy Shennan watched last night's drama-documentary Hillsborough with Anne Williams, mother of 15-year-old tragedy victim Kevin Williams

A handsome young man looks down on us as we sit watching television...

Powerful images from Jimmy McGovern's stunning drama-documentary flicker in front of our eyes, but our gaze keeps returning to an even more striking image above the screen – a framed photograph.

Just imagine that, all of you who were spellbound by Hillsborough. Try and imagine. And yet it's just an ordinary photograph, sitting on top of an ordinary television set in the ordinary living room of an ordinary house in Formby.

It's a photograph of Kevin Daniel Williams, taken six months before he died at Hillsborough. A boy who should have been sitting in this warm and welcoming living room watching the highlights of Liverpool v Nottingham Forest on the night of April 15, 1989, with his mother, Anne. He could have been sitting here with his mum on this night – he would be 23. Or perhaps he would be upstairs listening to his favourite Genesis records. But he isn't. Only his photograph is... and we can't take our eyes off it.

Anne, 45, lights up the first of what will be many cigarettes, as we sit together watching the harrowing programme. And yet, in a sense, she has seen it all before – over the many years she has fought for justice for Kevin. Thick folders of evidence are piled beside her armchair. "In a way I know too much about Hillsborough," says Anne, as she holds the "horn of life" chain around her neck – the chain Kevin was wearing when he died and the one she has worn ever since.

"I can't really be shocked anymore, because I have spent hours and hours looking at video footage – trying to spot Kevin on the pitch. But that was without sound. Seeing the pictures with the sound is more upsetting."

Like other parents, Anne is hoping the drama-documentary will lead to a new inquiry. "Then everyone can put Hillsborough behind them and get on with their lives." It doesn't sound much to ask.

"I just feel angry seeing it all again. You can see what SHOULD have happened, how the tunnel should have been blocked off."

And when Liverpool fans are shown ferrying the dead and injured on makeshift stretchers, Anne reveals: "The police even swore at them to stop ripping up the advertising hoardings. But for the fans, many more would have died."

The scenes on the pitch and in the gym are the most upsetting for Anne – no wonder when you consider the evidence she has unearthed over the years.

Anne was featured on ITV's The Cook Report two years ago, in a programme called Kevin's Mum, which claimed the Formby High School pupil was still alive up to 45 minutes after the 3.15pm "cut-off" point when the victims were ruled clinically dead.

A former special WPC told the programme Kevin whispered "Mum" before dying in her arms at about 4pm. Anne says she also has evidence that Kevin did not die from traumatic asphyxia, but suffered a neck injury which caused swelling that slowly blocked his windpipe and killed him. "Three-quarters of an hour of his life has just been brushed away. He could have been saved."

Anne is about to make her fourth written submission to Attorney General Sir Nicholas Lyell in a bid to win a new inquest for her son and is also hoping to have the book she has written about her fight – When You Walk Through A Storm – published (it was, in 1999). But there is so much red tape, so much injustice, and so many lies to battle through. And it all started on the day of the tragedy…

As we sit and watch the crass and callous interview techniques used by the police in the immediate aftermath of the disaster, Anne says: "They were even asking 14-year-old lads 'Did you have a drink?'"

The telephone rings during News at Ten – it's one of Kevin's old school pals who wants to tell Anne he is thinking of her.

"They're lovely people," she tells me, "they still keep in touch."

In part two, an off-duty policeman says of a boy he was treating on the pitch: "He was convulsing. He was vomiting and he had a pulse. He was alive at half past three." Anne stares intently at the screen and says: "That's Kevin he's talking about." And then as the inquest verdict (the original inquest verdict) is about to be given, she lights another cigarette. But Anne, who has two other children – Michael, 25, and Sara, 17 – is still waiting for another inquest and another verdict.

It won't bring back her son, but it will finally give her peace of mind after so many years of heartache and struggle.

The programme is long finished, but Kevin's handsome face is still looking down on us as his mum puts out another cigarette and smiles at his memory.

"Kevin loved life so much and he had his life all planned out. He loved football and he loved music, but he also studied very hard. He wanted to work in banking.

"He wanted to go to university with his former girlfriend, Esther Leach, who was going to study law. Esther's a lovely girl and I'm so pleased that she did it – she went to university as they had planned. She's now studying for the bar.

"I'm sure Kevin would have done it as well."

But today, it's his mum who's trying to do something for him. The fight for justice goes on… Good luck, Anne – and God bless you, Kevin.

***

Suddenly, after the screening of Hillsborough, it seemed like people across the nation were waking up to the real truth about what happened on April 15, 1989. The Hillsborough Family Support Group had always campaigned tirelessly for the truth, justice and accountability and now, with renewed calls for a full inquiry, it had the wind in its sails.

Myself and many others sensed that a Labour government was on its way – which, foolishly, some of us assumed would lead to the justice campaign being brought to a relatively swift and satisfactory conclusion – while the wonderful Phil Hammond, then the vice-chairman of the HFSG, was the driving force behind the Hillsborough Justice Concert, which would take place at Anfield on May 10, 1997.

Labour had swept to power just days earlier, and in June, new Home Secretary Jack Straw appointed Lord Justice Stuart-Smith to conduct a "scrutiny of evidence".

What could possibly go wrong? We didn't have to wait long to find out. On October 6 that year, Stuart-Smith arrived at the Merseyside Maritime Museum at Albert Dock to meet with families – and immediately asked a bereaved father: "Have you got a few of your people here or are they like the Liverpool fans, turn up at the last minute?"

It was no surprise when, after apparently reviewing the new evidence not presented at the inquiry or inquests, as well as the 3.15pm cut-off point and instances of changed witness statements, he concluded there was "nothing significant" to warrant a new inquiry. Straw confirmed that assessment the following February.

On March 14, 2001, my weekly column included the following words: "New Labour is the party which seems to enjoy seriously disillusioning its hard-core supporters. With me and countless other Merseysiders, it took less than a year after Tony Blair came to power, when Home Secretary Jack Straw ruled out a fresh inquiry into Hillsborough."

***

In 2005, myself and my former *Echo* colleague Brian Reade

were honoured to be invited by Phil Hammond – who had taken over from Trevor Hicks as chairman of the HFSG the previous year – to give the readings during the memorial service at Anfield to mark the 16th anniversary of Hillsborough. My then colleague Tony Barrett, who is today head of club and supporter engagement at Anfield, told me: "Whatever else you are asked to do and whatever other accolades you may get in the future, you'll never receive a better tribute than that." I still can't argue with that.

As well as Tony's words, my next Wednesday column in the *Echo* included the following: "The skies may have been grey and the rain unrelenting, but the poignant and supremely well-organised service was a truly uplifting experience... Brian and I were understandably nervous – not just about the prospect of facing 6,000 people on the Kop but, much more importantly, because we didn't want to let some very special people and a very special occasion down. Apparently, we didn't, and the relief was immense." After giving our readings, we were able to sit back and listen to and applaud Phil Hammond as he made his position regarding a certain "newspaper" crystal clear. As I wrote: "His comments followed the recent, well-publicised, efforts of *The Sun* to make up for lost time – and sales – on Merseyside, by promising to dig deep into the Hillsborough story... but only once the families had accepted its too-little-too-late 'apology'.

"But why the condition? As Phil asked: 'Does *The Sun* have no sense of public duty to publicise and remedy miscarriages of justice?'"

***

After the service, Press Association reporter Mike Hornby handed me a copy of Phil's rain-soaked script, which I still treasure to this day. It also included the following words: "Whenever disasters strike, the media is not far behind. Every picture, every story and every film is of people and their suffering. And so it was in the aftermath of the Hillsborough disaster. Today, our readings have been done by Brian Reade and Paddy Shennan – two journalists of the utmost integrity, who have been unstinting in their support of Hillsborough families from the outset, both of whom have used their privileged positions to further the families' pursuit of justice. We thank you both from the bottom of our hearts."

No, thank you, Phil.

***

Phil Hammond, whose 14-year-old son, Philip junior, died at Hillsborough, had to step down as chairman of the HFSG after suffering a devastating brain haemorrhage a few days after Christmas, 2008.

At one point, doctors gave him no chance of survival. But Phil is a born fighter. He has never stopped fighting for his son.

Ahead of the publication of the Hillsborough Independent Panel's report in 2012, Phil told me: "The main thing is my son wasn't to blame for his own death and today's children need to be educated about that."

As well as campaigning for the whole truth of Hillsborough to be told, Phil always stressed the importance of educating our children and our children's children. It was vital, he told me on so many occasions, that the real truth was passed on – again and again and again.

Some of us who were already adults at the time of Hillsborough have, at times, assumed too much of too many people. I know I have definitely expected people around me to know the crucial facts of Hillsborough – whatever their age. I remember being taken aback during the second inquests – held in Warrington between 2014 and 2016 – when a young reporter, who had been following the reports of the hearings, earnestly told me that the fans definitely weren't to blame.

"No shit!" I might have told him, if I was less polite. I might have added: "Where the f*** have you been since 1989?" Then, of course, I would have stopped and realised he probably hadn't even started school.

Phil Hammond couldn't have been more right.

In 2012, when I spoke to Phil and his wife, Hilda, on the eve of the publication of the Independent Panel report, he told me: "People look at you and say 'Is he soft? Why is he going on about this all the time?' All Hilda and I have ever wanted is the truth – we want to know the whole story from the start. We can't speak for anybody else and different people may think different things, but this will be enough for us and will give us closure – because it will clear our son's name. Justice is the truth – the whole story.

"We want people, including future generations, to be

educated. Having all the facts out there will let them know what really happened at Hillsborough – that the fans were not drunken hooligans but decent and honest people."

***

"A quiet vindication... that's my hope for the day," September 11, 2012

It was the day that changed everything – the 20th anniversary of the Hillsborough disaster and a memorial service like no other. A record-breaking attendance of around 30,000, more than double the previous record of 14,000 for the 10th anniversary service, gathered at Anfield on a day marked out by its raw emotion, passion – and anger.

Many in the stadium had simply had enough of being fobbed off – and Andy Burnham, the then secretary of state for culture, media and sport, was about to feel the full force of their frustration.

He may be a Scouser and a football fan – on April 15, 1989, he was at Villa Park supporting Everton in that day's other FA Cup semi-final – but on April 15, 2009, he was a member of a Labour government which hadn't taken any action on Hillsborough since the then Home Secretary Jack Straw ruled out a new inquiry months after Labour swept into power.

Liverpool-born, Cheshire-raised Mr Burnham had been invited to speak by the then Lord Mayor of Liverpool Steve Rotheram, now Labour MP for Walton, and he provoked much applause – not least when praising those fans who helped the dying at Hillsborough and saluting Merseyside's sense of community, spirit and solidarity.

But there was also booing, barracking and cries of "hypocrite" which, after the minister had sat down, prompted Hillsborough Family Support Group president Trevor Hicks to apologise.

Yet today many may say the ends justified the means, as the call for full disclosure of the unseen Hillsborough files gathered pace that day – Mr Burnham has stressed that he, and Garston and Halewood MP Maria Eagle, had already been working on this. Today, recalling the 20th anniversary, Mr Burnham said: "I agonised about whether I should go. My main worry, and it seems strange saying this, was getting through my speech without crying."

He added: "Steve Rotheram asked me to be there and I could never have lived with myself if I'd not been there. I'd been thinking in the run-up that, in some way, this could be fate – that I was being put there for that moment in time. I was thinking 'Is there some way I can now open up Hillsborough again?' I felt more nervous than I had ever felt before in my life. But, knowing the city as I do, I thought I will take what comes – I'll deal with it as best I can. I sensed, 'This has to happen – this feeling people have of a huge sense of injustice and a lack of a resolution has to have its voice'."

Recalling his speech, he said: "It got very difficult when I mentioned Gordon Brown. I was there as his minister in the same way the Bishop represents the Queen on days like that. But I've always said, if I wasn't the minister, I'd have been one of those shouting at the minister.

"They were right. I don't hold anything against anyone who shouted at me that day. Hillsborough was in the spotlight then and when was it ever going to be in the spotlight again? Potentially this was one of the last times the country was going to focus on Hillsborough and the issues around it. People react to emotional situations in different ways. I don't think people had any need to apologise."

He added: "What people don't know is that literally minutes afterwards, I walked into the Centenary Stand and received a call from Gordon. He said 'That's a brilliant thing you've done. Thanks for doing it – you've done the right thing'. The next day we had a Cabinet meeting and I said to Gordon 'I'm going to raise Hillsborough'. It wasn't on the agenda and it wasn't on the Government's radar, and I asked him if he minded. He said 'No, I don't'. I said 'I'm not saying this just because I had a bad time yesterday.' To his eternal credit, Gordon Brown immediately backed me up and from that meeting came all the developments regarding the Hillsborough Independent Panel."

But, regarding the years of inaction, Mr Burnham said: "I understand and said it in the debate in the House of Commons – no political party can say they have done enough. Hopefully we are beginning to put that right."

Looking to the future, he said: "I am absolutely confident that we will now get the whole truth. I don't know what's in the panel's report but I know how it has gone about its job and so I am confident we will have the whole truth. And, as Bishop James Jones says – 'Truth has its own power'.

"The first thing is we need to hear the whole story and feel the impact of the whole story. People need to be allowed time to understand the enormity of it. I have called Hillsborough one of the greatest injustices of the 20th century. I can't think of a parallel situation where a tragedy has occurred on this scale and immediate efforts were made to shift the blame onto those who died and their fellow supporters, causing more anguish to the families involved."

He added: "Also, I don't think it will be the end of the story. There will be things that come from it. What they are depends on what's in the panel's report. I think we will get the truth. The question then is 'What is justice and how do we best get it?' These are the things that will be asked on September 13, 14, 15. But it's very important, on September 12, for the truth to be allowed to speak for itself and to be heard. I am very conscious the families may react in very different ways. Let's first of all focus on September 12, which I think will be a momentous day for the city. People always say 'Why are they still going on about that?' I think, slowly, what's going to come from here is that the rest of the country will say 'We finally understand why the city of Liverpool has been unable to let this go'.

"It won't be a victory but a quiet vindication. That's my hope for the day."

"It had the feel to me of an Establishment cover-up"

In June 1997, Jack Straw appointed Lord Justice Stuart-Smith to take a fresh look at the tragedy to see if there should be a new inquiry.

The following February, Mr Straw announced the review had found nothing to challenge the findings of Lord Justice Taylor or the inquest verdicts of accidental death, and there would be no new public inquiry. This prompted families to decide to take their own action.

Andy Burnham said: "I was very proud that Labour fulfilled the manifesto commitment (to take a fresh look at Hillsborough). But looking back there might have been a factor of a new government not being used to holding civil servants to account properly.

"I don't know the man (Stuart-Smith). I never met him. I never heard from him about his reasoning. It had all the feeling to me of an Establishment cover-up.

"I don't know how anyone could look again at it and think a 3.15pm cut-off was anything other than morally indefensible. I have a feeling that's what the panel will reveal. A fixed deadline couldn't possibly be brought down on it."

At the inquests, coroner Dr Stefan Popper had refused to hear details of anything which happened after 3.15pm on the day of the disaster, on the grounds that those who died had already received their fatal injuries by then. This was despite assertions by grieving families that some victims lived long after that time. The cut-off point denied them the opportunity to submit evidence that South Yorkshire Police failed to act quickly enough once the disaster was under way.

Mr Burnham added: "I wasn't an MP or minister at the time. I'm definitely not saying that Labour was part of a cover-up. What I am saying is that the full picture wasn't brought out at the time and it should have been. We were still in the pre-Freedom of Information age, but we're in a different era now when it comes to public information. Whether it was Stuart-Smith not wheedling out all the information or whether people didn't cooperate with him, I don't know. It felt to me that the Establishment closed ranks to frustrate Stuart-Smith, or he didn't want to fully expose things."

"I felt uneasy at Hillsborough the previous year"

On April 15, 1989, when early reports of the Hillsborough disaster began filtering through to Villa Park, where Everton played Norwich City in that day's other FA Cup semi-final, the thoughts of many fans – including a then 19-year-old Andy Burnham – turned to previous matches at Sheffield Wednesday's ground.

During the 1981 FA Cup semi-final between Spurs and Wolves, 38 Spurs fans were injured following crushing in the Leppings Lane end while, over the years, fans of other clubs – including Liverpool's after the 1988 semi-final – had voiced concerns about that part of the ground.

Mr Burnham said: "The thing I'd like to get over, because I think it's so relevant to what is about to come out, is my experience at Hillsborough for Everton's FA Cup third round tie against Sheffield Wednesday (on January 9, 1988)."

Everton salvaged a 1-1 draw thanks to a late Peter Reid equaliser, though that isn't the shadow health secretary's main memory of the day.

He explained: "I didn't watch anything on the pitch in

the second half because I was deeply uncomfortable. I was just 18 then and I thought 'If I feel like this, what are my brother, then 14, and my dad feeling?' I spent the whole of the second half watching them and as we sat in our car on the M6 after the FA Cup semi-final the following year, we all immediately started talking about that game. Instantly, we knew what had caused the tragedy.

"All the stuff about hooliganism was coming out, but we immediately knew that ground was fundamentally unsafe. This wasn't something new. I'm not saying it was inevitable that something was going to happen, but there had been many near misses at the ground down the years. I think it's so relevant.

"I remember coming out of that game (at Hillsborough) feeling physically ill. I was relieved when that game was over."

***

Like Andy Burnham, I was in the Leppings Lane end for that FA Cup third round tie in 1988, though I remember being more concerned at a far less well-attended league game at Hillsborough the following season. That FA Cup third round tie attracted 33,304, while just 21,761 were at Hillsborough for the league game between Sheffield Wednesday and Everton on November 5, 1988, which also finished 1-1.

Despite there being fewer Evertonians in the Leppings Lane that Saturday afternoon, I recall me and my friends discussing the lack of space and comfort as we felt the police had kept us as tightly herded together as possible – rather than allowing us to enjoy space by opening up more of that end.

***

A shocked Paddy Shennan reports from inside Liverpool Cathedral, September 12, 2012

April 15, 1989 to September 12, 2012.

Twenty-three years, four months and 28 days. It's a scandal that it has taken this long to get to this point but, of course, the Hillsborough families and survivors know all about scandals. And cover-ups. And a lack of accountability. And the denial of justice.

Today, though, the covers were off with hundreds of thousands of documents having been dusted down and distilled into a near 400-page report.

It may take days and weeks to fully absorb the weighty words carefully crafted by the diligent members of the Hillsborough Independent Panel. But to help people take on board some of their key findings, members of the panel addressed family members and survivors this morning before facing the media this afternoon.

There it was, in black and white, after all this time. All this campaigning. All this waiting. And my God, it was even worse than many of us had thought. The shocking lies and shifting the blame. The abhorrent and appalling attempts to denigrate the dead and the survivors.The rank amateurism and ineptitude of the emergency service response.

All of this is laid bare in the astonishing report, with sickening revelations coming thick and fast.

Bereaved family members said they wanted the whole story, warts and all – the word "warts" hardly does justice to some of the stomach-churning details documented by the panel.

More lives could have been saved and would have been had there been a "swifter, more appropriate, better focused and properly equipped response". This is an absolute scandal.

The ground modifications made after crushing at the 1981 semi-final between Spurs and Wolves actually increased the dangers at the Leppings Lane end of the stadium. Documents further showed that the risks were known and the tragedy at the 1989 semi-final was foreseeable.

This is an absolute scandal.

A document disclosed to the panel revealed an attempt was made to smear the reputations of the deceased by carrying out police computer checks on those with a non-zero alcohol level.

This is an absolute scandal.

The disclosed documents show blood alcohol levels were tested in some survivors who attended hospital, as well (we already know) as in all those who died.

This is an absolute scandal.

Access to cabinet documents revealed that in an exchange about the government "welcoming the (Taylor) report" Margaret Thatcher expressed her concern that the "broad thrust" of the report constituted a "devastating criticism of the police".

It is an absolute scandal if that was her main concern – how bad South Yorkshire Police would look.

Following the publication of the Taylor Report, Thatcher was briefed that the "defensive and at times close to deceitful behaviour by senior officers in South Yorkshire" was "depressingly familiar".

The Government did not seek to protect the South Yorkshire Police chief constable Peter Wright and it was considered inevitable that he would resign. His resignation, however, was rejected by the South Yorkshire Police Authority.

What a shameful state of affairs.

Regarding *The Sun's* tissue of lies, gleefully headlined "The Truth" by Kelvin MacKenzie, the panel revealed that the allegations (of course stated as fact by MacKenzie), were filed by Sheffield-based news agency Whites. They were based on meetings over three days between agency staff and several police officers, together with interviews with Irvine Patnick MP and the South Yorkshire police federation secretary Paul Middup.

It is an absolute scandal that such lies could be cooked up by such senior figures and then printed with such relish.

David Cameron issued what he called a "proper apology" – he could do nothing else looking at the sheer weight and scale of the damning evidence before him.

Some will say this report and the publicity surrounding it is also for the benefit of those who haven't been close to the story of Hillsborough. Those who, perhaps, weren't listening when Lord Justice Taylor delivered his damning verdict of the South Yorkshire Police so soon after the disaster. And those who, perhaps, were listening when shameless, hard-faced liars like MacKenzie were gleefully putting the boot in with no respect for the real truth.

Or the dead. Or their families. Or the survivors. Or their families.

Yes, the families, survivors and Merseysiders, in general, already knew so many key parts of this nightmare story and have known them for a long time but, after years of appalling political and judicial inertia, the setting up of the Hillsborough Panel represented a belated, but welcome, attempt to ensure every available scrap of information was made available. And, as has been said in the run-up to the report's publication, the truth has its own power.

In yesterday's *Echo*, Phil Hammond, the former chairman of the Hillsborough Family Support Group, said: "Justice is the truth – the whole story."

Have the families and survivors now got it – or, at least, now got a far better chance of getting it?

There are some gaps, but at this early stage and considering the amount of sterling work that the panel has obviously undertaken, this may be as much as we ever get. Shadow health secretary Andy Burnham, whose controversial appearance as the then sports minister at the 20th anniversary memorial service at Anfield led to the setting up of the panel, said this would be a momentous day for the city of Liverpool. It truly is.

There is still an enormous amount of material to absorb but, after 23 years, four months and 28 days, many people will now be daring to believe that this is the beginning of the end of a shameful chapter in this country's history – the beginning of the end of the scandal of covering up the real truth about a disaster which should never have happened.

***

The amazing week when the world realised what we've known for 23 years. Paddy Shennan reflects on a momentous week that changed Liverpool forever, September 15, 2012

What a week for the Hillsborough families. What a week for the survivors. What a week for truth and justice. What a week for the city of Liverpool.

This was a week for the good guys because this was a week when the bad guys went running for cover – if they weren't falling over themselves to try and get their way-beyond-belated apologies in first.

For more than 23 years campaigners had so often found themselves derided, defamed and damned by those who thought they knew better.

Better? They knew nothing.

But everything changed on September 12, 2012 – the day of judgement for so many people in so many positions of power in so many parts of this country. If it had been a boxing match, it would have been stopped in the early rounds. The "Establishment" took one hell of a beating, but still didn't attract, or deserve, an ounce of sympathy.

No one knows exactly where and when this story will

finish and reflecting on these past few days, it's impossible to know where to start.

There are so many things we will never forget. People wanted to be told the whole story and, in providing so many new lines, as well as so much confirmation and clarity, the Hillsborough Independent Panel very nearly achieved this impossible feat. The families and survivors accepted that with the new information would come new pain, but that was a price they were willing to pay to get a fuller picture of the events of April 15, 1989, and beyond.

But how many of us dared to believe that the day's events would be so dramatic, so damning of authority figures – and provide so much of a boost to the campaigners, by repeatedly confirming so many things they have been saying for so many years? I'll never forget hearing the first whispers of what was to come as I was standing in the car park at Liverpool Cathedral, waiting for the Lady Chapel to be opened to the nation's media.

The families and survivors were already inside hearing from the Panel and looking at its report and, if what we were hearing was correct, they must have been reeling. Police computer checks were carried out on those victims with a non-zero alcohol level? No, that had to be wild, wide-of-the-mark speculation.

Shamefully, it wasn't.

And knowing what we know now, it's a wonder only three family members fainted as they were being given this and other information.

I'll never forget the gasps of astonishment from journalists as they turned over the pages of the press release, executive summary and report. All left for us on the chairs of the Lady Chapel.

I'll never forget hearing one of the 75 TV, radio and print media people present saying "Jesus!" – about every 20 seconds – as he read each shocking revelation. I'll never forget turning in shock to the TV screens that had been placed in the chapel as David Cameron gave what really was a "proper apology". Many of us expected nothing better than a feeble expression of "regret".

I'll never forget the silence of the House of Commons chamber being punctuated by gasps of disbelief from MPs.

I'll never forget the feeling that, suddenly, everything had been turned on its head – vindication belonged to the families and condemnation belonged to those named and shamed in the report.

I'll never forget that this day, more than any other in the fight for justice, was a day of mixed emotions. People rightly celebrated being given the truth – but were left heartbroken by the horror of so much of it.

I'll never forget the big, beaming smiles on the face of Margaret Aspinall, chairwoman of the Hillsborough Family Support Group. And I'll never forget the big tears which rolled down her face.

I'll never forget the one-liners of Trevor Hicks, the group's president – or how he introduced legal adviser "Peter" Mansfield QC. "It's Michael," said Michael, as laughter swept through the chapel.

Kelvin MacKenzie? He, said Trevor, was "lowlife, clever

lowlife, but lowlife". Norman Bettison? "If he is anything of a man he should resign and scurry up a drainpipe."

Trevor was even brave enough to admit: "I was a big Maggie Thatcher fan until Hillsborough."

I'll never forget how one three-letter word sounded so incredibly powerful. Was this the biggest cover-up in British legal history? "Yes!" said Michael Mansfield. Nothing needed to be added.

I'll never forget Sheila Coleman, spokeswoman for the Hillsborough Justice Campaign, paying a tender tribute to John Glover, who lost his 20-year-old son Ian at Hillsborough and went to the cathedral in his wheelchair: "He's been my driving force for 23 years," said Sheila. "He didn't know the system but he knows it now and he learnt about it pretty quickly."

I'll never forget the smiles on people's faces, thumbs up, hugs and general scenes of solidarity and togetherness at the vigil on St George's Plateau.

I'll never forget how the day's events dominated the evening's and night's national news programmes. At last, the whole nation was talking about this grave injustice. At last, the whole nation knew what we have known here on Merseyside for so long. Sadly, I'll never forget how Norman Bettison felt the need to put the boot into Liverpool fans by releasing such an offensive and arrogant statement.

But I am so, so pleased to be able to say I will never forget the never-say-die words of the inspirational Phil Hammond, former chairman of the Hillsborough Family Support Group, who has always said: "Something will turn up."

You've been saying it for years, Phil. You said it in the *Echo* again on Tuesday – and, having never given up hope, you were proved right the very next day.

Well done to the Hillsborough Independent Panel. Well done to the Hillsborough families and survivors. Well done to the city of Liverpool. And well done to the countless Merseysiders who never gave up campaigning for the truth.

For more than 23 years, malicious and malignant members of the Establishment had it all their own way, but the tide turned on Wednesday.

This week belonged to us – and so does the future.

***

December 12, 2012

This day's *Echo* carried interviews I did with Anne Williams and her late son Kevin's former girlfriend.

Anne wasn't just delighted that Esther Leach was now a solicitor, but that she was actually working in partnership with her own solicitor, Elkan Abrahamson.

"It's nice to have that link," Anne told me.

While Esther said of Anne's son: "Kevin was really popular. He was great fun – the main thing about him is that he was a very funny person and a joker. He was also very bright – the teachers also adored him…

"I went out with him for about four months from around autumn 1988. We weren't going out at the time of Hillsborough, but were good friends. I still don't believe what happened. But I see Kevin in Anne and I get a lot of comfort from my relationship with her." And she adds: "Anne has been relentless in her campaigning – she has been an inspiration for people. She's never been intimidated by the Establishment. No mother could have done more."

***

Anne, however, was now in poor health – as explained in the following extract...

After the news that the Attorney General (Dominic Grieve) is going to the High Court to apply to quash the original inquest verdict, Anne told me: "I feel now that I'm going to see it through. I can picture being at a new inquest, where a jury will hear the truth. This news has given me a new lease of life. I've felt well since I heard."

After more than 23 years of intense campaigning, during which time she has been a brilliant thorn in the side of the Establishment, this should now be a better time for Anne Williams. Everything changed for those who have been relentlessly battling for justice on behalf of the 96 Hillsborough victims with the publication, on September 12, of the Hillsborough Independent Panel's report. Suddenly, after years of having doors slammed in their faces, the families and survivors were on the front foot.

But within a few short weeks, Anne – who had been in hospital in the lead-up to the report's publication – was diagnosed with terminal bowel cancer.

She recalls: "I wasn't well on September 12, although this was before I knew what was wrong with me. It was an effort to get through the day – I was living on adrenalin. When I looked out that evening and saw the crowd on St George's Plateau I couldn't believe it. That report was excellent and it was an overwhelming day."

Regarding her ill-health at the time of the report, she recalls: "I thought 'I should be getting a new suit – and I should be feeling well. Trust me to be ill now at the end when I should be enjoying this bit'."

***

April 18, 2013

Tragically, Anne died in the early hours of April 18, 2013, after a seven-month battle with cancer. She was 62.

Her relentless, brilliant and inspirational campaigning had been thoroughly vindicated by the panel report, and subsequent quashing of the "accidental death" verdicts. And she had told me the previous December: "I've always done it for Kevin and the other 95 victims. Kevin would have gone mad over the injustice – that's the sort of person he was." On the day of her death, in his excellent obituary, my colleague Dan Kay – a great friend of the Williams family – asked: "What kept Anne going despite having so many doors slammed in her face? The knowledge that Kevin was the awkward little boy who didn't fit into the picture painted by those wanting everyone 'still going on' about Hillsborough to go away. Her hard-won evidence, combined with a mother's death-defying love for her child, was the powerful cocktail that fuelled her to keep going – the woman just would not give up."

My own tribute on that sad day began with the words spoken by Everton chairman Bill Kenwright at the Hillsborough memorial service just three days earlier... "They picked on the wrong mums!"

He was talking about people like Anne Williams – loving, caring, tireless, fearless fighters for truth and justice who refused to let the powerful and poisonous Establishment grind them down. Anne, in a wheelchair, was there to hear that tribute – but while she didn't live to see the new inquests and hear the new verdicts, no one did more to help bring them about.

***

September 10/September 11, 2013

To mark the first anniversary of the publication of the Hillsborough Independent Panel's report, I thought it would be good to bring together Margaret Aspinall of the Hillsborough Family Support Group – whose son, James, 18, died at Hillsborough – and Andy Burnham, to reflect on that momentous occasion.

It was a brilliant afternoon.

***

Andy Burnham: Can you believe it's a year, Margaret? It's been manic for you since then.

Margaret Aspinall: It has. You're honoured to have me here!

Andy: I have to make a booking to get to see her these days!

Margaret: That morning, with all the families in Liverpool Cathedral, none of us knew what news we were going to get and we were all absolutely terrified. We were holding each other's hands. The first thing the (then) Bishop (James Jones, panel chairman) said to us was 'I know what's on all your minds – have we found anything new?' I took a deep breath and thought 'Please God, I hope you have' – and he just said three simple words: 'Yes, we have'. The minute I heard that I thought 'Oh thank God, our city has been exonerated. Liverpool was isolated in 1989. I always felt we were a lonely city for quite a few years. People were against us but the city was always behind us. That's why I felt so much joy – I'm so proud of this city.

Andy: The whole day was just overwhelming. I remember the night before ringing you late on, Margaret. And I said 'I'm feeling terrible, so I can't imagine what you're feeling'. Margaret thanked me for what I'd done and I had tears rolling down my cheeks. There was so much pent-up emotion. I was the only person who had permission to go to Downing Street to read the report, so I spent the morning in the splendour of No.10 reading it on my own. My emotions swayed from elation at the vindication of the thousands of people who were yearning for that vindication, to sheer anger. What sticks in my mind was the section about the police national computer (attempts were made to "impugn the reputations of the deceased" by carrying out criminal record checks on those with a non-zero alcohol level). It took me back to the night of the disaster when I was in a pub on the outskirts of Warrington, waiting for my Liverpool-supporting mates to come back and then hearing their stories. I kept thinking back to what the police were doing in Sheffield at the same time. I felt blind anger. Later, I couldn't concentrate on a word of Prime Minister's Questions, or David Cameron's apology.

Margaret: I can't say that was a nice surprise, because we lost 96 people, but I thought 'Gosh, he's given us a lot more than I thought he would'. We will always be grateful for that.

Andy: I back that up.

Margaret: I always say it's never too late to apologise for wrongs that have been done. What I do regret is that it could have been done years ago – and that would have given the families, survivors and the city a bit of comfort. A lot of family members have died without seeing the truth come out. I am lucky because I am still here and will hopefully see the job finished properly.

I must thank all the MPs who have been with us. I'm sorry to say this in front of Andy but I always blamed Labour for letting us down – promises were not fulfilled. I've known Andy for a number of years and I trust him, like I trust (Walton MP) Steve Rotheram, (Garston and Halewood MP) Maria Eagle, (Halton MP) Derek Twigg and (Wirral South MP) Alison McGovern. These are the new generation and I don't believe you can blame the sins of the fathers on their children.

The Vigil at St George's Plateau

Andy: I went from the Commons with Steve Rotheram and

got the train to Liverpool. It was an occasion which really brought everyone together.

Margaret: Absolutely.

Andy: I remember looking out from the steps and the sky was bright blue over Lime Street.

Margaret: It felt as if a dark cloud had been lifted. It was a wonderful, wonderful feeling.

Andy: The day had a dramatic effect on people who had been affected by Hillsborough. People were coming up and saying they had never spoken to anyone about it before. And we finished off in the Ship and Mitre pub. It was an unforgettable night.

April 15, 2009 – Andy Burnham is barracked at the 20th anniversary memorial service

Andy (as Margaret laughs uncontrollably): My brother, John, who was there, texted me afterwards and said 'Don't worry. We've had many bad afternoons (as Evertonians) at Anfield. This wasn't the first and won't be the last!' I agonised about going. Steve Rotheram (then Lord Mayor of Liverpool) engineered it a bit, didn't he Margaret? I think he had a sixth sense that this had to be the moment when we tried to do something, prompt something. He was clear I should do it.

Before the service (which attracted 30,000 people), my brother had texted saying 'I don't want to worry you but I am sitting in the Anfield Road End'. All sides of the ground were filling up. I look back at it as the best thing that ever happened. I think fate put me there. But you started the booing, didn't you Margaret?!

Margaret: Sorry, I can't stop laughing! He was taking all this stick and I could see Trevor (Hicks) next to me panicking. And I could see poor Andy standing there like a nodding donkey. Trevor said 'Do you want to get up and stop this or should I?' I said 'He's man enough, let him take it!' I was right – he was man enough.

Andy: (As a member of the then Labour government) I kind of expected what happened and I wanted it to carry on in a weird way. But afterwards, I did say to Steve Rotheram 'I am going home now'. But Steve, who is an incredible man and politician, said 'No, you're coming to talk to the families in the Town Hall (they were being awarded the Freedom of the City) – and that's when things changed. As I walked up the grand staircase the first people I saw were Kenny Dalglish, Alan Hansen, Steven Gerrard and Jamie Carragher. I was feeling bruised and Kenny said 'Oh God, you've not come to upset them all again, have you?!'

Margaret: That, to me, was the change of history. The change of everything. And to think you were a part of that, Andy, is something to be proud of. At the time you might have felt very nervous but, don't forget, we have all felt nervous. Poor Andy, it must have been one of his biggest learning curves... but he took our message back, kept his word and changed the story of Hillsborough.

Andy: It was everybody, wasn't it? If it hadn't been kept alive by people like you and (predecessors) Phil Hammond and Trevor Hicks and all the many other people who kept on going, then it wouldn't have happened. When I got to the Town Hall I knew I was committed to seeing it all the way through – and we will see it all the way through, although we've still got a long way to go.

Margaret: The job is not finished, but with the support we've got I don't think we can lose.

Achievements and what is still to come

Margaret: There has been a lot of progress and things are still going on now. So much happened in the short space of time between September 12, 2012 (the day the Hillsborough Independent Panel published its report) and the end of the year. We had the original inquest verdicts quashed (it was great to listen to those three top judges in the High Court) and the IPCC (Independent Police Complaints Commission) launching the biggest-ever independent investigation into police wrongdoing. We have always kept on fighting to get those verdicts quashed but we were told by many people that it would never happen.

Andy: You were always saying that to me, weren't you?

Margaret: I hope the doubters are reading all of this!

Andy: I was getting a lot of colleagues in Parliament saying to me 'You are raising expectations', but sometimes you have got to go for something with all your heart. And I've got to say without Steve Rotheram and Maria Eagle – particularly Steve, he was a great support to me because of that extra 'We can do this!' – we couldn't have done it. Now, sitting here, you can think it was all inevitable that it was going to happen. But Margaret and I had many an agonising phone call between 2009 and 2012.

Margaret: Andy's right. I don't want this just to be about what Andy has done, no disrespect! As he has said, this is also about what so many people have done. There are far too many to mention but they include people like Phil and Hilda Hammond, Trevor Hicks – who was chair for 15 years and is still very active in the campaign today – and all the families and survivors. And there's Jimmy McGovern with his drama-documentary, Phil Scraton, who wrote books, all the people of Merseyside who have supported us, Everton Football Club – look at what Bill Kenwright has done for us – and even Manchester United. Sir Bobby Charlton has been brilliant – as has the football community. It's like a football team, you all work for each other.

Andy: We have got our grievances with the Football Association, but at the grassroots level people have understood and supporters have been great.

Margaret: They knew this could have happened at any time.

Andy: They knew it could have happened to them.

Margaret: So we have come a long way but there is so much still to do. We have got to get the right verdicts at the new inquests next year. I don't want different verdicts. I think they have all got to be the same for all the 96. (Regarding the IPCC investigation) I've always said I'm not a vengeful person. Twenty years ago, I would have wanted them all hung, drawn and quartered. But you grow from that.

Nothing will bring the 96 back and nothing will ever, ever, ever alter what the families went through, but we have got to have accountability. That's a different word from justice – I don't believe there's any such thing as justice. There's no justice for a life. Hanging them all doesn't bring anyone back. But everyone who played a part in the cover-up needs to be named and shamed. They are a disgrace to this nation. Everyone knows who did what, where it began and where it ended and, hopefully, this will now all end with accountability. And if this could have been done to 96 people who have so many others fighting for them, what about all those lonely voices involved in other cases who have not had anyone to stand by them? That concerns me.

The Hillsborough families should be proud of what they have achieved for other people after taking on the Establishment – that's the legacy of the 96. But this is not the end of it and things have got to be done right from this point on. We have waited a long time to get to where we are now, so we have got to make sure we now get the job done properly.

Andy: We are not complacent. We are watching every step now. (Wirral South MP) Alison McGovern chairs the Hillsborough all-party working group and every development is being monitored. We are encouraged by the way the IPCC is going about things – it seems incredibly thorough to me. But I would say I think people need to be ready because I think there will be more things that will come out that will shock them.

Margaret: I've been to Warrington (to see the IPCC operation) and I was pleasantly surprised. So far, so good.

Andy: We will see it through, won't we? Nothing will be allowed to get in the way of getting what will be justice, of a kind, in the end. It's unstoppable now. You've got the whole country with you. It will come. But we can't be complacent for a second – and we're not.

Margaret Aspinall on Andy Burnham

I'll be honest – I absolutely love this guy to bits, and he knows it. I find him honest – the same as I do with Steve (Rotheram). I love him to bits, too. Andy is trustworthy – the most important thing for the families is to be trustworthy – and he will always do his best for the families. He is a person who believes in truthfulness, integrity and honesty. I trust him and he's a friend – a dear friend.

Andy Burnham on Margaret Aspinall

That's very nice, Margaret, thank you. I love the bones of Margaret and all the families.

We have formed a special bond over time. I think I speak for a lot of people when I say this – we identify with Margaret because we see in her something of our own mums and grandmothers.

Margaret: Grandmothers?! I've gone off him now. I don't mind 'mother' but he had to bring 'grandmother' into it!

Margaret has four grandchildren and tells me: "I'm very proud of them – but as long as people don't think I'm a great-grandmother!"

Andy: Anyone who comes from this city will know what I mean! I could fill your whole paper with this. I'm sitting next to an incredible person. Margaret, you always underplay what you do. You are forever understating the effect you have on people and understating your ability to communicate.

I am in awe of what you have achieved. I feel history will look at this as a pivotal moment. I think people will draw inspiration from the Hillsborough campaign for many years to come.

It won't be possible any more for people to treat others in the way these families have been treated. To do what the families have done, and with the dignity they have shown despite everything that has been thrown at them... this really is a moment in British social history when the underdog has won. And that's incredible – and Margaret embodies the mums, and grannies, of Merseyside!

Margaret: This lad is not going to get out of here with his legs!

***

February 20, 2014

Just a few months after that happy afternoon, I was delighted to see the Hillsborough families and campaigners topping the *Echo's* 100 Greatest Merseysiders poll, as voted for by our readers.

A poignant presentation was held in the *Echo* offices in Old Hall Street, with family members, who included representatives of the Hillsborough Family Support Group, Hillsborough Justice Campaign and Hope For Hillsborough (For Justice), being given specially-framed *Echo* front pages.

Reflecting the thoughts of the great many *Echo* readers who made them number one – above the likes of John Lennon, Paul McCartney, Ken Dodd and Bill Shankly – the front-page headline said: "YOU MAKE US PROUD!"

***

A day we will never forget: Paddy Shennan on the Hillsborough inquests verdicts, April 27, 2016

It wasn't a dream, was it?

11.13am, Tuesday April 26, 2016.

Remember the day? Remember the time?

No, there is no need for the fantastic Hillsborough families, survivors, campaigners and all their supporters – throughout Merseyside and beyond – to make a point of remembering the moment the truth was finally delivered.

For what happened, and the time it happened, in the large room of a modern building in a nondescript business park in Warrington – no disrespect to Birchwood Park or Warrington, because you will be in so many of our hearts forever – will never be forgotten by anyone who was there.

Back in the *Echo* offices in Old Hall Street, Liverpool, I was staring at a Google document into which this paper's dedicated – and brilliant – Hillsborough reporter, Eleanor Barlow, was writing a second-by-second report which was immediately transferred onto our website's live blog. I can only guess at the tension that existed inside that bright building in Cheshire. But in Old Hall Street, the tension certainly increased as the clock ticked towards the start of the final day of proceedings which had lasted for two years and 27 days – and a hush descended on the editorial floor at 11am.

Just 13 minutes later – ironic, perhaps, given this often delayed and tortuously slow inquest process – that big "YES" was delivered.

YES. The 96 Hillsborough victims HAD been unlawfully killed.

We knew this. We knew this at 11.12am yesterday, just before the forewoman of the jury said the word. For pity's sake, we knew it on the afternoon of April 15, 1989. But now, finally, a proper inquest had been held and a proper verdict delivered. The headline across pages two and three of yesterday's special late edition of the *Echo* said 'Were fans unlawfully killed? YES. Were fans to blame for the disaster? NO.' That's all it needed to say.

At 11.13am, when that "YES" appeared on my screen, I shouted out my own "YES!" – and then smashed my right fist onto my desk.

Was that unprofessional and unbecoming behaviour? I really couldn't care less. That simple three-letter word "Yes" had rarely sounded so powerful. The scene had been set just a minute earlier, with the jury's response – another "Yes" – to question five of 14.

It had been asked: "When the order was given to open the exit gates at the Leppings Lane end of the stadium, was there any error or omission by the commanding officers in the control box which caused or contributed to the crush on the terrace?" The forewoman said "Yes" – and added: "Commanding officers did not inform officers in the inner concourse prior to the opening of Gate C.

"Commanding officers failed to consider where fans would go.

"Commanding officers failed to order the closure of the central tunnel prior to the opening of Gate C".

And then came THAT question and THAT answer.

That momentous answer.

The jury was asked "Are you satisfied, so that you are sure, that those who died in the disaster were unlawfully killed?"

Then came that beautiful three-letter word…

"Yes".

There were cheers and there was applause in the courtroom.

The families, survivors and campaigners had waited 27 years and 11 days to hear this word. And when it was uttered the emotion poured out of all those in Warrington, in Liverpool and across Merseyside, and across the country and the world who had been waiting on the words (or word) of the jury forewoman.

The truth had finally been delivered. The insulting words "accidental death" had been wiped from the records.

That question had been question six. And the very next question was also of enormous importance.

"Was there any behaviour on the part of the football supporters which caused or contributed to the dangerous situation at the Leppings Lane turnstiles?" The forewoman answered "No."

More applause – and another outpouring of emotion.

The questions were put and answered between 11.08am and 11.22am – 14 minutes which changed everything in the story of Hillsborough.

Anybody who had been a part of this day of days – whether they were in Warrington, or following the proceedings on the *Echo's* live blog back home in Liverpool or anywhere else in the world – will never forget it.

And they will certainly never forget the moment they heard that particular word at 11.13am.

It was delivered clearly, if relatively quietly. But other people – in Warrington and elsewhere – repeated it immediately afterwards in a much more emphatic fashion. YES!

At long bloody last, things had been made crystal clear to the world.

A special tribute to the 96 – in the words of their families, May 4, 2016

The second Hillsborough inquests started to hear the first pen portraits of the victims from their loved ones on April 3, 2014.

With tears in my eyes, I read them on my phone as I waited to board a flight to Jersey that afternoon at Liverpool John Lennon Airport.

They were so beautiful and moving that I decided there and then that I would approach *Echo* editor Ali Machray as soon as I got back in the office – to ask him if we could publish a special *Echo* supplement containing each and every tribute once the inquests were over.

He said yes. Of course he did.

It was without doubt the best thing I was ever involved in during my 33 years at the *Echo*.

In my column of May 4, 2016, I wrote: "The *Echo* has printed millions of words relating to the Hillsborough disaster, but I don't think it will publish anything more important than the commemorative edition that is now in the shops. The 96 – In The Words of Their Families is a supplement which includes the pen portraits, or tributes, which were read out by family members at the start of the new inquests in memory of their loved ones.

"It was a privilege to work on this edition – which costs £2, with all *Echo* profits being shared equally between the Liverpool FC Foundation and Everton in the Community charities – just as it was to be in Birchwood Park in Warrington to hear some of the tributes being given. They were heartbreaking but full of humanity – upsetting, yet uplifting.

"Steve Kelly of the Hillsborough Justice Campaign, whose brother, Michael, 38, died at Hillsborough, told me how he had changed his mind about the portraits: 'Hillsborough has been so public for all the families I was hoping we could have some privacy, even during the inquests. But listening to the families over the past weeks, it's brought their loved ones to life. We were just the vehicles delivering the words – the 96 were fighting for themselves.'

"It wasn't easy for the families to stand up in court and

deliver these moving tributes, and no one will find it easy to read the words written about those whose lives were cut so cruelly short.

"But there are no words relating to Hillsborough which will ever mean more."

***

At the inquests, Steve Kelly's powerful tribute to his brother began: "Hillsborough victim, one of the 96, in death he became body number 72. Also, the last Hillsborough victim to be claimed by his family. Yet another statistic. All descriptions that identify body number 72.

"His name was Michael David Kelly. He was born on March 1, 1951, St David's Day. Mike's dad's name was Patrick, his mum was Jean, his sister was Joan, who remained an avid campaigner until her own sudden and untimely death, February 8, 2001. He also had a brother, Stephen. I am Stephen, and one of the 96 was my brother.

"In life, he was an individual. In death, he is a number. I want to remove that sequence of numbers from him. I am here today waiting to reclaim my brother."

And his lengthy, poignant tribute ended with the following words: "I said earlier I have come here to reclaim him. I hope the decision of this inquest allows me that. Only then can Mike rest in peace. Thank you."

***

Andrew Devine – the 97th victim. A tribute

For so many years, as documented in so much of this chapter, it had been "the 96" – but this changed following a further tragic death.

On July 28, 2021, a coroner's inquest ruled Andrew Devine – who died the previous day – was unlawfully killed as a result of the injuries he suffered 32 years earlier at Hillsborough, making him the disaster's 97th victim.

His family released a statement, which read: "It is with great sadness and a sense of immense loss that we can confirm that Andrew Devine passed away yesterday at the premature age of 55.

"Our collective devastation is overwhelming, but so too is the realisation that we were blessed to have had Andrew with us for 32 years since the Hillsborough tragedy.

"We welcome the conclusion of the coroner, Mr Andre Rebello, made today at Liverpool Coroner's Court, that Andrew was unlawfully killed, making him the 97th fatality of the tragic events that occurred on April 15, 1989.

"In the intervening years, Andrew has been a much loved son, brother and uncle. He has been supported by his family and a team of dedicated carers, all of whom devoted themselves to him.

"As ever, our thoughts are with all of those affected by Hillsborough."

On April 15, 2014, the *Echo* carried my interview with Andrew's family – it was the only interview they have ever given, and was headlined: **The Hillsborough survivor – a born fighter who has repeatedly proved doctors wrong.** I reproduce it here, in its entirety.

Andrew Devine suffered horrendous injuries at Hillsborough – his chest was crushed and his brain deprived of oxygen – and wasn't expected to survive the day. Having made it through the first crucial 24 hours, his mum and dad were warned he would probably be dead within six months.

Later still, they were told nobody who had suffered such injuries had survived beyond eight years.

Today, 25 years on, Andrew is attending his first Hillsborough memorial service at Anfield – and is living proof of the power of unbreakable, unbeatable and unconditional love.

On April 15, 1989, the devoted Liverpool FC fan, from Mossley Hill, was a carefree 22-year-old.

On April 15, 2014, the now 47-year-old remains confined to a wheelchair, unable to speak and able to eat only puréed food – though, despite having seen more than his fair share of hospital wards, he lives in the family home with his devoted parents. His dad, retired police inspector Stanley, 74, mum Hilary, 72, sisters Wendy, 44, Julie, 40, Gill, 32, and brother Graham, 36, could be forgiven for being overcome by sadness and consumed with bitterness and anger.

But speaking to the *Echo* for the first time, and on behalf of the family, Wendy and Graham stress this wouldn't do Andrew any good.

Sitting in her home in Halewood, Wendy says: "There have been a lot of tears over the years, but we are lucky.

"Andrew survived, he is living at home with his mum and dad – and with 24-hour professional care – and is loved and cared for by his family. He is the centre of the family and the glue which holds us together.

"We are a tremendously close family and Andrew is a big part of that. A lot of families break apart, with family members living and working in different parts of the country, but we've remained together for Andrew. And family feuds are not an option for our family, because we have something far more important to do – be there for Andrew, the most important member of the family."

Graham adds: "It's not just day to day life, it's everything – Christmas arrangements for example. Everything is geared towards Andrew."

They also dismiss any idea of Andrew having been "forgotten" outside the family, with Wendy stressing: "He's not been forgotten. It's just that people don't know, and part of that is because mum and dad decided to stay away from the Press. To say he's forgotten sounds bitter, and we're not."

And on the 25th anniversary of the disaster, she adds: "Our hearts always go out to those families who lost loved ones and we have always supported them – and we're so glad that Andrew will be with us at this year's memorial service, because it's important to show that support."

Wendy and Graham say they are lucky, but so is Andrew – lucky to be part of such a warm, caring, devoted and loving family.

Andrew has had two very different lives – before and after

Hillsborough. Graham, 11 years his junior, recalls: "Because he was the oldest, he was kind of in charge of the rest of us, after mum and dad. He loved his football and was an avid Red who followed them around Europe. And he also loved going fishing."

Wendy, just three years younger, adds: "He had a big gang of mates and was very popular – he went to Dovedale Primary in Mossley Hill and the Blue Coat School. He was very much the outdoor type and would spend time with friends on a canal boat and riding his bike. He had a girl-friend and I think he would definitely have wanted kids. He was great with kids and still is."

Graham says: "He's a lot older than me and Gill but always played with us. We were really close."

Andrew worked for Post Office Counters, but was training in accountancy with the aim of moving into that line of work.

And recalling the night before Hillsborough, Wendy says: "I was 19 and moved in the same social circles as Andrew but we hadn't seen a lot of each other in the weeks leading up to the game.

"But the night before he came in as I was about to go to bed and we ended up having a really good catch-up. I have always been very grateful for that."

Regarding the next morning, Graham says: "I remember him winding me up! I'd started getting into football two or three years earlier and Andrew had taken me to the Alan Hansen testimonial game the previous year.

"We were having a bit of banter and I was saying 'Can

you get me a ticket?' He told me to go and make him a cup of tea!"

Andrew had been at Hillsborough for the 1988 semi-final, while he was also at Heysel – so Wendy says the family already had experience of ringing an emergency helpline. "I told my mum 'You know we won't be able to get through'," recalls Wendy. "But, unlike some families, we were fortunate to get some information early, about 6 or 7pm. A friend of dad's – a sergeant who was on duty in Liverpool – came round to the house."

Mr Devine then rang a number in Sheffield and after asking about his son was told: "If you don't come shortly, you won't see him alive."

Wendy says: "It's difficult not knowing what happened to Andrew. We were once told he had been taken onto the pitch but it turned out he had been taken to the back of the ground."

On hearing their son had received very serious crush injuries and wasn't expected to survive the day, Andrew's parents went straight to Sheffield's Royal Hallamshire Hospital – and were there for the next six weeks, as Andrew, who was on a life support machine in intensive care, defied all the odds. He was later transferred to Walton Hospital and then the young disabled unit at Fazakerley Hospital, while he also had spells at the Royal Hospital for Neurodisability in Putney, London. Throughout all this, family members were always by his side. After about two years, Andrew was able to be cared for at home, although there would still be times when he had to go into hospital.

"Everything has just evolved," explains Wendy. "At first, it was hour by hour and then it was day by day. I initially thought things were black and white – that Andrew was going to die or wake up and be OK. We thought he might be in a wheelchair but somehow didn't envisage him being like he is now.

"He was in a deep coma at first but his eyes opened after a few months. Everything has been such a gradual process. He is conscious.

"He sleeps and wakes and though we can't have a full knowledge of his level of understanding because he can't communicate verbally, we so often know when he is happy or unhappy. And he is able to eat puréed food – which he hadn't been for a few years, during which time mum and dad were told he had no swallow reflex and would choke if they tried to feed him.

"Andrew has made tremendous progress and his ongoing treatment includes physio and spending time in a hydro-therapy pool and a sensory room. Mum and dad have been absolutely fantastic. They have shown how strong and loving they are as parents. They have fought for Andrew all the way, while always having time for the rest of us." Graham adds: "They have never wallowed, which would have been so easy. Getting Andrew home was a huge thing and they fought so hard to do that."

Looking ahead, Wendy says: "Andrew is totally immobile and to keep a totally immobile man in his late 40s healthy is no mean feat.

"The priority now is to keep him healthy and give him the

best possible quality of life – and he does have a good life, which includes spending time in a caravan in North Wales, while we are able to take him to a few Liverpool games early and late in the season when the weather is good."

And today, Andrew is an uncle, with his four nephews and two nieces being Georgia, 16 (who last year spearheaded her school form's charity campaign to raise money for the Hillsborough Family Support Group), Alex, 13, Fraser, 11, Christopher, seven, Freya, two and Dylan, two – and Graham says: "When the young ones climb all over Andrew, his arms relax so we know he enjoys that part of family life."

Hillsborough has taken so much from the Devine family – it took a healthy son and brother.

But Andrew Devine survived, and continues to enjoy the best possible quality of life – thanks to his incredible parents, sisters, brother, extended family and a brilliant supporting cast.

All he needs is love, and he will never be short of that.

***

Finally, I want to give my thanks to all the family members, survivors and campaigners who have been kind enough to speak to me over the years.

I came to appreciate their help and openness even more when I heard the words of one family member – Steve Kelly, who I am proud to call a friend – in an interview he gave me which was headlined **Hillsborough never gives back, but it takes so much.**

Here are some extracts…

January 23, 2017

"Hillsborough never goes away… You can't escape it – trust me, I've tried. I've tried to move my life on but I can't sit still on it, and lots of people are the same. We have all tried to move on. We all want to move on…,

"Some people may think that the story of Hillsborough goes away during those periods it's not in the news, but I will sit in the house in the evening on the computer talking to other families – because this is our life…

"Sometimes, some of us will stand in front of a TV crew – or be speaking to the *Echo*. We want to keep on at people and want to keep the story going, but this aspect is also a difficult thing for us.

"When I attended the inquests, I used to dread that walk of 200 to 300 yards from the car park into the court – I'll never forget it. On many days, there would be masses of cameras and people shouting out for quotes. My stomach would be churning, and inside I was trying my best to be this actor.

"I was coming out with statements and praying to God that I had got things right because I didn't want to upset anybody. The pressure on you in these situations – including doing this – is tremendous because you don't want to let anybody down.

"And, being selfish, I don't want to let our Mike down (Steve's brother, who was 38 when he died at Hillsborough). And I don't want to let my mum (Jean, who died in 1994) down. Or my sister, Joan Sinclair, who died in 2001. Or my son, David, who died six years ago of a heart attack when he was just 29. Or my partner, Pam, who died four years ago...

"After this interview is over, I will sit back and breathe a sigh of relief because I will be able to say 'I've done it, I got through it'. But, again, it will have taken something out of me – something I will never get back.

"Every time I speak to the media, I lose a little bit of myself. I think every one of us is the same, but I'm not sure if people realise that.

"Hillsborough never gives back, but it takes so much."

Acknowledgements

THE TALK of Liverpool wouldn't be in your hands but for the help and support of too many people to mention – but I'll mention a few!

My thanks to Darren Thwaites, marketplace publisher for Reach plc's North West region, for giving this book his blessing by approving the use of *Liverpool Echo* copyright content.

Once this was secured, I approached Steve Hanrahan, managing director of the Reach Sport empire, which includes Mirror Books.

Happily, Steve and his executive editors, Paul Dove and Rick Cooke, loved the idea. My thanks to you all for the expert help, guidance and skills which turned it into a reality. My gratitude also goes to Claire Brown, the company's marketing and communications expert, and Richard Williamson – a former *Echo* colleague and fellow long-suffering Evertonian – who undertook editing duties.

Daily Mirror writer Brian Reade, a former colleague of mine in the Liverpool Echo's features department – and the nearby Cross Keys pub – kindly provided the foreword. This was a great honour for me, as I have revered Readey's writing for decades. It's just a shame he's a Liverpool fan – and lager drinker.

I was able to source the vast majority of my original

articles from the boxes in my loft, but there were missing pieces to the jigsaw. I am indebted to Jan Grace, a wonderfully-helpful archivist at the Liverpool Record Office, and my dear pal Cheryl Mullin, *Liverpool Echo* audience editor, for locating them.

Regular *Echo* readers won't be surprised to see various Half Man Half Biscuit lyrics adorning these pages – thanks to my good friend, Nigel Blackwell, for allowing me to use them.

Second, third and fourth pairs of eyes, even before a book's official editing process begins, are so important. My thanks to two friends who took the time and trouble to help – Eleanor Barlow, the former *Echo* reporter who covered the Hillsborough inquests, kindly proofread the chapter on Hillsborough, while ex-*Echo* sports editor Dave Prentice kindly proofread the chapter about individuals associated with our beloved Everton. And, most of all, thanks to my wife, Sandra – yet another former *Echo* colleague! – who proofread the entire book.

I am so grateful to so many former colleagues. Thank you to the countless feature writers and reporters who I enjoyed working and laughing alongside (definitely a decent percentage – and hopefully they know who they are). My gratitude also goes to the sub-editors who worked on my copy, the photographers who provided the brilliant images which sat alongside the words, and the editors, news editors and feature editors (so many feature editors) who, as well as asking me to write certain stories and feature articles, gave me the freedom to write about so many of my favourite subjects. And thanks to all those staffers who often get overlooked at times like these – including the all-important receptionists and library, canteen and security staff (yes, kids, the *Echo* used to have a canteen).

For my last year in the office, Lorna Hughes and I were the *Echo's* print/feature writers (before Covid lockdown, working from home, furlough and then – for Lorna – a new job in another part of the Reach empire and – for me – voluntary redundancy). I'm sure she won't mind me claiming the title of the *Echo's* last print/feature writer, as she was enjoying her new job by the time I signed off. We were in the same boat during furlough (Lorna's eight measly weeks was no match for my 20), and helped keep each other afloat via frequent messaging and phone chats. A strange and stressful time. Thanks pal.

Thank you to all the people I've temporarily forgotten (it's old age, you'll understand).

And finally, thank you to the most important individuals of all – the people who were generous enough to allow me to interview them, and the people who were generous enough to buy the paper to read the results.

Thirty-three years? It really didn't seem like it.